Stakeholders, Sustainable Development Policies and the Coal Mining Industry

This book identifies the impact of internal and external stakeholders on the implementation of sustainable development policies in the coal mining sector in Europe and the Commonwealth of Independent States.

The book assesses what activities and conditions need to be improved so that sustainable development policies can be more effectively and efficiently implemented. With a specific focus on the hard coal and lignite mining sectors, it examines a broad range of case studies from Eastern European countries and the Commonwealth of Independent States, including Russia, Ukraine, Poland, Kazakhstan, Germany, Spain, France and the United Kingdom, among many more. Beginning with an introduction to sustainable development and stakeholder theory, Part II then examines internal stakeholders, including owners, managers, employees and trade unions. Part III examines external stakeholders, touching upon those directly related to the mining industry, such as customers and mining enterprises, and those not directly associated such as local and regional communities and environmental organisations. The book concludes by proposing a model approach to the management of stakeholders involved in mining enterprises, focusing on improving the process of implementing sustainable development in the mining sector and strengthening the effects of this process.

This book will be of great interest to students and scholars of the extractive industries, natural resource management and policy and sustainable development.

Izabela Jonek-Kowalska is Associate Professor in Mining Economics and Director of Institute of Economics and Computer Science at Silesian University of Technology, Poland.

Radosław Wolniak is Full Professor in Management Sciences in the Faculty of Organization and Management at Silesian University of Technology, Poland.

Oksana A. Marinina is Associate Professor in the Department of Economics, Organization and Management at Saint-Petersburg Mining University, Russia.

Tatyana V. Ponomarenko is Full Professor in the Department of Economics, Organization and Management at Saint-Petersburg Mining University, Russia.

Routledge Studies of the Extractive Industries and Sustainable Development

Resource Extraction, Space and Resilience
International Perspectives
Juha Kotilainen

Our Extractive Age
Expressions of Violence and Resistance
Edited by Judith Shapiro and John-Andrew McNeish

The Impact of Mining Lifecycles in Mongolia and Kyrgyzstan
Political, Social, Environmental and Cultural Contexts
Edited by Troy Sternberg, Kemel Toktomushev and Byambabaatar Ichinkhorloo

Oil and National Identity in the Kurdistan Region of Iraq
Conflicts at the Frontier of Petro-Capitalism
Alessandro Tinti

The Anthropology of Resource Extraction
Edited by Lorenzo D'Angelo and Robert Jan Pijpers

Andean States and the Resource Curse
Institutional Change in Extractive Economies
Edited by Gerardo Damonte and Bettina Schorr

Stakeholders, Sustainable Development Policies and the Coal Mining Industry
Perspectives from Europe and the Commonwealth of Independent States
Izabela Jonek-Kowalska, Radosław Wolniak, Oksana A. Marinina and Tatyana V. Ponomarenko

For more information about this series, please visit: www.routledge.com/Routledge-Studies-of-the-Extractive-Industries-and-Sustainable-Development/book-series/REISD

Stakeholders, Sustainable Development Policies and the Coal Mining Industry

Perspectives from Europe and the Commonwealth of Independent States

Izabela Jonek-Kowalska, Radosław Wolniak, Oksana A. Marinina and Tatyana V. Ponomarenko

LONDON AND NEW YORK

from Routledge

First published 2022
by Routledge
4 Park Square, Milton Park, Abingdon, Oxon OX14 4RN

and by Routledge
605 Third Avenue, New York, NY 10158

Routledge is an imprint of the Taylor & Francis Group, an informa business

© 2022 Izabela Jonek-Kowalska, Radosław Wolniak, Oksana A. Marinina
and Tatyana V. Ponomarenko

British Library Cataloguing-in-Publication Data
A catalogue record for this book is available from the British Library

Library of Congress Cataloging-in-Publication Data
Names: Jonek-Kowalska, Izabela, author. | Wolniak, Radosław, author. |
Marinina, Oksana A., author. | Ponomarenko, Tatyana V., author.
Title: Stakeholders, sustainable development policies and the coal mining
industry : perspectives from Europe and the commonwealth of independent
states / Izabela Jonek-Kowalska, Radosław Wolniak, Oksana A. Marinina and
Tatyana V. Ponomarenko.
Description: Abingdon, Oxon ; New York, NY : Routledge, 2022. |
Series: Routledge studies of the extractive industries |
Includes bibliographical references and index. |
Identifiers: LCCN 2021048158 (print) | LCCN 2021048159 (ebook) |
ISBN 9780367549008 (hbk) | ISBN 9780367549046 (pbk) |
ISBN 9781003091110 (ebk)
Subjects: LCSH: Coal trade--Government policy--European Union
countries. | Coal mines and mining--Government policy--European Union
countries. | Sustainable development--European Union countries. |
Coal trade--Government policy--Europe, Eastern. | Coal mines and
mining--Government policy--Europe, Eastern. | Sustainable
development--Europe, Eastern.
Classification: LCC HD9555.E82 J66 2022 (print) |
LCC HD9555.E82 (ebook) | DDC 338.2/7240947--dc23/eng/20211207
LC record available at https://lccn.loc.gov/2021048158
LC ebook record available at https://lccn.loc.gov/2021048159

ISBN: 978-0-367-54900-8 (hbk)
ISBN: 978-0-367-54904-6 (pbk)
ISBN: 978-1-003-09111-0 (ebk)

DOI: 10.4324/9781003091110

Typeset in Bembo
by Taylor & Francis Books

Contents

Figures

Tables

Introduction

The main aim of the research and considerations conducted in the monograph is to identify the impact of internal and external stakeholders on the implementation and effects of sustainable development policy in the coal mining sector. This approach combines the theory of stakeholders with sustainable development policy, and thus allows the development of new conclusions and recommendations directed at improving stakeholder management, in order to achieve better results in the implementation of sustainable development principles in the mining sector. According to the authors, this is an important and current task, although in practice it is very difficult to achieve, due to the very serious social, ecological and economic controversies related to the functioning of this sector in the economy.

The approach proposed here does not focus on one group of stakeholders or one selected aspect of sustainable development, which, in the last part of the monograph, allows us to view the analysed problems holistically, i.e. through the prism of all stakeholder groups in the context of many threads of sustainable development. This view includes: (1) conclusions from detailed analyses, carried out in relation to individual stakeholders in each of the following chapters, and (2) a synthesis in the form of a mining enterprise stakeholder management model, taking into account their goals, bargaining power, impact on the functioning of enterprises and the entire sector, mutual interactions and role in implementing sustainable development in the mining sector.

The main research problems posed in each of the chapters regarding internal and external stakeholders are the following: (1) How does a given group contribute to strengthening or destroying the principles of sustainable development in the mining industry? and (2) What activities, attributes and conditions should be strengthened or levelled in order to implement the principles of sustainable development more effectively and efficiently?

Considerations and research are carried out in relation to the hard coal and lignite mining sector (deep or open pit). The geographical scope of research refers to the European states, as well as countries forming the Commonwealth of Independent States, in which this raw material is or has been extracted. Therefore, the research group includes countries such as Russia, Ukraine, Kazakhstan, Georgia, Poland, Germany, Czech Republic, Slovakia, Romania,

DOI: 10.4324/9781003091110-1

Spain, Turkey, United Kingdom, France, Greece, Hungary, Bulgaria, Slovakia, and Slovenia.

The research methodology in each of the chapters on individual stakeholders assumes the use of two research perspectives:

- a macro perspective covering the analysis of statistical data, describing the scale of the phenomena studied in a given country (e.g. number of employees; number of private and state mines; level of air pollution),
- a micro perspective covering case studies (authors' own – developed on the basis of our own original materials, as well as surveys and expert interviews conducted in Poland and Russia, and follow-up – derived from available reports, articles and publications on other countries).

In Part I of the monograph, the authors present in-depth literature studies on the two main research trends of stakeholder theory and sustainable development.

These studies are an introduction to research and analysis of the importance of individual stakeholder groups in the mining sector. They are of dual thread nature. The first thread refers to fundamental issues of a universal nature (genesis and key assumptions of stakeholder theory and sustainable development; categorisation and stakeholder analysis models; Sustainable Development Goals; Global Reporting Initiative). The second thread enables the narrowing down of the above considerations to the mining industry, thus constituting a sectoral perspective referring to previous research and considerations on sustainable development and stakeholder theory in mining enterprises.

The monograph is divided into four parts, containing a total of 14 chapters. The first part contains two introductory chapters on issues related to sustainable development and stakeholder theory in general, as well as industry terms. The second part focuses on internal stakeholders (*consubstantial stakeholders*) and includes: owners, managers, employees and trade unions. The third part is dedicated to external stakeholders. First of all, reference is made to those stakeholders who are directly related to mining enterprises, namely the suppliers, customers and competitors (*contractual stakeholders*). Then, stakeholders from further environment are analysed, that is: the country, local and regional communities, as well as ecological organisations (*contextual stakeholders*). The fourth part is a summary of the considerations under which subsequent comparative analyses are carried out. In addition, Part IV proposes a model approach to the management of stakeholders of mining enterprises, focusing on improving the process of implementing sustainable development in the mining sector and strengthening the effects of this process.

The features that distinguish this study from available publications are:

- a unique research perspective that allows the analysis of sustainable development from the perspective of individual groups of stakeholders of mining enterprises,
- a wide subject and object scope of analyses and research,

- a two-tier research perspective covering statistical analyses (macro perspective), case studies and surveys, as well as expert interviews (micro perspective),
- development of a mining management stakeholder model to improve the process of achieving sustainable development priorities in the mining sector.

Due to the theoretical and practical content contained in individual chapters, the recipients of the book can be both scientists involved in management in the mining industries and managers employed in such industries. Practitioners who can use publications are located in all those countries where natural resources are extracted, which enables international collection of publications. In the case of students, the book can be used as inspiration for diploma theses in the field of management and economics of mining industries.

Part I

Introduction to research and considerations

1 Sustainable development in mining enterprises

Fundamentals and main research results

Origins and essentials of sustainable development in enterprises' management

The concept of sustainable development appeared for the first time in 1972 in the Stockholm Declaration. This definition was then adopted at the second session of the UNEP Governing Council (United Nations Environment Programme). The concept was introduced into world circulation in particular in 1987, when the so-called Brundtland Report was published. The essence of the Brundtland Report was the message that in order to ensure further existence of humankind on Earth and meet its needs in the long term, it is necessary to develop sustainability in all areas of human life and activity (Rogers et al., 2008; Idowu et al., 2019).

Brundtland defined sustainable development as that which meets the needs of the present without compromising the ability of future generations to meet their own needs (Brundtland, 1987). Brundtland's concept was then adopted and developed at the Earth Summit in Rio de Janeiro in 1992. One of the key declarations of this summit was that today's development must not negatively affect the ability of future generations to meet their own needs.

This concept emerged in response to the growing concern about the limited possibilities of the terrestrial ecosystem to lift the pressure of human activity. Its goal was to eliminate the imbalance that occurs between the socio-economic development of humanity and the natural environment. Humans have not taken responsibility for their actions for too long, which has led to a decrease in the quality of their own life and that of other living things.

In the following years, the concept of sustainable development has evolved into a more practical approach, focusing on economic development and environmental responsibility. At the Earth Summit in Johannesburg in 2002, three basic components of sustainable development were identified: economic development, social development and environmental protection.

The change in the area of awareness of human attitudes towards nature and the appearance of the concept of sustainable development can be presented in the form of a three-stage process:

DOI: 10.4324/9781003091110-3

- the first stage – natural technocratism – was the most aggressive towards resources, it consisted in an unrestricted use of natural resources;
- the second stage – the minimum ecological period – the importance of ecological problems began to be considered and selected ecological principles were implemented into business practice;
- the third stage – sustainable development – a period characterised by an equitable connection of the forces of nature with the socio-economic development of society.

(Trzepacz, 2012)

The idea of sustainable development has been shaping the policy of international organisations, countries, regions, as well as smaller territorial units for over twenty years. It exerts a growing impact on the functioning of economies, at both the macro- and micro-economic levels.

The application of the principles of sustainable development in business practice should take into account the following features:

- immaterialisation (tertiary economy) – qualitative growth consisting in increasing the share of intangible production in global production, increasing the importance of the service sector,
- dematerialisation – ecological efficiency, separating the relationship between environmental damage and tangible production,
- decarbonisation – separating the relationship between economic growth and the increase in CO_2 emissions,
- decoupling – separating the relationship between economic growth and the increase in transport needs,
- comprehensiveness – including many different variables into management,
- adaptive management – connecting natural systems into the management process, while taking into account their high level of uncertainty,
- legal issues – striving to introduce issues arising from the principles of sustainable development into legal legislation at the national and supranational level,
- sustainability indicators – determining the level of sustainable development by using various types of numerical indicators to measure the phenomenon of sustainable development.

(Kamaljit and Seidler, 2009; Sachs, 2015)

Implementing the concept of sustainable development allows the setting of new rules for the organisation's functioning. It is very important, in this case, to recognise the limits of the functioning of the market mechanism. In this way, the classic concept of economic development can be modified, hitherto determined by economic indicators, such as GDP. In the case of sustainable development, it is important to combine moderate levels of consumption with strong social institutions and a healthy society. In this way, it will be possible to achieve long-term development that will not lead to depletion of our planet's resources (Kamaljit and Seidler, 2009; Idowu et al., 2019).

In order to determine how individual entities are involved in sustainable development, various types of indicators should be used to measure this phenomenon. For EU countries, the type of indicator often used is SDI (Sustainable Development Index), as defined by Eurostat. The indicator is used to monitor the objectives of implementing the Sustainable Development Strategy (Hass et al., 2002; Ledoux et al., 2005; Hickel, 2020). The most important leading indicators used in the SDI index include (Sustainable Development Index, 2020): real GDP per capita, resource efficiency, risk of poverty or social exclusion, employment rate of older workers, life expectancy and healthy life years, greenhouse gas emissions, consumption of energy from renewable sources, energy consumption of transport relative to GDP, abundance of common birds, conservation of fish stocks, official development assistance.

The implementation of the principles of sustainable development in mining practice should involve the integration of activities in three key areas, which are illustrated in Figure 1.1:

- technical and economic, ensuring economic growth,
- ecological, guaranteeing the protection of raw materials and the natural environment,
- social, ensuring concern for an employee in the workplace and in the development of the local community in the vicinity of a given mining plant.

The basic feature of sustainable development is the fact that it is a continuous process, not just ad hoc. It should have clearly defined goals and the means to achieve them in each of the three areas. It can be assumed that the weight of

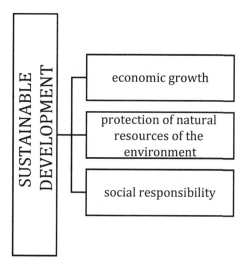

Figure 1.1 Areas of sustainable development
Source: study based on Dubiński, 2013

each individual area is identical. A brief description of these individual areas is presented in Table 1.1.

The latest document presenting trends in sustainable development is the so-called 2030 Agenda for Sustainable Development adopted by the UN General Assembly on 25 September 2015. On this basis, the European Union has committed itself to striving towards an economically sustainable Europe, in which people live well within the limits of our planet. The *2030 Agenda* is a programme of activities defining a model of sustainable development at the global level (Sachs et al., 2019). The initiator and spokesperson of the Agenda decree was the United Nations, at which a High-Level Panel on the Development Agenda was established. The Agenda consists of: preambles, declarations and 17 goals of sustainable development with their corresponding tasks (Arredondo et al., 2020; Juergensen et al., 2020; Walsh et al., 2020; Wiktor-Mach, 2020).

The most important goals of sustainable development resulting from the *2030 Agenda* include:

- end poverty,
- no hunger,
- good health and quality of life,
- good quality of education,
- gender equality,
- clean water and sanitation,
- clean and available energy,
- economic growth and decent work,
- innovation, industry and infrastructure,
- less inequality,

Table 1.1 Characteristics of sustainable development areas

Area	Characteristics
Economic growth	Achieving long-term stability by the mining plant both in terms of the planned production volume and meeting the needs of recipients, as well as achieving economic efficiency obtained from the sale of extracted raw material.
Protection of raw material resources and the natural environment	Care for the deposit manifests itself through rational sourcing and savings in extraction. This area also covers activities that minimise the negative impact of various processes related to the extraction of mineral resources on various forms of the geological environment and the natural environment on the surface.
Social responsibility	Ensuring safe working conditions, but also the care of mining entrepreneurs in the social aspects of this work, including mining families, the surroundings of the mining plant etc.

Source: study based on Dubiński et al., 2007, Dubiński, 2013

- sustainable cities and communities,
- responsible consumption and production,
- action on the climate,
- life below water,
- life on land,
- peace, justice and strong institutions,
- partnership for goals.

(*2030 Agenda*, 2015)

Many of the activities listed are directly related to the mining industry and the mining industry must take measures to meet the goals of the *2030 Agenda* (Monteiro et al., 2019; Moomen et al., 2019).

Sustainable development in extractive industries: difficult implementation or utopia?

The concept of sustainable development is particularly important in the case of mining. The basic principle of sustainable development in mining must be the rational and economical acquisition and use of mineral resources, because they are non-renewable resources and their excessive extraction will deprive future generations of the possibility of using them. Mining must also pay attention to environmental and social issues, in line with the three pillars of sustainable development outlined in the previous subsection. Today, care for the natural environment is one of the most important elements that determine whether mining activities will gain social acceptance.

Mining enterprises, in order to achieve long-term economic success, must have social permission to conduct mining operations (Owusu et al., 2019). They can only achieve this by engaging key stakeholders in a constant dialogue, while conducting far-reaching environmental protection measures. Therefore, they have to get involved in the implementation of the sustainable development strategy (Ogrodnik and Mieszaniec, 2013).

From the historical side, mining is one of the oldest and best documented types of human activity. Human activities in mining began in the Neolithic era (Reardon, 2011). In ancient times, many mines were exploited for iron, lead, copper, gold and other metals. Numerous mines are known to this day and some of them operated for many centuries (Fernández-Lozanoa et al., 2019). For several millennia, people have benefited from acquiring the earth's natural resources. With the passage of time, mining began to extract fossil fuels, in particular coal. Mineral resources, which have been extracted and used by humans for centuries, have been an important factor in the economic and civilisation development of many societies and countries.

The rapid development of the mining industry occurred in the 19th and 20th centuries as a result of the use of explosives and the mechanisation of the production process. During this period there was a huge increase in the amount of extracted raw materials. In the last 25 years of the 20th century, fossil fuels began to be extracted from previously inaccessible places, such as the bottom of the sea and polar regions.

Rational and economical management of natural resources is a key element in ensuring sustainable management of natural resources. Meanwhile, humans have got used to the high availability of mineral resources over the past two centuries, often forgetting about the fact that they are non-renewable resources.

The mining sector with the largest share in the world, in terms of production, is the extraction of oil and natural gas. Oil extraction has fully developed during the last century. These activities have a significant impact on the natural environment, in particular in the form of oil spills into the seas, and soil pollution (Chang et al., 2014; Nwachukwu et al., 2017; Dino et al., 2020).

Other important environmental problems concerning the extraction of oil and natural gas relate to the removal of scale from pipe cleaning, which is highly radioactive, and the sands depoisted at the bottom of oil tanks contain metals and radionuclides in high concentrations, which can have a very negative effect on the natural environment.

Coal is the particular fossil fuel on which this book is focused. In the 19th and 20th centuries, coal was the most important energy source in many industrial processes around the world. In the second half of the 20th century, it began to be replaced by natural gas and oil. Currently, coal is responsible for satisfying about 1/3 of the world's energy demand (IEA, 2019). Coal reserves are estimated at 892 trillion tonnes. If the current level of consumption is maintained, they would last for about 110 years. In the case of oil and natural gas reserves, these resources, at the current level of use, would last for approximately 52–54 years (World Coal Association, 2020).

Coal combustion has a negative impact on the environment. The problems related to sustainable development in the mining industry, in this respect, result from the fact that each mining activity – to a lesser or greater extent – affects the state of the natural environment (Angelakoglou and Gaidajis, 2020). In particular, the following negative environmental effects resulting from mining activities can be mentioned:

- surface deformations in the form of depressions, horizontal displacement or discontinuous deformations,
- mining-induced seismicity,
- changes in water level,
- soil depletion,
- gas and dust emissions,
- noise.

(Dubiński and Turek, 2006; Drebenstedt 2008)

Negative environmental effects resulting from the combustion of coal in terms of emissions to the atmosphere include:

- increase in the level of carbon dioxide in the atmosphere,
- increase in the level of greenhouse gases in the atmosphere (nitrogen oxide N_2O and methane CH_4),
- emission of radioactive substances,
- emission from toxic metals.

(IYan et al., 2012, Carvalho et al., 2014; Peralta et al., 2016; UNSCEAR, 2017; EA, 2020)

These factors affect global warming and are responsible for current climate change. For this reason, actions are currently underway around the world to reduce the level of emissions of these gases into the atmosphere (Carvalho, 2017; Huang et al., 2017; Tuokku et al., 2019). Many countries in the world, in particular in the European Union, are trying to reduce coal burning due to its negative environmental impact.

A very important factor of sustainable development in mining is the issue of occupational health and safety in mining. It can be understood as:

- care for the employee's health and life in the workplace,
- care for employees' professional development, their competences and skills,
- ensuring job stability,
- the level of remuneration ensuring fair living conditions of miners' families.

In the case of work safety in mining, it should be taken into account that this industry, especially in the case of underground mining, belongs to the sectors of the economy where there is high level of risk of accidents (Braun et al., 2017).

Another issue related to sustainable development in the case of the mining industry is paying attention to relations with the local community residing in the vicinity of the mine (Borujeni and Gitnavard, 2017). This is particularly important because, in democratic societies, it is necessary to obtain the community's acceptance for the operation of the mine.

Research conducted in Polish mines has helped to identify the following key factors, relevant to sustainable development:

- limiting the waste of resources and the amount of waste generated by the mine, in particular hazardous waste,
- management improvement for the reclamation of degraded landscapes as a result of mining activities,
- limiting the impact of mining activities on the surface,
- reducing the amount of wastewater, in particular saline water from mine drainage,
- reducing dust emissions and gaseous pollutants into the atmosphere, in particular reducing greenhouse gas emissions,
- reduction of energy consumption by the mine,
- effective storage of methane released from the rock mass in order to minimise its emission into the atmosphere, as well as the prevention of

hazards related to underground methane in order to ensure an improvement in the safety of miners' work,

- continuous increase of the economic use of methane discharged and extracted to the surface,
- reduction of noise emission to the environment.

(Burchart-Korol et al., 2014; Willmer and Scholtz, 2018)

Because energy is needed for the functioning of modern civilisation, it is necessary to draw it from some kind of natural resources. It seems that, despite environmental problems regarding the extraction and burning of fossil fuels, it is not possible to maintain the current level of civilisation development without using them. This is confirmed by the analysis of the data presented in Figure 1.2, which shows Total Primary Energy Supply in the years 1990–2017. The analysis of the data shows that coal, oil and natural gas are still the basic sources of energy in the world.

In the last 30 years, there has been an increase in the use of nuclear energy and energy coming from the burning of biofuels, but it is still too little to stop, or even significantly reduce, the burning of fossil fuels. In the future, in order to protect the environment and balance energy consumption, the use of energy from other sources must increase (Brown, 2011; Michaelides, 2012). However, at present, there are no sources ensuring the possibility of drawing energy on such a scale and as cheaply as is the case with energy coming from burning fossil fuels. It is also worth noting that Smil's research on quality of life has shown that the *Human Development Index* shows a high level of quality of life, only if a given society exceeds a certain high level of energy consumption (2004). For this reason, it will be difficult to significantly reduce energy consumption on a global scale in the short term, as this would result in a decrease in people's quality of life.

However, in the future, the principles of sustainable development should be introduced in mining operations as much as possible, in a way that does not

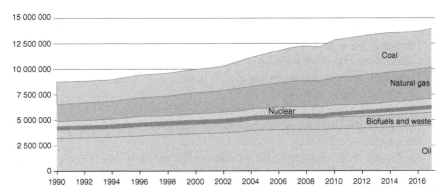

Figure 1.2 Total Primary Energy Supply (TPES) by source – years 1990–2017
Source: IEA, 2020

excessively use these resources. Attention should also be paid to the negative environmental effects of the business, as well as its impact on people's health. Investments should be planned in such a way as to cause as little as possible harm to the environment and local communities. Mining enterprises must plan activities for sustainable development right at the inception stage of their missions. When assessing the environmental impact of a given mining investment, the entire mine life cycle analysis should be used and a detailed assessment of its possible negative impact on the natural environment should be made. Life cycle analysis must take into account all hidden costs associated with conducting mining activities. The responsibility for this type of activity should be clearly defined and suitable measures should be ensured to deal with all problems encountered.

For currently operating mines, procedures should be implemented to protect the environment and health. In order to ensure the implementation of the concept of sustainable development in mining, legislative changes should be sought that force appropriate action on the part of mine owners.

Socially responsible mining companies should implement good practices in this area to reduce the environmental impact of their operations as much as possible. An important factor in this respect may be the introduction of robots, which will cause significant changes in the functioning of the entire mining industry. In particular, this may be an opportunity due to the fact that work at the mine is dangerous to the health and life of miners. Robotisation and implementation of the concept of Industry 4.0 – known as the fourth industrial revolution – in mining can contribute to the development of such technologies that will eliminate the negative effects of mining processes on the health and life of mining crews. Technological development may also allow the development of technology to repair existing environmental effects in such a way, that they can be restored for further use.

Certainly, the implementation of the concept of sustainable development in mining is difficult due to its strong negative environmental impact and the fact that we are dealing with non-renewable resources. However, this does not mean that the concept of sustainable development cannot be implemented in this industry. On the contrary, we believe that this is the only opportunity, on the one hand, to ensure the energy resources necessary for the functioning of modern civilisation and, on the other, to deal with the negative effects of mining activities, the effects of which can be observed, e.g. in the form of climate changes.

Reporting on Social Corporate Responsibility in extractive industries: rules and results

The concept of corporate social responsibility (CSR) is a modern management concept that effectively combines many theoretically contradictory values (Hąbek, 2014). This concept combines enterprise development with ethical and social issues (Dahlsrud, 2006). The concept of CSR appeared in the mid-20th century. It is understood as a long-term strategic management process

(Bowen, 1953), where social goals are compatible with financial goals, and one of them is gaining the trust of the communities in the environment of the projects (Drucker, 2010).

Implementation of the CSR concept in enterprises is related to the issue of its reporting. Over the past 30 years, we have witnessed public pressure to increase social and environmental information provided by enterprises. The increased need in this area was influenced by many factors, such as increased public awareness, stakeholder pressure and social concerns regarding labour exploitation practices or ecological disasters (Carrots and Sticks for Starters, 2006).

Socially responsible mining enterprises believe that the concept of CSR should be implemented in order to improve the quality of life, diversify local economies, improve employee engagement, or build more sustainable communities (Sari and Setiahadi, 2019). Researchers are also of the opinion that mining companies should become increasingly socially responsible (Jonek-Kowalska, 2016; Jonek-Kowalska and Zieliński, 2018; Zieliński and Jonek-Kowalska, 2020). As compensation for the extraction of natural resources, they should reduce poverty and support employment in local communities (Pegg, 2006; Alizar and Scott, 2009). Most of the activities undertaken by mining organisations towards sustainable development are focused on community development, environmental protection and stakeholder involvement. The concerns of communities living in mining areas are increasingly being paid attention to by mining companies (Kepore and Imbun, 2011; Tang et al., 2020).

In the longer term, mining companies should focus on determining what socially responsible development effects are delivered to given communities (Jenkins, 2004). Mining companies should improve their relations with the local community and improve their social image (Kemp, 2010; Essah and Andrews, 2016). This can be done by implementing a wide range of corporate social responsibility concepts (Ponomarenko et al., 2016).

Based on the experience of mining enterprises implementing social responsibility into their practice, three main issues can be identified:

- the need for a more proactive approach on the part of mine managers to addressing environmental issues, social problems and strengthening social relations of the mines,
- the need to embed CSR in the mining enterprise's organisational culture, its strategy and compliance with the company's image,
- including issues related to corporate social responsibility in the organisation's strategies, so that this activity becomes a daily practice and is not only taken in response to events that have a negative impact on the company's image.

(Harfst and Wirth, 2011; Zhiguo et al., 2011; Mutti et al., 2012; Rakowska and Cichorzewska, 2012; Dobele et al., 2014; Narula et al., 2017)

Reporting of non-financial data, such as data on the organisation's involvement in the implementation of the CSR concept, is becoming more and more popular every year. To date, there is no uniform standpoint on social responsibility accounting. As a consequence, different entities may use different standards, norms, guidelines and recommendations when reporting (Wiśniewska and Chojnacka, 2016; Marinina, 2019).

There are many types of standards, initiatives, guidelines, guides or norms in the world for reporting CSR data. The most important are:

- Global Reporting Initiative – GRI Guidelines,
- UN Global Compact Communication of Progress,
- AA1000 Accountability Standards
- ISO 26000,
- OECD guidelines for multinational enterprises,
- CERES Principles,
- Carbon Disclosure Project,
- Sustainability Global Reporting Programme,
- SA 8000 Standard,
- International Federation of Accountants – Sustainability Framework,
- European Federation of Financial Analysts Societies – ESG Framework.

(Hąbek and Wolniak, 2013; Hąbek and Wolniak, 2016)

The guidelines most often used in the world are those contained in the Global Reporting Initiative. GRI is working intensively on improving and disseminating sustainable reporting among enterprises around the world (Jones and Jonas, 2011; Hilson et al., 2019). GRI not only includes in its guidelines indicators related to economic, social and environmental performance. The scope of guidelines on how to prepare reports is much larger (Singhal and Dev, 2016). The purpose of the guidelines is to help organisations in presenting key sustainable development results. Sustainable reporting guidelines primarily include a list of detailed rules on defining the content of the report and ensuring its quality. The guidelines are developed in such a way that they can be used by various organisations, regardless of their business, size, or country in which they operate (GRI, 2020; Ramaganesh and Bathrinath, 2020; Zhou, 2020).

Environmental supplements are designed to help enterprises in presenting significant aspects of their activities related to the specificity of the sector in which they operate. Each sector has some special features. For example, the mining activity sector of particular interest to us in this book is closely related to a number of issues related to the natural environment (Technical Protocol, 2011). The guidelines contained in GRI regarding the reporting of enterprises from the mining and metals sector appeared for the first time in 2010 (Mathu and Scheepers, 2016). The guidelines add four elements in the social area: small mining and craft activities, displacement, decommissioning planning, and materials management. Eleven MM (*Mining and Metals*) indicators were also introduced and included in the group of basic indicators. Particularly important, from the point of view of mining activities, proposed indicators can include:

- the size, area of land, intended for mining activities, damaged, disturbed or reclaimed land,
- the total amount of workload, rock, operational mining waste, sludge, silt and associated types of risk,
- the number of strikes and breaks from work lasting more than a week,
- the extent to which complaint mechanisms have been used in resolving disputes regarding land ownership, the local community and indigenous peoples, the results of the mechanism,
- the number and percentage of enterprises operating in areas where small mining and craft activities related to mining and in adjacent areas take place, resulting and related types of risk, as well as actions taken to mitigate the effects of these types of risk.

(Sarkar, 2013; Kudełko et al., 2016; GRI, 2020)

CSR reports published according to GRI guidelines should, in particular, take into account the following issues:

- Vision and Strategy – to present the strategy of the organisation reporting on sustainability issues, including a management declaration.
- Profile – review of the structure and activities of the reporting organisation and the scope of the report.
- Structure and Management System – a description of the organisational structure, action programmes and management systems, including those involving stakeholders in the company's activities.
- GRI Content Indicator (GRI Index) – a table indicating where the information is in the organisation's report.
- Results Indicators – assessment of the effect or impact of the reporting organisation, including integrated, economic, environmental and social performance indicators.

(G4, 2013; GRI, 2020)

Organisations using the GRI methodology are required to present the adopted strategy of sustainable development in the dimension under consideration and present their results in relation to more general conditions and objectives of sustainable development. Reporting in accordance with GRI guidelines is characterised by a high level of quality when the principles of balance, comparability, accuracy, timeliness, transparency and reliability are observed (Donaldson and Preston, 1995; Morsing and Schultz, 2006).

To date, mining companies, and in particular in developing countries, have had a dubious reputation for implementing CSR (Peck and Sinding, 2003; Dashwood, 2007; Dashwood, 2012; Fonseca et al., 2014). The growing pressure on reporting social activity in mining enterprises has caused these companies to introduce a social responsibility strategy as part of the company's element of global strategy (Günther et al, 2007; Ventura and Saenz, 2015; Dong and Xu, 2016). CSR activities undertaken by mining companies must be appropriately reported. Informing the stakeholders about pro-social and pro-ecological activities is a must. Nowadays, mining companies not only include CSR activities in their business strategies, but also publish relevant reports (Wolniak, 2019).

For example, in Poland, two coal mining companies submit annual CSR reports. In their reports, they refer to various issues of social responsibility, such as:

- organisational order,
- human rights,
- work practices,
- the environment,
- fair operating practices,
- consumer issues,
- social commitment.

(Kijewska and Bluszcz, 2016; Woźniak and Jurczyk, 2020)

In the countries of the European Union, in accordance with Directive 2014/95/EU from 2016, in all member countries, enterprises employing more than 500 people will be required to report on corporate social responsibility, in particular in the field of:

- obligations to provide information on environmental, social and labour matters, human rights, the fight against corruption and fraud,
- describing their business model, results and risk policies related to the above subjects, as well as diversity policy in the context of the composition of the management board and the supervisory board,
- encouragement to use recognised CSR reporting guidelines, in particular GRI.

Interesting studies on the comparability of CSR reports from mining enterprises from various countries around the world were carried out by Boral and Henri. Based on their analyses, it can be concluded that there are many problems with the comparability of reports, which – to a large extent – are divergent and present a different range of information. The main problems occurring in the case of CSR reporting in the mining sector include:

- the qualitative nature of many GRI indicators,
- the use of different scales in various indicators and in reports of various mining enterprises,
- incomplete information,
- the lack of many indicators in individual reports,
- because reports are a marketing tool, they try to present the enterprise's activities in an excessively positive way, negative information is usually omitted,
- many reports lack information that allows verification of data reliability,
- there is no external verification of many reports.

(Boral and Henri, 2015)

Reporting on corporate social responsibility is certainly necessary to show that mining enterprises are actually involved in implementing a sustainable development strategy. However, as the analyses show, as of today, this reporting is incomplete and does not completely accomplish its function. In the future, particular attention should be paid to the compatibility of reports and ensuring that all mining sector organisations report exactly the same information, using the same measures. This will not only ensure greater comparability of reports, but also – in such a situation – it will be much more difficult to hide data that is inconvenient for the organisation, as they will not be able to omit it in the reports.

Bibliography

2030 Agenda (2015). https://www.gov.pl/web/rozwoj-technologia/agenda-2030 [access date: 24. 04. 2020].

Alizar, A.M., Scott, R. (2009). Working at the Local Level to Support Sustainable Mining. *Canadian Mining Journal*, 130 (3), 24–25.

Angelakoglou, K., Gaidajis, G. (2020). A Conceptual Framework to Evaluate the Environmental Sustainability Performance of Mining Industrial Facilities. *Sustainability*, 12 (5), 2135.

Arredondo, A., Recamán, A.L., Castrejón, B. (2020). Universal Health Coverage in the Framework of the 2030 Global Agenda for Sustainable Development: Agreements and Challenges. *Journal of Global Health*, 10 (1), 010316.

Boral, O., Henri, J.F. (2015). Is Sustainability Performance Comparable? A Study of GRI Reports of Mining Organizations. *Business & Society*, 56 (2), 1–30.

Borujeni, M.P., Gitnavard, H. (2017). Evaluating the Sustainable Mining Contractor Selection Problems: An Imprecise Last Aggregation Preference Selection Index Method. *Journal of Sustainable Mining*, 16 (4), 207–218.

Bowen, H. (1953). *Social Responsibility of the Businessman*. Harper & Row: New York.

Braun, T., Henning, A., Lottermoser, B.G. (2017). The Need for Sustainable Technology Diffusion in Mining: Achieving the Use of Belt Conveyor Systems in the German Hard-rock Quarrying Industry. *Journal of Sustainable Mining*, 16 (1), 24–30.

Brown, L. R. (2011). *World on the Edge: How to Prevent Environmental and Economic Collapse*. W.W. Norton & Company: New York, London.

Brundtland, G.H. (1987). *Our Common Future*. https://www.are.admin.ch/dam/are/en/dokumente/nachhaltige_entwicklung/dokumente/bericht/our_common_futurebrundtlandreport1987.pdf.download.pdf/our_common_futurebrundtlandreport1987.pdf [access date: 24. 04. 2020].

Burchart-Korol, D., Krawczyk, P., Czaplicka-Kolarz, K., Turek, M. (2014). Development of Sustainability Assessment Method of Coal Mines. *Journal of Sustainable Mining*, 13 (4), 5–11.

Carrots and Sticks for Starters (2006). *Current Trends and Approaches in Voluntary and Mandatory Standards for Sustainability Reporting*. UNEP & KPMG.

Carvalho, F.P., Oliveira, J.M., Malta, M. (2014). Exposure to Radionuclides in Smoke from Vegetation Fires. *Science of the Total Environment*, 472, 421–424.

Carvalho, F.P. (2017). Mining Industry and Sustainable Development: Time for Change. *Food and Energy Security*, 6 (2), 61–77.

Chang, S.E., Stone, J., Demes, K., Piscitelli, M. (2014). Consequences of Oil Spills: A Review and Framework for Informing Planning. *Ecology and Society*, 19, 26–36.

Dahlsrud, A. (2006). How Corporate Social Responsibility Is Defined: An Analysis of 37 Definitions. *Corporate Social Responsibility and The Environmental Protection*, 15 (1), 1–23.

Dashwood, H.S. (2007). Towards Sustainable Mining: The Corporate Role in the Construction of Global Standards. *Multinational Business Review*, 15 (1), 47–66.

Dashwood, H.S. (2012). CSR Norms and Organizational Learning in the Mining Sector. *Corporate Governance*, 12 (1), 118–138.

Dino, G.A., Cavallo, A., Rossetti, P., Garamvölgyi, E., Sandor, R., Coulon, F. (2020). Towards Sustainable Mining: Exploiting Raw Materials from Extractive Waste Facilities. *Sustainability*, 12 (6), 2383.

Dobele, A.R., Westberg, K., Steel, M., Flowers, K. (2014). An Examination of Corporate Social Responsibility Implementation and Stakeholder Engagement: A Case Study in the Australian Mining Industry. *Business Strategy and the Environment*, 23 (3), 145–159.

Donaldson, T., Preston, L.E. (1995). The Stakeholder Theory of the Corporation: Concepts, Evidence, and Implications. *Academy of Management Review*, 20 (1), 65–91.

Dong, S., Xu, Lei. (2016). The Impact of Explicit CSR Regulation: Evidence from China's Mining Firms. *Journal of Applied Accounting Research*, 17 (2), 237–258.

Drebenstedt, C. (2008). Responsible Mining – Approaches and Realization. *Proceedings 22nd World Mining Congress – Innovations and Challenges in Mining*, 1, Istanbul, 135–147.

Drucker, P. (2010). *The Changing World of the Executive*. Harvard Business Press: New York.

Dubiński, J. (2013). Sustainable Development of Mining Mineral Resources. *Journal of Sustainable Mining*, 12 (1), 1–6.

Dubiński, J., Turek M. (2006): Proces restrukturyzacji a ochrona środowiska na terenach górniczych. *Bezpieczeństwo Pracy i Ochrona Środowiska w Górnictwie*, 12, 4–9.

Dubiński, J., Czaplicka-Kolarz, K., Stańczyk, K., Świadrowski, J. (2007). Produkcja paliw ciekłych i gazowych z węgla – szanse i perspektywy, *Wiadomości Górnicze*, 58(5), 273–278.

Essah, M., Andrews, N. (2016). Linking or De-linking Sustainable Mining Practices and Corporate Social Responsibility? Insights from Ghana. *Resources Policy*, 50, 75–85.

Fernández-Lozanoa, J., Palao-Vicente, J.J., Blanco-Sánchez, J.A., Gutiérrez-Alonso, G., Remondo, J., Bonachea, J., Morellón, M., González-Díeza, A. (2019). Gold-bearing Plio-Quaternary Deposits: Insights from Airborne LiDAR Technology into the Landscape Evolution during the Early Roman Mining Works in North-west Spain, *Journal of Archaeological Science: Reports*, 24, 843–855.

Fonseca, A., McAllister, M.L., Fitzpatrick, P. (2014). Sustainability Reporting among Mining Corporations: A Constructive Critique of the GRI Approach. *Journal of Cleaner Production*, 84, 70–83.

G4 Sector Disclosures. Mining and Metals (2013). Global Reportive Initiative: Amsterdam. https://cdn2.hubspot.net/hubfs/2642721/Recursos/Guias%20y%20Estandares/Suplem entos%20sectoriales%20G4/GRI-G4-Mining-and-Metals-Sector-Disclosures%20(1).pdf [access date: 30. 03. 2021].

Global Reporting Initiative (2020). https://www.globalreporting.org/ [access date: 24. 04. 2020]

Günther, E., Hoppe, H., Poser, C. (2007). Environmental Corporate Social Responsibility of Firms in the Mining and Oil and Gas Industries: Current Status Quo of Reporting Following GRI Guidelines. *Greener Management International*, 53, 7–25.

Hąbek, P. (2014). Evaluation of Sustainability Reporting Practices in Poland. *Quality & Quantity*, 48, 1739–1752.

Hąbek, P., Wolniak, R. (2013). Analysis of Approaches to CSR Reporting in Selected European Union Countries. *International Journal of Economics and Research*, 4 (6), 79–95.

Hąbek, P., Wolniak, R. (2016). Assessing the Quality of Corporate Social Responsibility Reports: The Case of Reporting Practices in Selected European Union Member States. *Quality & Quantity*, 50 (1), 339–420.

Harfst, J., Wirth, P. (2011). Structural Change in Former Mining Regions: Problems, Potentials and Capacities in Multi-level-governance Systems. *Procedia-social and Behavioral Sciences*, 14, 167–176.

Hass, J.L., Brunvoll, F., Hoie, H. (2002). Overview of Sustainable Development Indicators Used by National and International Agencies. ECD Statistics Working Papers. OECD: Paris.

Hickel, J. (2020). The Sustainable Development Index: Measuring the Ecological Efficiency of Human Development in the Anthropocene. *Ecological Economics*, 167, 1–10.

Hilson, G. (2002). An Overview of Land Use Conflicts in Mining Communities. *Land Use Policy*, 19, 65–73.

Hilson, A., Hilson, G., Dauda, S. (2019). Corporate Social Responsibility at African mines: Linking the past to the present. *Journal of Environmental Management*, 241, 340–352.

Huang, J., Tian, Ch., Xing, L., Bian, Z., Miao, X. (2017). Green and Sustainable Mining: Underground Coal Mine Fully Mechanized Solid Dense Stowing-Mining Method. *Sustainability*, 9 (8), 1418.

Idowu, S.O., Schmiedpeter, R., Liangrong, Z. (2019). *The Future of the UN Sustainable Development Goals: Business Perspectives for Global Development in 2030*. Springer.

IEA [International Energy Agency] (2019). World Energy Balances. https://www.iea.org/regions/eurasia [access date: 24. 04. 2020]

IEA [International Energy Agency] (2020). Data and Statistics. https://www.iea.org/data-and-statistics?country=WORLD&fuel=Energy%20supply&indicator=Total%20primary%20energy%20supply%20(TPES)%20by%20source [access date: 29. 03. 2021].

Jenkins, H. (2004). Corporate Social Responsibility and the Mining Industry: Conflicts and Constructs. *Corporate Social Responsibility and Environmental Management*, 11 (1), 23–34.

Jonek-Kowalska, I. (2016). Sustainable Development as a Challenge for Polish Coal Mining Enterprises. *Scientific Papers of Silesian University of Technology. Organization and Management Series*, 95, 131–145.

Jonek-Kowalska, I., Zieliński, M. (2018). Social and Economic Aspects of CSR in Employment Restructuring of the Polish Coal Mining. In: *Aktualne problemy podnikovej sféry 2018. Zborník vedeckych prac*. Stefan Majtan a kolektiv. Ekonomicka Univerzita v Bratislave. Fakulta Podnikoveho Manazmentu. Katedra Podnikovohospodarska. Bratislava: Vydavatel'stvo Ekonom, 589–598.

Jones, A., Jonas, G. (2011). Corporate Social Responsibility Reporting: The Growing Need for Input from the Accounting Profession. *CPA Journal*, 81 (2), 65–78.

Juergensen, L., Premji, S., Wright, B., Holmes, D., Bouma, G. (2020). "A Time to Lead". Efforts to Promote Social Justice: The Promise and Challenges of the United Nations 2030 Agenda and Sustainable Development Goals for Nurses. *International Journal of Nursing Studies*, 104, 103533.

Kamaljit, S.B., Seidler, R. (2009). *Dimensions of Sustainable Development*. Eolss Publisher: Oxford.

Kemp, D. (2010). Community Relations in the Global Mining Industry: Exploring the Internal Dimensions of Externally Orientated Work. *Corporate Social Responsibility and Environmental Management*, 17 (1), 1–14.

Kepore, K.P., Imbun, B.Y. (2011). Mining and Stakeholder Engagement Discourse in a Papua New Guinea Mine. *Corporate Social Responsibility and Environmental Management*, 18 (4).

Kijewska, A., Bluszcz, A. (2016). Kierunki zmian w sprawozdawczości przedsiębiorstw górniczych. Studia Ekonomiczne. *Zeszyty Naukowe Uniwersytetu Ekonomicznego w Katowicach*, 267, 43–54.

Kudełko, J., Hop, N., Kozłowska-Pęciak, W., Bachowski, C. (2016). Raportowanie społecznej odpowiedzialności biznesu w przemyśle wydobywczym według wytycznych Global Reportive Initiative. *Nauki o Zarządzaniu*, 28 (3), 72–92.

Ledoux, L., Mertens, R., Wolff, P. (2005). EU Sustainable Development Indicators: An Overview. *Natural Resources Forum*, 29, 392–403.

Marinina, O. (2019). Analysis of Trends and Performance of CSR Mining Companies. *IOP Conference Series: Earth and Environmental Science*, 302 (1), 012120.

Mathu, K.M., Scheepers, C. (2016). Leading Change Towards Sustainable Green Coal Mining. *Emerald Emerging Markets Case Studies*, 6 (3).

Michaelides, E.E.S. (2012). *Alternative Energy Sources*. Springer: New York.

Monteiro, N.B.R., da Silva, E.A., Moita Neto, J.M. (2019). Sustainable Development Goals in Mining. *Journal of Cleaner Production*, 228, 509–520.

Moomen, A.-W., Bertolotto, M., Lacroix, P., Jensen, D. (2019). Inadequate Adaptation of Geospatial Information for Sustainable Mining Towards Agenda 2030 Sustainable Development Goals. *Journal of Cleaner Production*, 238, 117954.

Morsing, M., Schultz, M. (2006). Corporate Social Responsibility: Communication, Response and Involvement Strategies. *Business Ethics: A European Review*, 15 (4), 323–334.

Mutti, D., Yakovleva, N., Vazquez-Brust, D., Di Marco, M.H. (2012). Corporate Social Responsibility in the Mining Industry: Perspectives from Stakeholder Groups in Argentina. *Resources Policy*, 37 (2), 212–222.

Narula, S.A., Magray, M.A., Desore, A. (2017). A Sustainable Livelihood Framework to Implement CSR Project in Coal Mining Sector. *Journal of Sustainable Mining*, 16 (3), 83–93.

Nwachukwu, M.A., Ronald, M., Feng, H. (2017). Global Capacity, Potentials and Trends of Solid Waste Research and Management. *Waste Management Research*, 35 (9), 923–934.

Ogrodnik, R., Mieszaniec, J. (2013). Górnictwo węgla kamiennego w kontekście zrównoważnego rozwoju. *Research Papers of Wrocław University of Economics*, 219, 116–125.

Owusu, O., Banash, K.J., Mensah, A.K. (2019). "Small in Size, but Big in Impact": Socio-environmental Reforms for Sustainable Artisanal and Small-scale Mining. *Journal of Sustainable Mining*, 18 (1), 38–44.

Peck, P., Sinding, K. (2003). Environmental and Social Disclosure and Data Richness in the Mining Industry. *Business Strategy and the Environment*, 12, 131–146.

Pegg, S. (2006). Mining and Poverty Reduction: Transforming Rhetoric into Reality. *Journal of Cleaner Production*, 14 (3), 376–387.

Peralta, S., Sasmito, A.P., Kumral, M. (2016). Reliability Effect on Energy Consumption and Greenhouse Gas Emissions of Mining Hauling Fleet Towards Sustainable Mining. *Journal of Sustainable Mining*, 15 (3), 85–94.

Ponomarenko, T.V., Wolniak, R., Marinina, O.A. (2016). Corporate Social Responsibility in Coal Industry (Practices of Russian and European Companies). *Journal of Mining Institute*, 222, 882–891.

Rakowska, A., Cichorzewska, A.M. (2012). Instances of Corporate Social Responsibility in Coal Mining: An Example of Chosen Polish mines. In: V. Dermol, N.T. Sirca, G. Dakovic, U. Lindav, T. Vukasovic (Eds.), *Knowledge and Learning: Global Empowerment*. Proceedings of the Management, Knowledge and Learning International Conference 2012, 20–22 June 2012, Celje, Slovenia, 393–401.

Ramaganesh, M., Bathrinath, S. (2020). Analysing Environmental Factors for Corporate Social Responsibility in Mining Industry Using ISM Methodology. *Advances in Intelligent Systems and Computing*, 1057, 349–360.

Reardon, A.C. (Ed.) (2011). *Metallurgy for the Nonmetallurgist*. 2nd ed. ASM International: Materials Park: OH, USA.

Rogers, P.P., Jalal, K.F., Boyd, J.A. (2008). *An Introduction to Sustainable Development*. Glen: London.

Sachs, J., Schmidt-Traub, G., Kroll, C., Lafortune, G., Fuller, G. (2019). *Sustainable Development Report 2019*. Bertelsmann Stiftung and Sustainable Development Solutions Network (SDSN): New York.

Sachs, J.D. (2015). *The Age of Sustainable Development*. Columbia University Press: New York.

Sari, S.R.K., Setiahadi, R. (2019). How Important CSR to Mining Companies: Empirical Case in Indonesia. *IOP Conference Series: Earth and Environmental Science*, 347 (1), 012121.

Sarkar, A.N. (2013). Review of Strategic Policy Framework for Re-Evaluating "CSR" Programme Impacts on the Mining-Affected Areas in India. *International Business, Sustainability and Corporate Social Responsibility*, 11, 217–261.

Singhal, N.S., Dev, A. (2016). Global Reporting Initiative; Sustainability Reporting. Proceedings of the 6th International Conference on Operation and Technology of Offshore Support Vessels, Singapore.

Smil, V. (2004). World History and Energy. In: C. Cleveland (Ed.) *Encyclopedia of Energy*, Vol. 6, Elsevier: Amsterdam, 549–561.

Sustainable Development Index (2020). https://www.sustainabledevelopmentindex. org/about [access date: 29. 03. 2021].

Tang, P., Yang, S., Yang, S. (2020). How to Design Corporate Governance Structures to Enhance Corporate Social Responsibility in China's Mining State-owned Enterprises? *Resources Policy*, 66, Article 101609.

Technical Protocol Applying the Report Content Principles (2011). Global Reporting Initiative.

Trzepacz, P. (2012). *Zrównoważony rozwój – wyzwania globalne*. Instytut Geografii i Gospodarki Przestrzennej UJ: Kraków.

Tuokku, F.X., Kpinpuo, S.D., Hinson, R.E. (2019). Sustainable Development in Ghana's Gold Mines: Clarifying the Stakeholder's Perspective. *Journal of Sustainable Mining*, 18 (2), 77–84.

United Nations Environment Programme. https://www.un.org/youthenvoy/2013/08/ unep-united-nations-environment-programme/ [access date: 24. 04. 2020].

UNSCEAR, (2017). *Sources, Effects and Risks of Ionizing Radiation*. United Nations Scientific Committee on the Effects of Atomic Radiation. UNSCEAR 2016 Report to the General Assembly, with Scientific Annexes. United Nations: New York.

Ventura, J., Saenz, S. (2015). Beyond Corporate Social Responsibility. Towards a Model for Managing Sustainable Mining Operations. Qualitative Research Based upon Best Practices. *Social Responsibility Journal*, 11 (3), 605–621.

Walsh, P.P., Murphy, E., Horan, D. (2020). The Role of Science, Technology and Innovation in the UN 2030 Agenda. *Technological Forecasting and Social Change*, 154, 119957.

Wiktor-Mach, D. (2020). What Role for Culture in the Age of Sustainable Development? UNESCO's Advocacy in the 2030 Agenda Negotiations. *International Journal of Cultural Policy*, 26 (3), 312–327.

Willmer, F.W., Scholtz, R.W. (2018). What Is the Optimal and Sustainable Lifetime of a Mine? *Sustainability*, 10 (2), 480.

Wiśniewska, J., Chojnacka, E. (2016). Weryfikacja danych pozafinansowych przedsiębiorstw odpowiedzialnych społecznie - wyniki badania ankietowego. *Studia Ekonomiczne*, 284, 97–107.

Wolniak, R. (2019). The Corporate Social Responsibility Practices in Australian Mining Sector. In: I. Jonek-Kowalska (Ed.), *Contemporary Management in Extractive Industries: Multidimensional and Practical Approach*. Wydawnictwo Politechniki Śląskiej: Gliwice, 205–217.

World Coal Association (2020). https://www.worldcoal.org/coal/where-coal-found [access date: 29. 03. 2021].

Woźniak, J., Jurczyk, W. (2020). Social and Environmental Activities in the Polish Mining Region in the Context of CSR. *Resources Policy*, 65, 101554.

Yan, G., H.-M. Cho, I. Lee, and G. Kim. (2012). Significant emissions of 210Po by coal burning into the urban atmosphere of Seoul, Korea. *Atmospheric Environment*, 54, 80–85.

Zhiguo, G., Luo, X., Chen, J., Wang, F.L., Lei, J. (Eds.) (2011). *Emerging Research in Web Information Systems and Mining: Communications in Computer and Information Science*. Springer: Berlin.

Zhou, Y. (2020). Integrating Corporate Social Responsibility and Sustainability for Deep Seabed Mining. In: W. Leal Filho, P. Borges de Brito, F. Frankenberger (Eds.) *International Business, Trade and Institutional Sustainability*. World Sustainability Series. Springer: Cham, 499–514.

Zieliński, M., Jonek-Kowalska, I. (2020). Profitability of Corporate Social Responsibility Activities from the Perspective of Corporate Social Managers. *European Research Studies Journal*, 23 (2), 264–280.

2 Stakeholder theory

From a theoretical to mining perspective

Stakeholder theory in the context of sustainable development

Stakeholder theory as an independent trend in the research of general and strategic management has been actively discussed in academic literature for several decades. Such a long and steady interest in this problem indicates, on the one hand, its theoretical and practical significance, and on the other hand, the incompleteness and partial inconsistency of the approach. Over this period, the stakeholder concept has become known to large companies, primarily in resource-based industries.

We agree with the largest Russian institutionalist V. L. Tambovtsev (Tambovcev, 2008) that the initial, implicitly formulated stakeholder concept arose in the early 1930s in A. Berle and M. Dodd's discussion (Berle, 1931; Dodd, 1932). A. Berle believed that corporate management should only care about the wealth of shareholders, whereas M. Dodd emphasized that the goals of the corporation also include safe working places for employees, better product quality for consumers, and benefit to the welfare of the local community. Thus, we can talk about attempts to reconsider the target function of the company. It can be assumed that such reconsideration was associated with the Great Depression of the 1930s and the need to stabilize the lives of workers and cities.

The next step in the development of the stakeholder concept was G. Simon's development of the contribution-inducements model in the 1950s as a logical basis for the formation of organizations. According to the model, potential participants in an organization (entrepreneur, employee, consumer) are offered some incentives for joining it (sales revenue, salaries, goods and services), in exchange for their contribution to the company (Simon, 1952). The model limited the range of potential company participants, but identified their interests.

Since the 1960s, the neoclassical concept of the company has been weakening. As a key development factor, it considers only economic value, which is created by effective allocation and use of resources. The shareholder theory based on this approach considers the company as the means to efficiently transform external resources and achieve economic results, that are assigned to the owners, and only then can be shared with society (inside-out model). This

DOI: 10.4324/9781003091110-4

approach gives grounds for reactive strategies, focused on environmental considerations and impact mitigation.

A dynamically changing environment, with the increasing speed of changes and uncertainty, determines the change of attitudes towards company development. The company concept turns from its internal resources and environment (previously explained by neoclassical theory and the resource dependence approach) to the requirements of the external environment, its subjects, their expectations and demands, that the company must satisfy (outside-in model). Company operation is formed largely by the external environment; the company's strategy becomes proactive, influencing the environment and interacting with it. The behavioural theory of the company (Cyert and March, 1963) states that companies are the result of negotiations between different groups with divergent interests, not strictly related to shareholder wealth maximization. A new paradigm that meets the needs of the time is the new institutional theory (Coase, 1992; Williamson, 1996), in which the company is regarded as a "bundle of contracts" and is closely linked with stakeholder theory.

Since the 1980s, the strengthening social interest in the problem of sustainable development in a broad (macro-level) and narrow sense (the company, the area of presence) has given impetus to the rapid development of the stakeholder concept. This strong external factor forces companies to revise their business goals and stakeholders' interests, and to transform the developed strategies for greater sustainability. The need to change the dominant concept of the company is theoretically justified in the reports on sustainable development (WCED, 1987).

The origin of the company-stakeholder (CS) concept is mainly linked to the Brundtland Report's (WCED, 1987) definition of "sustainable development" and it entails the incorporation of the triple bottom line long-term economic prosperity, social equity, and environmental responsibility into company operational and management practices. Likewise, the CS concept has also been defined as a heuristic multi-criteria approach, composed by economic, social and environmental performance dimensions (Schaltegger and Burritt, 2010).

Freeman's fundamental works have given impetus for conceptualization and the subsequent formation of stakeholder theory in the mid-1980s (Freeman and Reed, 1983; Freeman, 1984; Freeman and Gilbert, 1987; Freeman and Evan 1990). R. Mitchell, B. Agle and D. Wood, T. Berman, A. Wicks, S. Kotha, T.M. Jones, M.C. Jensen, O.E. Williamson (Blagov, 2010; Mitchell et al., 1997), and many other researchers developed various approaches to analyse company–stakeholder relationships, defining the term stakeholders and their identification, and disclosing factors that determine the nature of stakeholder interaction and methods of its management. Back in 1995, the number of publications on the topic exceeded more than 100 articles and more than 10 monographs (Donaldson and Preston, 1995). The interest in this topic has further intensified.

The subject of the stakeholder concept includes three inter-related aspects: definition and classification of stakeholders, identification of their interests, methods and strategies of their actions.

Mitchell et al. (1997) introduced the chronological development of the definition "stakeholder" for the period 1963–1995 and introduced their own classification of stakeholders. Among the 26 definitions, we have distinguished several periods with dominant views:

- 1963–1986 – the period of "nucleation", in which the definition of stakeholders was based on identification and characteristics of "influence" in a broad sense, but little attention was paid to their organizational framework, the classifications were purely empirical;
- 1987–1993 – the period of "formation" with a search for the basis of "influence", much emphasis is put on its contractual nature in the broad sense, the normative basis for classification is applied;
- 1994–1995 – the period of "conceptual development", in which the contractual nature of stakeholder "influence" interpreted the interactions and relationships between the company and its stakeholders as the foundation for the company's value.

At the first stage the concept of stakeholders has been further evolved. It was claimed that the initial stakeholders' priorities should not be only economic. The company should respect all points of view and build the balance of interests to become sustainable. At this preliminary stage the groups of stakeholders have been normalised, changing the approach of analysing them from empirical to analytical.

Various classifications are presented in the framework of the stakeholder concept: primary or secondary stakeholders; as owners and non-owners of the company; as owners of capital or owners of less tangible assets; as actors or those acted upon; as those existing in a voluntary or an involuntary relationship with the company; as rights-holders, contractors, or moral claimants; as resource providers to or dependents of the company; as risk-takers or influencers; and as legal principals, to whom agent-managers bear fiduciary duty (Mitchell et al., 1997). Various theories constitute the basis for the classifications: the agency, behavioural, ecological, institutional, resource dependence, and transaction cost theories of the company. But the attributes are not clarified, thus, classifications can be formed on different grounds.

Stakeholders can be defined in both broader and narrower senses. In a broad sense, stakeholders are any groups or individuals that influence the achievement of company goals (Freeman and Reed, 1983), the attribute of the goal somewhat specifies the managerial nature of stakeholders.

In general, the broad interpretation coincides with the early definition of the Stanford Research Institute (1963), which relates the identification of stakeholders to the survival and continuation of the company's activities (see Steurer et al., 2005). From this definition we can conclude that the list of real stakeholders is open and can be supplemented by potential new ones. It is theoretically acceptable and gives an idea of the whole theoretical universe of stakeholders, however, it is not realistic for practical use.

In the narrow sense (Cornell and Shapiro, 1987), stakeholders are distinguished by specific features, such as risk:

> Voluntary stakeholders bear some form of risk as a result of having invested some form of capital, human or financial, something of value, in a company. Involuntary stakeholders are placed at risk as a result of a company's activities. But without the element of risk there is no stake.
>
> (Clarkson, 1994, p. 5)

Of course, the relationship of risk and interest is the most important, but not the only feature that allows the identification and classification of stakeholders. The identification of risks has great practical significance for the specific conditions of the internal and external environment of the company. Stakeholders, as potential beneficiaries bearing the risk of the company's activity, are the following: owners, buyers, resource providers, employees, the local community, various community groups, the state.

Primary categories of stakeholders (distinguished on the basis of resource assessment and risk) include persons most interested in the company's activities (investors, personnel, customers, suppliers); without them, the company cannot operate. Secondary categories of stakeholders may not support company policy; therefore, their influence is less significant.

At the second stage, the concept evolves both qualitatively and quantitatively. Researchers intensively analysed interests and needs of stakeholders, as well as assessed and measured the company's response to their expectations. The concept of corporate social responsibility (CSR) is formed to explore the company–society interaction (Raza et al., 2012; Jones, 1980; Carroll, 1999; Carroll, 1991; Gilbert and Uoorhis, 2003); its object is the social group of stakeholders that have more than just economical claims. The main methodological problem of this stage is the attempt to quantify and evaluate expectations and results, which is not always possible. For example, Kujala et al. (2016, p.28) demonstrate that "the responsiveness approach seeks to identify the most important stakeholders, analyse the interests and needs of these stakeholders, and measure responses to stakeholder expectations. Measures for analysing the connection between social responsibility and social performance have also been developed" (e.g., Berman et al., 1999; Kobeissi and Damanpour, 2009; Orlitzky et al., 2003).

At the third stage (by the mid-1990s), the stakeholder theory tools were gradually formed, and fundamental works were published. These works have significantly affected further development of stakeholder theory. For example, summarizing a 10-year context and development experience, Mitchell et al. (1997) made an important contribution to the stakeholder theory by defining the principle of who and what really counts in stakeholder management. They identified three attributes that serve as a basis for stakeholder salience: power of the stakeholder, urgency of the demand made by the stakeholder, and the legitimacy of the stakeholder demand. Their theoretical framework, the salience model, is one of the best-known models. It is dynamic and enables the company to manage interactions with stakeholders.

Thus, by the mid-1990s, the fundamental principles of today's stakeholder theory had developed:

- the company has relationships with a large number of groups and individuals (stakeholders) that make up its environment (internal and external) and influence or are influenced by the company's decisions;
- stakeholder theory explores the nature of these relationships (the processes that accompany the relationship and the results of the resource exchange for the company and its stakeholders);
- the interests of all stakeholders are potentially entitled to be taken into account and satisfied;
- stakeholder theory can be used in management when making management decisions.

(Jones and Wicks, 1999)

When identifying stakeholders, it is essential to consider the fact that any individual or group interested in the company's activities is surrounded by a huge number of other groups and individuals, who also associate their interests with the company. It is impossible to take into account all existing and potential interests. It is also impossible to agree on the interests and responses to them with all other subjects. Therefore, there is a need to select the most important entities from the set of those groups and individuals. This raises the core problem of identifying stakeholders and their significance.

When identifying the interests of stakeholders, it has been found that stakeholders are the owners of "certain" resources for the company and they also acquire "certain" results from it. Different interpretations of the resource theory can explain the nature of their interests. The methods and strategies of stakeholders' behaviour determine the ways of influence to best serve the interests of stakeholders. The ability to implement a specific strategy is directly related to the nature of the resource relationship.

The next 25 years of dynamic large-scale development of stakeholder theory focus on several areas overlapping with other concepts and form the current trends of its development:

1   Corporate sustainability research that takes into account the relationship with sustainable development concepts (Ivashkovskaya, 2009); Antolín-López et al., 2016).
2   Corporate Social Responsibility (CSR) research that takes into account the relationship with the concepts of corporate social responsibility (Blagov, 2010; Ponomarenko and Marinina, 2017).
3   Theoretical justification for creating company value that takes into account the relationship with the concept of shared value (Porter and Kramer, 2006, 2011).

4   Application in management, taking into account the relationship with the theory of strategic management (Tambovcev, 2008; Katkalo, 2008).
5   Application in corporate management, taking into account the relationship with contractual theory and the concept of residual income rights and control of stakeholders (Barkhatov et al., 2014).
6   Applications of stakeholder theory.

In addition, stakeholder theory is currently criticized in some aspects. For example, the authors Narbel and Muff (2017) identified two key limitations:

1   The need to measure public needs through the economic performance of companies;
2   The need to develop a regulatory mechanism for negative externalities.

Indeed, value creation is in the focus of stakeholder theory. But the issues of determining and measuring the social and economic value in the short and long term and establishing their balance do not have a satisfactory solution. And this is further complicated by the existence of the unlimited range of stakeholders, whose interests must be taken into account.

As noted in the study by Narbel and Muff (2017), the transformation of stakeholder theory is carried out in the direction from the actual social problems to win–win solutions for the company and society. The main results (based on the combination of the sustainable development concept and stakeholder theory) formulate and clarify the core objective of any company as "creating value for all stakeholders", studying ways to measure value and develop tools for its growth, justifying methods to increase corporate sustainability.

There is, hitherto, no single approach to understanding corporate sustainability as an economic category, but there are many tools for measuring it (Antolín-López et al., 2016). So, it should be noted that, although the CS concept has received growing attention from academics (e.g. Schaltegger and Burritt, 2010) and practitioner scholars (e.g. Porter and Kramer, 2011) over the past decade, research has been mainly focused on understanding the adoption drivers of CS practices (e.g. Berrone and Gómez-Mejía, 2009; Delmas and Montiel, 2009). Other relevant aspects of CS, such as corporate sustainability performance measurement (CSPM), remain underexplored despite its prominence in the business arena (Chelli and Gendron, 2013; Maas and Reniers, 2014). There have been relatively few attempts to provide insights on how to measure sustainability performance (e.g. Krajnc and Glavič, 2005; Searcy and Elkhawas, 2012), and most of them focus on a more macro level. Furthermore, most of the studies addressing sustainability performance at the corporate level have analysed a single dimension of CS, mainly environmental sustainability (e.g. Delmas and Montiel, 2009; Herva et al., 2011).

There are many definitions of CS associated with numerous interests of various stakeholders, and the discussion on the conceptualization of sustainable development for the corporate level continues (Searcy and Elkhawas, 2012; van

Marrewijk, 2003) with some consensus. The following questions remain unaddressed: Which components of the economy, environment, and society should be measured? How to determine the results? How to choose weights and take into account sector specifics of companies? How are activities of companies reflected in CS.

The analysis of publications on the topic showed that the very definition of CS developed on the basis of the evolution of sustainable development ideas. Gladwin et al. (2006) defined the term "sustaincentrism" as the process of achieving human development in an inclusive, connected, equitable, prudent, and secure manner. Sustainable development components are:

a   inclusiveness (environmental and human systems, near and far, present and future),
b   connectivity (world problems interconnected and interdependent),
c   equity (fair distribution of resources and property rights),
d   prudence (duties of care and prevention), and
e   security (safety from chronic threats).

It should be noted, that a long discussion in the scientific literature for sustainability of the corporate level reflects the discussion for the global level, where, above all, issues of ecologically sustainable development were raised. At the global level, environmental issues of sustainable development dominated in 1970–1990. As a result, the concepts of strong and weak sustainability (Costanza and Daly, 1992; Costanza et al., 1997) were formed. For the development of the economy, the concepts of the anthropocentric approach, ecological economy, "green economy", and the "three-tiered approach" were substantiated (Biely et al, 2018; Hjorth and Bagheri, 2006; Di Maio and Rem, 2015). Since 1995, after a large-scale discussion in the *Academy of Management Review* special issue (see Donaldson and Preston, 1995), the concept of "environmental sustainability" has become theoretically significant for the corporate level.

Since the mid-1990s, various views on corporate sustainability have been formulated and attempts have been made to integrate them into the development strategies of companies aimed at creating common value. An important methodological problem that has not been resolved to date is the inconsistency of SD indicators at the macro and micro levels, as has been termed by Dyllick and Muff (2015) as the "big disconnect". They emphasized that it is necessary to answer two questions: first, what contribution does corporate sustainability make to sustainable development at the macro level, and second, under what conditions does a business become sustainable. The authors propose a new typology of corporate sustainability strategies to answer these questions: Business Sustainability 1.0 (Refined Shareholder Value Management) to Business Sustainability 2.0 (Managing for the Triple Bottom Line) and to Business Sustainability 3.0 (True Sustainability).

We agree with the authors that the requirements of global sustainable development have a strong influence on company strategies. This can be observed in large

Russian companies of the mineral resource complex, which choose goals from the SDG-2030 (https://www.undp.org/sustainable-development-goals) and formulate corporate strategies in terms of these goals. In corporate reporting, it is noted that the implementation of SD requirements provides both tangible benefits and intangible results: for example, "tangible benefits in the form of reduced costs and risks of doing business, as well as through intangible benefits in the form of increased brand reputation, increased attractiveness to talent, and increased competitiveness" (Haanaes et al., 2012; UN Global Compact & Accenture, 2010). "But this good news is not reflected in studies monitoring the state of our planet" (Dyllick and Muff, 2015).

Despite the lack of results reflecting the relationship between CS and SD at the macro level, there is no doubt that achieving CS is impossible without the interconnected development of economic, natural and social capital, taking into account the irreplaceability and irrevocability of the latter (Blagov, 2011). Scholars seem to agree that CS is composed of three dimensions, namely economic, social and environmental, otherwise referred to as the 3Ps approach to business (Profit, People, Planet) or the "triple bottom line" (e.g. Elkington, 1998; Hart and Milstein, 2003; Antolín-López et al., 2016). Such interpretations agree well with the concept of SD, resource and institutional theories, and link the stakeholder concept with them.

We hold the view that stakeholder theory is the ideological foundation of the concept of corporate social responsibility, which can influence the behaviour of a business (Ponomarenko et al., 2016). Therefore, both the stakeholder concept and the CSR concept explain the partial shift of the company's goals from maximization of shareholders' benefits to multi-objective maximization of stakeholders' benefits. According to M. Jensen (2002), the target function of a company, which takes into account the interests of all categories of its stakeholders, cannot be clearly described and specified. Instead of maximizing one indicator, one should consider the value search function, or multidimensional quantity.

Many studies have shown that, with a focus on creating value for stakeholders, strategic management must be changed, and some tools have been proposed. Shrivastava (1995) proposed that the way to achieve sustainability was through the integration of four mechanisms:

a   total quality environmental management,
b   ecological sustainable competitive strategies,
c   technology-for-nature swaps, and
d   corporate population impact control (Antolín-López et al., 2016).

Blagov (2006) defined "corporate sustainable development" as a tridimensional construct composed of:

a   economic prosperity achieved through value creation,
b   social equity through corporate social responsibility, and
c   environmental integrity through corporate environmental management.

C. Laszlo's model (Blagov, 2011) of the development of the "sustainable company" justifies the creation of sustainable value, which is formed when the company creates value for shareholders, without encroaching on other stakeholders' interests. Thus, the company creates new opportunities (through profile raising, product differentiation, staff motivation, cost improvement, entering new markets) and reduces risks (loss of customers, strengthening of state regulations and penalties, reducing market share). These processes aim at achieving goals, fulfilling the interests of stakeholders, and improving their satisfaction as a result of stakeholder interaction management.

The interdependence of stakeholders' interests and goals with the company's goals and results determines their motivation and potential opportunities to act as resources for the company (Ponomarenko and Sergeev, 2012). The interaction between stakeholders and the company has a complex and predominantly non-financial nature, but it relies on a resource basis.

Porter and Kramer (2011) made a new attempt to revise the concept of CSR and the stakeholder concept. Called the Concept of Shared Value (CSV), their theory was developed in the continuation of the authors' previous research in the field of strategic management (Porter and Kramer, 2006). CSV can be defined as policies and operating practices that enhance the competitiveness of a company while simultaneously advancing the economic and social conditions in the communities in which it operates. Shared value creation focuses on identifying and expanding the connections between societal and economic progress (Porter and Kramer, 2011). Porter and Kramer's publication received a great response in the academic environment, including a number of critical works (Crane et al., 2014; Meyer, 2018). Significant shortcomings of the new concept were the lack of a definition of "social value", the impossibility of measuring it, and the weak theoretical validity of the new concept. It was underlined that the author argued that, in the absence of a general definition, social value consisting of outputs and outcomes can only be legitimately created and measured if there is agreement amongst relevant stakeholders, which crucially includes public policy-makers (Beschorner, 2013).

The work of Post, Preston, and Sachs (2002) emphasizes the importance of interactions with stakeholders, especially for complex "extended enterprises" (corporations, in the modern sense) that are becoming "the most important asset and the ultimate source of organizational wealth." Werther and Chandler (2005) suggest that the right balance of company strategy, intangible asset management, and CSR leads to a sustainable competitive advantage of the corporation.

Different stakeholder groups may have competing interests that fail to meet the purpose of maximizing the fundamental value. A number of studies (Ivashkovskaya, 2008, 2009) have shown that the account of stakeholders' interests is a condition for maximizing shareholder value in the long run and higher added value for key stakeholders. Such a model "solves the problem of creating a harmonious company, in which the management cycle is subordinated to the structuring of multiple interests and achieving a balance in it.

Balanced interests form a special quality of relationships with stakeholders" (Ivashkovskaya, 2009, p. 201).

The company's responsibilities to stakeholders comprise four levels (Blagov, 2011). The first level includes the development of a value system to improve the welfare of stakeholders (consumers, other primary stakeholders, and others). At the same time, the company forms a model for meeting the expectations of the most important stakeholders. The second level involves ensuring the stability and balance of interaction with stakeholders in a changing environment. The third level requires an active position of the managers or owners to the stakeholders. Finally, the fourth level implies ethical leadership.

The interests of stakeholders have a decisive influence on the implementation of the selected business model and the achievement of the strategic goals of the company. Inattention to them usually leads to problems with the strategy implementation, based on a conflict of interests. Therefore, the development of a pro-stakeholder strategy ensures a compromise between various groups interested in the company's activities, provides added value for owners and other stakeholders, and fulfils social commitments.

Fundamental stakeholder classifications

Classifications of stakeholders in the present-day scientific literature (Freeman, 1984; Newbould and Luffman, 1989; Savage et al., 1991; Clarkson, 1995; Mitchell et al., 1997; Harrison, 1998; Dauling, 2003; Androsenko, 2007; Rodriguez et al., 2002; Nikitina, 2010; Ponomarenko et al., 2016; Zil'bershtejn et al., 2016; Jonek-Kowalska et al., 2018; Finogeeva, 2019) depend on the goals and objectives set in different periods of time. As already noted, the classification can be based on various conceptual approaches to the company.

On the basis of stakeholder identification, the methods are divided into descriptive (empirical) and normative. On the basis of detecting stakeholders' interests, the methods can be divided into analytical and reconstructional.

Among empirical methods, the following classifications are distinguished:

1   Classification based on the environment (Freeman, 1984; Clarkson, 1994; Harrison, 1998) ranking internal and external stakeholders. It is comparable with the classification of the internal and external environment (direct and indirect actions) in management. A simplified list of stakeholders includes owners, consumers, consumer rights protection, competitors, the media, employees, Special Interest Group (SIG), environmentalists, suppliers, government, and local communities (Blagov, 2011).

2   Classification based on the main resource functions of stakeholders (Newbould and Luffman, 1989; Dauling, 2003; Androsenko, 2007; Konstantinov, 2009; Nikitina, 2010):

- a group of stakeholders financing the organization (shareholders, investors, lending institutions);

- organization management;
- main employees;
- economic partners (suppliers, buyers).

3 This classification involves ranking according to basic functions necessary for the company's operability. The financial function combines stakeholders with different interests, while the interests of the state are not included.

4 Classification based on supporting functions of stakeholders (Dauling, 2003):

- authorizing: state bodies, shareholders, board of directors;
- current: employees, suppliers, service organizations;
- diffuse: media, special interest groups, local community, non-profit organizations;
- consumers.

5 This classification combines the resource-based view, functions and various types of the environment.

6 Classification based on types of influence on the company (Rodriguez et al. 2002):

- substantial: shareholders, investors, employees, strategic partners;
- contractual: suppliers, associate contractors, buyers, financial institutions;
- contextual: state and administrations, local community, public organizations; public opinion makers.

7 This classification relies on contractual and institutional theory of the company.

8 Classification based on the influence and functions of stakeholders (Yakubov, 2014):

- regulatory groups: government authorities, industry associations, tripartite commissions, professional associations;
- consumers;
- functional groups: shareholders, owners, top management, managers, employees, investors, creditors, competitors, suppliers, intermediaries, service organizations and dealers;
- diffuse: media, non-profit organization, special interest groups.

9 An important advantage of this classification is the expansion of the list of stakeholders in regulatory groups.

10 Classification based on significance, functions, types of influence and environment (Finogeeva, 2019), as well as the specifics of the functioning of integrated companies:

a internal or intra-group strategic stakeholders (determining and influencing strategic and operational activities):

- shareholders/owners of the company;

- management of both the holding company and its subsidiaries and affiliates;
- employees of all categories of personnel: direct labour, engineers, employees, non-industrial staff, managers and specialists;
- all employees (including employees of the holding company, subsidiaries and affiliates) and external part-time employees, as well as employees who previously worked at enterprises of the group and potential employees and their families;
- subsidiaries and affiliates that are part of a corporation or holding;

b external strategic and operational stakeholders (groups affecting the sustainable development of the company, operating activities of the holding, uninterrupted manufacture and product sales):

- buyers / customers / clients (products, works, services sold both on behalf of the holding company and on behalf of subsidiaries and affiliated companies independently);
- business partners, including suppliers and contractors, strategic project partners;
- institutional investors;

c external regulatory and controlling stakeholders (establishing and regulating the legal framework of the organization, affecting the strategic development of the holding):

- state authorities, regional and municipal administrations;
- lending organization;
- stock market;
- non-profit organizations, public associations;

d other external stakeholders that determine the company's reputation and market position, affect its strategic development:

- industry competitors (on the Russian and world markets);
- media;
- scientific community and educational institutions;
- local community.

11 This classification fully reflects the specifics of integrated companies with many different stakeholders.

Apart from different functions, goals and interests, stakeholders hold different positions in value hierarchy. This approach presents classifications based on stakeholders' level of interest and influence (Lindenberg and Crosby, 1981), cooperation and competition (Freeman, 1984), cooperation and threat (Savage et al., 1991), urgency, legitimacy and influence (Mitchell et al., 1997).

Cameron et al. (2011) defined a process for ranking stakeholders based on needs and the relative importance of stakeholders to others in the network.

Fletcher et al. (2003) defined a process for mapping stakeholder expectations based on value hierarchies and key performance indicators. Turner et al. (1999) have developed a process of identification, assessment of awareness, support, and influence, leading to strategies for communicating and assessing stakeholder satisfaction, and determining who is aware or ignorant and whether their attitude is supportive or opposing.

The prevailing approach to classifying stakeholders' value is introduced by Mitchel's model (Mitchell et al., 1997). It characterizes stakeholders in terms of the presence of one or more attributes, such as power, legitimacy and urgency of their claim. The classification is presented as a management tool where stakeholders are divided into the following groups:

- definitive,
- dangerous,
- dependent,
- dominant,
- dormant,
- discretionary,
- demanding.

The combination of the three listed attributes – power, legitimacy and urgency – defines stakeholder salience. Stakeholders with one attribute are the least influential and belong to the latent class; possessing two attributes belong to the "expectant" class; possessing all three attributes form the most influential categorical group. This approach has an undeniable advantage as it allows the formation (or adjustment) of a behaviour strategy for each stakeholder.

The analysis of literature sources showed that sector specifications in the classifications are insufficiently presented. This means that individual sectors cannot identify specific groups of stakeholders, their resources, their power and interests. Therefore, the implementation of entrepreneurial or project activities in such sectors (primarily resource-oriented) often encounters company–stakeholder problems. Projects and activities of companies can be stopped or terminated if the stakeholder interests are not fully identified or their dynamic pattern is not considered.

The researchers Jonek-Kowalska et al. (2018) and Ponomarenko et al. (2016) supplement the analytical method with the mineral sector specifications reflecting the complexity of the organizational structure, the influence of logistic, infrastructural and market factors, the high level of state regulation of mining companies, the single-industry (within the sector) focus of mining companies, work in single-industry towns and interaction with the local community. For example, the identification of specific groups (local community, territories of presence) is relevant to all coal mining companies, since the nature of their activities is associated with the use and development of a huge safety exclusion area.

Sustainable development from the perspective of the mining industry

As emphasized many times in the sustainable development and corporate social responsibility, primarily the need to balance economic, social and environmental goals has been stressed, which is largely due to the need to include all stakeholder groups in company management. This idea, however, stands in strong contrast to traditional and well-established economic concepts in which the main goal of the enterprise's operation is to achieve financial profits, and without which it is difficult to think about the survival and development of the enterprise. In many cases, such a view still dominates and shapes the managerial hierarchy of the company's goals, which in turn impedes and sometimes prevents the effective implementation of social responsibility principles. Changing habits and the way of thinking in practice is not easy and requires the ability to put long-term benefits over short-term financial profits. Nevertheless, without changing attitudes and prioritising current consumption, the existence of future generations will be seriously threatened.

In mining companies, the concept of *homo oeconomicus* seems to be very deeply rooted, and results from two key circumstances. First of all, the natural resources extracted by these enterprises are rare, and can be depleted, but they are necessary for the operation of most industries around the world. The temptation to achieve above average profits is in this case very strong and supported by the possibility of monopolizing commodity markets in the region and the world. Most natural resources do not have direct substitutes, therefore mining companies – in addition to maximizing profits from a product made available by nature – also have the opportunity to gain a strategic market position giving them power in shaping the market situation.

Secondly, the activity of mining companies in a given region or country depends on the sufficiency of deposits of a given raw material. After the depletion of geological resources, these enterprises leave the area of their current activity and look for another lucrative location. Therefore, their life cycle is significantly limited by the abundance of deposits and the profitability of their extraction. In such circumstances, long-term relationships with stakeholders are difficult to build. This can cause them to be ended at any time. Therefore, mining companies do not see the sense and benefits accompanying the involvement of stakeholders in the process of creating the value of a mining company, all the more so, as this usually means the necessity of incurring additional financial outlays on social or environmental investments, thinning financial profits.

The economization of mining activities is extremely bright in regions that have a less developed economy and civilization (e.g. Africa, Central and South America, Asia). Very often there is serious social and environmental malpractice. Authorities and local communities do not have the same bargaining power as mining companies. They do not have proper legal regulations. They do not have the adequate business experience. In such regions, usually mining companies are the driving force of the local economy and are a large, if not the largest local employer, therefore they feel they can go unpunished, and without major obstacles and protests, to maximize economic profits, pushing aside or completely ignoring environmental and social goals. In developed economies, in European countries or in the USA, such behaviour is not common, because the mining industry must take into account the opinions and consent of local communities and environmental organizations.

The obstacle to implementing the principles of sustainable development and the rules of social responsibility in the mining industr is not only the pursuit of maximizing economic profit at the micro (enterprise) and meso (region) levels, but also at the macro level on a state level. The extraction of natural resources in many countries is an industry of strategic economic importance, which creates many jobs and is an important stimulus for economic growth and development. This not only applies to emerging markets, such as China or India, but also to such economic powers as the USA or Russia.

It should also be emphasised that in addition to the strong economization of the mining industry, the environmental burden of this industry is what makes the hope of implementing SD and CSR in world mining seem utopic. While social problems can be negotiated and possibly eliminated or neutralised, ecological threats will always accompany mining operations and are simply inevitable. These negative effects can be partially limited, but there are no effective ways to eliminate them completely. At the same time, they are visible and felt many years after the terminating of operations and often pose a threat to human health and life.

Can we therefore talk about sustainable development in mining at all? According to the authors of this monograph, this is not an abstract and utopian topic. It may not be possible to achieve fully sustainable development in the mining industry, but it is worth writing about it and stressing its practical significance. Failure to implement social responsibility in mining companies may well result in further economization of these entities, but ignoring their environmental and ecological problems, taking into account the scale of their operation and impact, may have catastrophic consequences in the form of pauperization of mining regions and/or ecological disasters. An escalation of these consequences is also a threat to individual economies and, consequently, to the whole world. Therefore sustainable development is an opportunity for mining enterprises to take long-term actions that will provide society and economies with access to economically necessary natural resources while minimizing the negative impact on local and regional communities and the natural environment.

In the next part of this monograph, the role of individual stakeholder groups in the implementation and fulfilment of sustainable development principles in the mining industry is analysed. At the same time, a narrower understanding of stakeholders is adopted, in which not only being involved in the activity of a mining company is highlighted, but also bearing the risk associated with the existing relationship, and the expected specific results of being a stakeholder. For each of the identified groups, the goals and scope of involvement in the activities of mining companies, including the fulfilment of the concept of sustainable development, are defined. The adopted division of stakeholders first includes four groups integrally associated with the mining company that are directly involved in its operation and which have the greatest impact on it. These stakeholders are: owners, managers, employees and trade unions. Then, the analysis covers groups operating in the environment of mining companies, which include: suppliers and recipients, competition, local communities and ecological organizations.

Bibliography

Androsenko, N.V. (2007). *Ocenka rezul'tativnosti sistemy menedzhmenta kachestva v organizaciyah na osnove balansa potrebnostej zainteresovannyh storon.* SPb.

Antolín-López, R., Delgado-Ceballos, J., Montiel, I. (2016). Deconstructing Corporate Sustainability: A Comparison of Different Stakeholder Metrics. *Journal of Cleaner Production*, March, 135, 5–17.

Barkhatov, V., Nikolaeva, E., Pletnev, D. (2014). The Possibilities of Positive Use of Residual Control and Income Rights of Stakeholders in the Corporation. *Social and Behavioral Sciences*, 124, 521–527.

Berezhnoj, S.E. (2020). *Promyshlennye kompanii i korennye narody. Opyt Rossijskoj Federacii.* http://www.pandia.org/text/77/295/81354.php. [access date: 30. 03. 2021].

Berle, A.A., Jr. (1931). Corporate Powers as Powers in Trust. *Harvard Law Review*, 44, 1049–1074.

Berman, S.L., Wicks, A.C., Kotha, S., Jones, T.M. (1999). Does Stakeholder Orientation Matter? The Relationship Between Stakeholder Management Models and Firm Financial Performance. *Academy of Management Journal*, 42(5), 488–506.

Berrone, P., Gómez-Mejía, L. R. (2009). Environmental Performance and Executive Compensation: An Integrated Agency-Institutional Perspective. *Academy of Management Journal*, 52(1), 103–126.

Beschorner, T. (2013). Creating Shared Value: The One-Trick Pony Approach. *Business Ethics Journal Review*, 1(17), 106–112.

Biely, K., Maes, D., Passel, S.V. (2018). The Idea of Weak Sustainability Is Illegitimate. *Environment, Development and Sustainability*, 20(1), 223–232.

Blagov, Y.U.E. (2010). *Korporativnaya social'naya otvetstvennost': evolyuciya koncepcii.* Vysshaya shkola menedzhmenta.

Blagov, Y.U.E. (2006). Genesis of the concept of corporate social responsibility. *Bulletin of St. Petersburg University.* Management Series. 2, 3–24.

Blagov, Y.U.E. (2011). Evolution of the CSR concept and the theory of strategic management. *Bulletin of St. Petersburg university.* Management Series. 1, 3–26

Cameron, B.G., Seher, T., Crawley, E.F. (2011). Goals for Space Exploration Based on Stakeholder Value Network Considerations. *Acta Astronautica*, 68, 11–12.

Carroll, A. (1991). The Pyramid of Corporate Social Responsibility: Toward the Moral Management of Organizational Stakeholders. *Business Horizons*, 34(4), 34–48.

Carroll, A. (1999). Corporate Social Responsibility: Evolution of Definitional Construct. *Business and Society*, 268–295.

Chelli, M., Gendron, Y. (2013). Sustainability Ratings and the Disciplinary Power of the Ideology of Numbers. *Journal of Business Ethics*, 112(2), 187–203.

Clarkson, M. (1994). A Risk Based Model of Stakeholder Theory. Proceedings of the Second Toronto Conference on Stakeholder Theory. Centre for Corporate Social Performance & Ethics, University of Toronto: Toronto.

Clarkson, M.A. (1995). Stakeholder Framework for Analyzing and Evaluating Corporate Social Performance. *The Academy of Management Review*, 20(1), 92–117.

Coase, R.H. (1992). The Institutional Structure of Production. *The American Economic Review*, 82(4), 713–719.

Cornell, B., Shapiro A.C. (1987). Corporate Stakeholders and Corporate Finance . *Financial Management*, 16, 5–14.

Costanza, R., d'Arge, R., de Groot, R. (1997). The Value of the World's Ecosystem Services and Natural Capital. *Nature*, 387.

Costanza, R., Daly, H.E. (1992). Natural Capital and Sustainable Development. *Conservation Biology*, 6(1), 37–46.

Crane, A., Palazzo, G., Spence, L.J., Matten, D. (2014). Contesting the Value of "Creating Shared Value". *California Management Review*, 56(2).

Cyert, R., March, J. (1963). *Behavioral Theory of the Firm*. Blackwell: Oxford.

Dauling, G. (2003). *Reputaciya firmy: sozdanie, upravlenie i ocenka effektivnosti*. Konsaltingovaya gruppa «IMIDZH-Kontakt»: INFRA-M. http://pr.pstu.ru/wp-content/uploads/2013/11/Dauling-Grem-Reputaciya-firmy.pdf [access date: 09. 05. 2020].

Delmas, M., Montiel, I. (2009). Greening the Supply Chain: When Is Customer Pressure Effective? *Journal of Economics and Management Strategy*, 18(1), 171–201. doi:10.1111/j.1530-9134.2009.00211.x

Di Maio, F., Rem, P.M. (2015). Recycling, Recycling Rate, Innovation, Policy, Resource Efficiency, Indicators. *Journal of Environmental Protection, 6(10)*.

Dodd, E.M., Jr. (1932). For Whom Are Corporate Managers Trustees? *Harvard Law Review*, 45, 1145–1163.

Donaldson, T., Lee, E.P. (1995). The Stakeholder Theory of the Corporation: Concepts, Evidence, and Implications. *The Academy of Management Review*, 20(1), 65–91.

Donaldson, T., Preston, L.E. (1995). The Stakeholder Theory of the Corporation: Concepts, Evidence, and Implications. *Academy of Management Review*, 20 (1), 65–91.

Dyllick, T., Muff, K. (2015). Clarifying the Meaning of Sustainable Business: Introducing a Typology From Business-as-Usual to True Business Sustainability. *Organization & Environment*, 1–19.

Elkington, J. (1998). *Cannibals with Forks: The Triple Bottom Line of 21st Century Business*. Stony Creek, CT: New Society.

Finogeeva, A.I. (2019). *Formirovanie mekhanizma upravleniya klyuchevymi stekkholderami korporacji*. Moskva.

Finogeeva, A.I. (2019). *Formirovanie mekhanizma upravleniya klyuchevymi stekkholderami korporacii*. Moskva.

Fletcher, A., Guthrie, J., Steane, P. (2003). Mapping Stakeholder Perceptions for a Third Sector Organization. *Journal of Intellectual Capital*, 4(4), 505–527.

Freeman, R.E. (1984). *Strategic Management: A Stakeholder Approach*. Boston: Pitman. doi:10.1017/CBO9781139192675.003

Freeman, R.E., Evan, W. (1990). Corporate Governance: A Stakeholder Interpretation. *The Journal of Behavioral Economics*, 19(4), 337–359.

Freeman, R.E., Gilbert, D.R. (1987). Managing Stakeholder Relationships. In S.P. Sethi, C.M. Falbe (Eds.), *Business and Society: Dimensions of Conflict and Cooperation*. Lexington, MA: Lexington Books.

Freeman, R.E., Reed, D.L. (1983). Stockholders and Stakeholders: A New Perspective on Corporate Governance. *California Management Review*, 25(3), 93–94.

Gilbert, N., Uoorhis, R.A. (2003). Changing Patterns of Social Protection. *International Social Security Series*, 9. New Brunswick (USA) and London (UK): Transaction Publishers.

Gladwin, T., Krause, T., Kennelly, J. (2006). Beyond Eco-efficiency: Towards Socially Sustainable Business. *Sustainable Development*, 3(1), 35–43.

Haanaes, K., Reeves, M., von Streng Velken, I., Audretsch, M., Kiron, D., Kruschwitz, N. (2012). *Sustainability Nears a Tipping Point* (MIT Sloan Management Review and BCG Research Report). Boston, MA: Boston Consulting Group.

Harrison, J.S. (1998). *Strategic Management of Organizations and Stakeholders: Concepts and Cases*. Cincinnati: South-Western College Publishing.

Hart, S.L., Milstein, M.B. (2003). Creating Sustainable Value. *Academy of Management Perspectives*, 17(2), 56–67.

Herva, M., Franco, A., Carrasco, E.F., Roca, E. (2011). Review of Corporate Environmental Indicators. *Journal of Cleaner Production*, 19(15), 1687–1699.

Hjorth, P., Bagheri, A. (2006). Navigating Towards Sustainable Development: A System Dynamics Approach. *Futures*, 38(1), 74–92.

Ivashkovskaya, I.V. (2008). Model of Strategic Cost Analysis of the Firm. *Economic Science of Modern Russia*, 3, 115–127.

Ivashkovskaya, I.V. (2009). *Modelirovanie stoimosti kompanii. Strategicheskaya otvetstvennost' sovetov direktorov*. INFRA-M.

Jensen, M.C. (2002). Value Maximization, Stakeholder Theory, and the Corporate Objective Function. *Business Ethics Quarterly*, 12, 235–256. doi:10.2307/3857812

Jonek-Kowalska, I., Ponomarenko, T.V., Marinina, O.A. (2018). Problems of Interaction with Stakeholders during Implementation of Long-Term Mining Projects. *Journal of Mining Institute*, 232, 428–437.

Jones, T.M., Wicks, A.C. (1999). Convergent Stakeholder Theory. *Academy of Management Review*, 24, 206–221.

Jones, T.M. (1980). Corporate Social Responsibility Revisited, Redefined. *California Management Review*, 22, 59–67.

Katkalo, V.S. (2008). *Evolution of the Theory of Strategic Management*. 2nd edn. St. Petersburg: House of St. Petersburg University, 546.

Kobeissi, N., Damanpour, F. (2009). Corporate Responsiveness to Community Stakeholders Effects of Contextual and Organizational Characteristics. *Business & Society*, 48(3), 326–359.

Konstantinov, G.N. (2009). *Strategicheskij menedzhment. Koncepcii: uchebnoe posobie*. Biznes Elajnment.

Krajnc, D., Glavič, P. (2005). How to Compare Companies on Relevant Dimensions of Sustainability. *Ecological Economics*, 55(4), 551–563. DOI: 10.1016/j.ecolecon.2004.12.011

Kujala, J., Myllykangas, P., Lehtimäki, H. (2016). Toward a Relational Stakeholder Theory: Attributes of Value-creating Stakeholder Relationships. Academy of Management Annual Meeting Proceedings. Tampere University Press.

Lindenberg, M.M., Crosby, B.L. (1981). *Managing Development: the Political Dimension*. West Hartford, CT: Kumarian Press.

Maas, S., Reniers, G. (2014). Development of a CSR Model for Practice: Connecting five Inherent Areas of Sustainable Business. *Journal of Cleaner Production*, 64, 104–114.

Meyer, H. (2018). *Operationalising CSV Beyond The Firm*. University of Cambridge. https:// soundcloud.com/cambridgejbs/creating-shared-value-operationalising-csv-beyond-the-firm [access date: 09. 05. 2020].

Mitchell, R.K., Agle, B.R., Wood, D.J. (1997). Toward a Theory of Stakeholder Identification and Salience: Defining the Principle of Who and What Really Counts. *Academy of Management Review*, 22(4), 853–888.

Narbel, F., Muff, K. (2017). Should the Evolution of Stakeholder Theory Be Discontinued Given Its Limitations? *Theoretical Economics Letters*, 7, 1357–1381.

Newbould, G., Luffman, G. (1989). *Successful Business Politics*. London.

Nikitina, L.M. (2010). Klassifikaciya stejkkholderov v processe formirovaniya social'no otvetstvennogo povedeniya kompanii. *Vestnik Severo-Kavkazskogo federal'nogo universiteta*, 2, 157–162.

Orlitzky, M., Schmidt, F.L., Rynes, S.L. (2003). Corporate Social and Financial Performance: A Meta-analysis. *Organization Studies*, 24(3), 403–441.

Pletnev, D.A. (2014). Ostatochnye prava kontrolya i dohoda sub"ektov korporacii: razvitie stejkkholderskogo podhoda. *Korporativnye Finansy*, 1(29), 48–60.

Ponomarenko, T.V., Marinina, O.A. (2017). Corporate Responsibility of Mining Companies: Mechanisms of Interaction with Stakeholders in Projects Implementation. *Journal of Applied Economic Sciences*, 12(6), 1826–1838.

Ponomarenko, T.V., Sergeev, I.B. (2012). Obosnovanie strategicheskih investicionnyh reshenij v integrirovannyh gornyh kompaniyah na osnove stejkkholderskoj teorii firmy. *Gornyj zhurnal. Izvestiya vuzov*, 7, 23–31.

Ponomarenko, T.V., Sergeev, I.B. (2013). Integrirovannaya korporativnaya otchetnost' gornyh kompanij v kontekste stejkkholderskoj teorii. *Zapiski Gornogo Instituta*, 205, 232–237.

Ponomarenko, T.V., Wolniak, R., Marinina, O.A. (2016). Corporate Social Responsibility in Coal Industry (Practices of Russian and European Companies). *Zapiski Gornogo instituta*, 222, 882–891.

Porter, M.E., Kramer, M.R. (2006). Strategy and Society: The Link between Competitive Advantage and Corporate Social Responsibility. *Harvard Business Review*, 84(12), 78–92.

Porter, M.E., Kramer, M.R. (2011). Creating Shared Value. *Harvard Business Review*, 89 (1–2), 62–77.

Post, J.E., Preston, L.E., Sachs, S. (2002). Managing the Extended Enterprise: The New Stakeholder View. *California Management Review*, 45(1), 5–28.

Post, J.E., Preston, L.E., Sachs, S. (2002). *Redefining the Corporation: Stakeholder Management and Organizational Wealth*. Stanford, CA: Stanford University Press.

Raza, A. (2012). Relationship between Corporate Social Responsibility (CSR) and Corporate Financial Performance (CFP): Literature Review Approach. *Elixir Financial Management*, 46, 8404–8409.

Rodriguez, M., Ricart, J., Sanchez, J. (2002). *Sustainable Development and Sustainability of Competitive Advantage: A Dynamic and Sustainable View of the Firm*. Barcelona, Spain: University of Navana.

Savage, G.T., Nix T.W., Whitehead C.J., Blair J.D. (1991). Strategies for Assessing and Managing Organizational Stakeholders. *Academy of Management Executive*, 5(2), 61–75.

Schaltegger, S., Burritt, R. (2010). Sustainability accounting for companies: Catchphrase or decision support for business leaders? *J. World Bus.*, 45(4), 375–384. doi:10.1016/j.jwb.2009.08.002

Searcy, C., Elkhawas, D. (2012). Corporate sustainability ratings: An investigation into how corporations use the Dow Jones Sustainability Index. *Journal of Cleaner Production*, 35, 79–92.

Simon, H.A. (1952). Comments on the Theory of Organizations. *American Political Science Review*, 46(4), 1130–1139.

Steurer, R., Langer, M.E., Konrad, A., Martinuzzi, A. (2005). Corporations, Stakeholders and Sustainable Development I: A Theoretical Exploration of Business–Society Relations. *Journal of Business Ethics*, 61, 263–281. doi:10.1007/s10551-005-7054-0

Tambovcev, V.L. (2008). Stejkkholderskaya teoriya firmy v svete koncepcii rezhimov sobstvennosti. *Rossijskij Zhurnal Menedzhmenta*, 6(3), 3–26.

Turner, J.R., Grude, K.V., Thurloway, L. (1999). *The Project Manager as Change Agent: Leadership, Influence and Negotiation*. McGraw-Hill.

UN Global Compact & Accenture. (2010). *A New Era of Sustainability*. UN Global Compact – Accenture CEO Study 2010. https://archive.epa.gov/wastes/conserve/tools/stewardship/web/pdf/accenture.pdf [access date: 09.05.2020].

Van Marrewijk, M. (2003). Concepts and Definitions of CSR and Corporate Sustainability: Between Agency and Communion. *Journal of Business Ethics*, 44(2–3), 95–105.

Werther, W.B. Jr., Chandler, D. (2005). Strategic Corporate Social Responsibility as Global Brand Insurance. *Business Horizons*, 48, 317–324.

Williamson, O.E. (1996). *The Mechanisms of Governance*. Oxford: Oxford University Press.

WCED (World Commission on Environment and Development) (1987). Brundtland Report. https://www.are.admin.ch/are/en/home/media/publications/sustainable-development/brundtland-report.html

Yakubov, B.A. (2014). *Sovershenstvovanie organizacii vzaimodejstviya predprinimatel'skih struktur v ramkah koncepcii stejkkholder-menedzhmenta*. Velikij Novgorod.

Zil'bershtejn, O.B., Nevstruev, K.V., Semenyuk, D.D. (2016). *Analiz stejkkholderov na primere rossijskih predpriyatij* [Elektronnyj resurs]. http://naukovedenie.ru/PDF/42EVN316.pdf [access date: 09. 05. 2020].

Part II

Internal stakeholders in SD of mining enterprises

3 State and private ownership and their strengths and weaknesses

Private and state ownership in extractive industries in Europe and the Commonwealth of Independent States

In this chapter, mining enterprises will be considered in the context of the form of ownership and its impact on the implementation of sustainable development principles. The considerations – in accordance with the title of the monograph – will be geographically limited to Europe and the Commonwealth of Independent States (CIS).[1] Detailed issues and case studies on this subject will be described after a brief introduction on the hard coal market in the world and in the regions analysed. This will allow a better understanding of the significance and scale of the studied socio-economic trends and phenomena.

Hard coal (steam or coking) is a raw material extracted and consumed on virtually all continents. Steam coal is mainly used in energy and heating. Hard coal and bituminous coal are the most common varieties of this mineral. Hard coal has a higher calorific value and lower moisture content, which means that it is a better solid fuel than bituminous coal. The noblest type of steam coal is anthracite, which is the most transformed hard coal variety with the highest calorific value. Anthracite deposits are very valuable; however, they are relatively rare (Weisenberger et al., 2020).

Coking coal is used to produce steel. After extraction, it is processed into coke through coke plants. In practice, four types of coke are distinguished: blast furnace coke, metallurgical coke, foundry coke, and heating coke. Coke is mainly used for smelting iron in blast furnaces, where it acts as a fuel, reducer and scaffolding, allowing the passage of gases arising during the smelting process (Mohanty et al., 2019; Zhuo and Shen, 2020).

Hard coal (steam and coking) can be extracted using the deep mining method and the open-pit method. In the case of the deep method, raw material deposits are made available by drilling mining shafts and underground dog headings. In the open-pit method, access to the deposits takes place from the surface after removing the upper layers of soil and rocks. Open-pit coal mines usually extract bituminous coal due to its young geological age and low coal beds. Although in the USA, Australia or South Africa, this method is also used for hard coal mining (Wang et al., 2018).

DOI: 10.4324/9781003091110-6

It is worth noting that open-pit coal mining generates lower operating costs due to the lack of the need to produce and maintain cost and capital-intensive low underground infrastructure. However, it is more damaging to the natural environment due to the scale and extent of surface degradation and the resulting interference with ecosystems (Zhang et al., 2019; Ghose and Majee, 2000; Trigg and Dubourg, 1993). However, this does not mean that deep mining does not cause environmental damage. In this case, we usually deal with mining damage on the surface and disturbances to the hydrosphere. Existing and decommissioned mines require systematic drainage of unsecured dog headings to protect them against flooding. A side effect of this type of mining is also air pollution and surface water contamination (most often brine discharged from mines) (Liu and Li, 2019; Liu et al., 2018; Meng et al., 2009).

Since the beginning of the 1980s, the largest and increasing hard coal mining has been carried out in the Asia-Pacific region (Figure 3.1). The key extractors of this raw material are China, India and Australia. China and India are also major coal consumers in this area. Australia is primarily an exporter of this raw material (Mendelevitch et al., 2019; Oei and Mendelevitch, 2019; Bai et al., 2018; Balat, 2009).

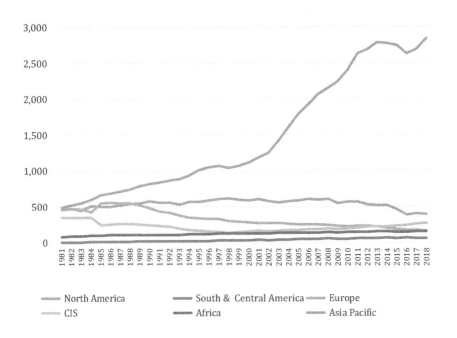

Figure 3.1 Hard coal production around the world in the years 1981–2018 [in million Mtoe]

Source: own study based on the data of the BP Statistical Review of World Energy, 2019

In other regions, hard coal mining in the last decade did not exceed 500 million Mtoe. In North America (Arora and Shi, 2016) and Europe it is slowly decreasing over time, due to the depletion of deposits, unprofitability of mining and decarbonisation policy. It is growing slightly in the Commonwealth of Independent States and Africa (Ahamad, 2016) due to the need to ensure the still existing demand for this raw material in countries resigning from hard coal mining and in less or medium developed countries (Greenberg, 2018; Oguejiofor, 2009).

As already mentioned, the largest amount of hard coal is consumed in the Asia-Pacific region (Figure 3.2), including China, India, Japan, South Korea and Australia. In other regions, the use of coal in the economy is definitely smaller and has been systematically decreasing over time since 2010 (Jiang et al., 2018; Zhang et al., 2017; Kim and Yoo, 2016).

In Europe, the largest producers of hard coal currently are Poland, Germany, Turkey, the Czech Republic and Serbia. To a lesser extent, this raw material is also extracted in Bulgaria, Greece, Hungary, Romania and Spain. Hard coal mining in the CIS is the largest in Russia, Kazakhstan and Ukraine. Coal is also mined in Uzbekistan and Georgia and, to a very small extent, in Kyrgyzstan. The volume of extraction in the four largest European countries and the CIS in 2018 is presented in Figure 3.3, which shows that the leader in hard coal

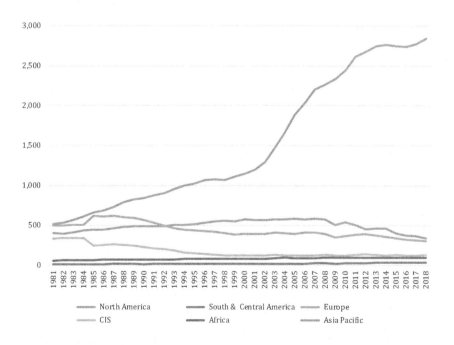

Figure 3.2 Hard coal consumption around the world in the years 1981–2018 [in million Mtoe]
Source: own study based on the data of the BP Statistical Review of World Energy, 2019

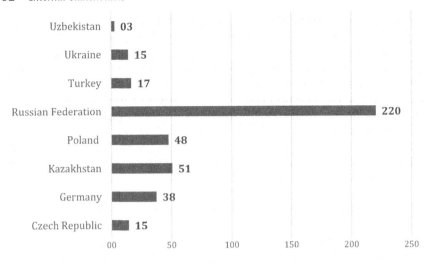

Figure 3.3 Hard coal production in selected European countries and the CIS in 2018 [in million Mtoe]
Source: own study based on the data of the BP Statistical Review of World Energy, 2019

production is definitely Russia, where extraction in 2018 exceeded the production volume by more than four times as compared to the next in the ranking Poland (Martus, 2019; Artobolevskiy, 2003).

The volume of consumption in the four largest European countries and the CIS in 2018 is presented in Figure 3.4. The group of the largest European hard coal consumers currently includes Germany, Poland, Turkey, the Czech Republic and Spain, which are, therefore, also the largest producers of this raw material in this region. Coal is also used in Austria, Belgium, Bulgaria, Estonia, Finland, Greece, Hungary, Italy, the Netherlands, Romania, Slovakia and Sweden. In the CIS, coal consumption is highest in Russia, Kazakhstan, Ukraine and Uzbekistan. Russia consumes the most hard coal in the group of countries presented in Figure 3.4, but it is only 40% of the volume of extraction in this country in 2018. Slightly less coal is used by Germany, Poland, Turkey and Kazakhstan (Jin and Kim, 2016).

Further considerations will analyse the situation in 10 European countries and in 7 countries belonging to the CIS. Detailed statistical data, selected case studies, and survey results will come from this group. The place of coal in the energy balance of these countries and the synthetic characteristics of the mining industry for the studied regions are presented in Table 3.1.

According to the information contained in Table 3.1, coal is the dominant source of energy in Bulgaria, the Czech Republic, Germany, Poland and Serbia. These countries are heavily dependent on the supply of this raw material. Other European countries use it in quite diverse energy mixes, but it is not

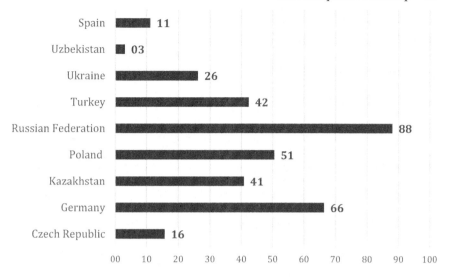

Figure 3.4 Hard coal consumption in selected European countries and the CIS in 2018 [in million Mtoe]
Source: own study based on the data of the BP Statistical Review of World Energy, 2019

Table 3.1 Strategic energy sources, as well as the type and method of coal mining in selected European and CIS countries

Country name	Strategic energy sources	Type of coal mined	Mining method
Europe			
Bulgaria	bituminous coal and lignite (over 48%) nuclear energy (over 34%) renewable sources (over 16%)	bituminous coal and lignite	open pit (less often deep pit)
Czech Republic	bituminous coal, hard coal and lignite (over 36%) nuclear energy (over 18%) oil (over 21%) gas (over 15%)	bituminous coal and lignite, hard coal	deep and open-pit
Greece	bituminous coal, hard coal and lignite (over 20%) oil (over 45%) gas (over 18%)	bituminous coal and lignite	open pit
Spain	bituminous coal, hard coal and lignite (over 7%) nuclear energy (over 20%) gas (over 20%) wind (over 18%) hydropower (over 13%)	hard coal, bituminous coal and lignite	deep and open-pit

(Continued)

Table 3.1 Continued

Country name	Strategic energy sources	Type of coal mined	Mining method
Germany	bituminous coal, hard coal and lignite (over 33%) nuclear energy (over 17%) gas (over 6%)	bituminous coal and lignite, hard coal	open pit
Poland	bituminous coal, hard coal and lignite (over 47%) oil (over 28%) gas (over 15%)	mainly hard coal, additionally: bituminous coal and lignite	deep pit (less often open pit)
Romania	bituminous coal, hard coal and lignite (over 26%) hydropower (32%) oil and gas (over 17%) nuclear energy (over 6%) renewable sources (over 22%)	bituminous coal and lignite, hard coal	deep and open-pit
Serbia	bituminous coal and lignite (over 71%) hydropower (26%)	bituminous coal and lignite	open pit
Turkey	bituminous coal, hard coal and lignite (over 29%) oil (over 28%) gas (over 28%)	bituminous coal and lignite, hard coal	deep and open-pit
Hungary	oil (over 29%) gas (over 31%) nuclear energy (over 15%) renewable sources (over 10%) coal (over 8%)	bituminous coal and lignite, hard coal	open pit
CIS★			
Kazakhstan	coal (over 45%) hydropower (over 1%) oil (over 19%) gas (over 35%) renewable sources (over 1%)	bituminous coal and lignite, hard coal	deep and open-pit
Kyrgyzstan	coal (over 23%) hydropower (over 31%) oil (over 42%) gas (over 7%)	bituminous coal and lignite	deep and open-pit
Tajikistan	coal (over30%) oil (over 25%) hydropower (over 45%)	bituminous coal and lignite	deep and open-pit
Uzbekistan	coal (over 7%) hydropower (over 2%) oil (over 7%) gas (over 86%)	bituminous coal and lignite	deep and open-pit
Russia	coal (over 15%) hydropower (over 2%) oil (over 21%) gas (over 53%) nuclear energy (over 7%) renewable sources (over 1%)	bituminous coal and lignite, hard coal	deep and open-pit

Country name	Strategic energy sources	Type of coal mined	Mining method
Ukraine	coal (over 29%) hydropower (over 0.8%) oil (over 14%) gas (over 27%) nuclear energy (over 25%) renewable sources (over 3%)	bituminous coal and lignite, hard coal	deep and open-pit
Moldova	coal (over 3%) oil (over 42%) gas (over 51%) hydropower (over 0.6%)	–	–

Source: own work on the basis of data from Euracoal and IEA World Energy Balances 2019

*Note: In Russia and the CIS, coal is classified into the following types: brown coal, mineral coal, anthracite and graphite. In the EU, it is classified into lignite coal, sub-bituminous coal and bituminous coal, hard coal and graphite, respectively.

a key source of energy. Currently, mainly bituminous coal and lignite are extracted in Europe in open-pit mines, due to their economic profitability and ease of operation. Deep coal mines only operate in the Czech Republic, Poland, Romania and Turkey. It is also worth adding that, in the past, hard coal was extracted in many deep mines in Europe, including in countries where mining does not currently exist, such as Great Britain or France (Strangleman, 2018; Burrell, 2017). The main reasons for decommissioning mines in Europe were:

- increasing mining costs negatively affecting efficiency,
- limiting and then withholding state aid to the mining sector,
- and progressive decarbonisation of economies and support for the development of renewable energy sources.

Coal is not the key energy source for most of the CIS countries. Only in Kazakhstan, the share of coal in energy consumption is dominant (45%). In terms of the structure of energy balance of Ukraine and Kyrgyzstan, coal makes up 20%. Russia, Georgia, Uzbekistan and Moldova use gas or oil as the main source of energy, while coal makes up only 3–15%.

The CIS countries, except Moldova and Georgia, extract coal within their territories, without depending on coal imports (Moldova imports a small amount of coal, while Georgia uses 30% of imported coal for energy purposes).

Three CIS republics (Russia, Kazakhstan, Ukraine) provide about 99.7% of the total volume of extracted black (bituminous) coal in the region. The share of Russia in the total volume of brown (lignite) coal production of the CIS countries is 89%, Kazakhstan – 6.8%, Uzbekistan – 3.1%, Kyrgyzstan – 0.9%, Ukraine – 0.2%. In the total production of anthracite (hard coal), the share of Russia is about 62.3%, Ukraine – 25.0%, Kazakhstan – 12.7% (Plakitkina, 2013).

In the period 1998–2018, in Russia, the increase in coal production amounted to more than 150%, in Tajikistan 200%, while in Ukraine the decrease in coal production amounted to more than 80%.

The open-pit method dominates in the Russian coal mining industry (more than 75%, 2019): in the period 1995–2019, open-pit coal production doubled. Underground mining remained stable at the level of 100–110 million tonnes per year (1995–2019). The main reasons for the dominance of the open-pit mining method in Russia are: its efficiency at relatively low capital and current costs, the presence of proved coal reserves with favourable mining and geological conditions, as well as a sharp increase in productivity due to modern mining technologies. Coal extraction by underground or open-pit methods in the CIS countries depends on historical, geographical and territorial factors, as well as mining and geological restrictions of the coal bed.

From 1995 to 2017, the global trade volume of coal grew 2.7 times. Over this period, Russian coal export volumes increased 6.3 times, with Russia's share in the global coal market growing up to 14% (2.3 times). In 2017, Russian coal was shipped to 77 countries (Yanovsky, 2019).

Bearing in mind the subject of this chapter, the following part of considerations focuses on the analysis of ownership forms of mining enterprises in the analysed European countries and those belonging to the CIS. Introductory data on this subject is contained in Table 3.2.

The data contained in Table 3.2 show that, in Western European countries (Germany and Greece), mining enterprises are privately owned, which is partly due to long free-market traditions in these economies and partly due to the systematic privatisation in this sector, carried out over the last several years, and focused on improving the profitability of mining (Jonek-Kowalska and Turek, 2011). It should be added that, in Spain, the repair process was not carried out successfully, which led to the decommissioning of all mines in the years 2018–2019 (Zafrilla, 2014).

State ownership of European mining enterprises is more common in former socialist countries, which is certainly a remnant of the previous political and economic system. Most of the mining sector belongs to the state in countries such as: Poland, Romania and Serbia (Jonek-Kowalska, 2017). Private ownership only appears in these regions in the case of small- or, at most, medium-sized mining enterprises. The group of countries with the dominant state share in the mining sector also includes Turkey, a country with strong national traditions and a well-established state authority. However, it should be added in this case, that – for several years – the Turkish authorities have been systematically privatising hard coal mines due to the need to improve mining efficiency and to become independent from electricity imports. Turkey is its largest importer in the study group, which negatively affects its energy independence (Jonek-Kowalska, 2019; Yılmaz, 2009; Balat, 2006).

The privatisation process of mining enterprises has definitely accelerated the EU ban on co-financing from the state budget introduced in 2010 by the decision of the *European Commission on state aid to facilitate the closure of uncompetitive coal mines (2010/787/EU)*. Pursuant to the provisions contained therein, the state may only grant support in the event of decommissioning unprofitable mining plants for the following categories of expenses:

Table 3.2 Ownership of mining enterprises in selected European and CIS countries

Country name	Mining enterprises and ownership
Bulgaria	**LIGNITE** MINI MARITSA IZTOK EAD: state owned STANYANTSI JSC: privately owned BELI BYRAG JSC: privately owned **BITUMINOUS COAL** VAGLEDOBIV BOBOV DOL EOOD: privately owned OTKRIT VAGLEDOBIV MINES EAD: privately owned BALKAN MK OOD: privately owned Vitren mine: privately owned Cherno More mine: privately owned
Czech Republic	**HARD COAL** OSTRAVSKO-KARVINSKÉ DOLY (OKD): state owned **BITUMINOUS COAL** SEVEROČESKÉ DOLY: state owned VRŠANSKÁ UHELNÁ: privately owned SEVERNÍ ENERGETICKÁ: privately owned SOKOLOVSKÁ UHELNÁ: privately owned
Greece	PUBLIC POWER CORPORATION (PPC): privately owned LIGNITIKI MEGALOPOLIS SA: privately owned West Macedonia Lignite Centre (WMLC): privately owned Megalopolis Lignite Centre (MLC): privately owned
Spain	**BITUMINOUS COAL AND LIGNITE** Hard coal and bituminous coal mines were closed in Spain and decommissioned in 2018 and 2019.
Germany	**BITUMINOUS COAL AND LIGNITE** LAUSITZ ENERGIE BERGBAU AG: privately owned MITTELDEUTSCHE BRAUNKOHLENGESELLSCHAFT mbH (MIBRAG): privately owned ROMONTA GmbH: privately owned
Poland	**HARD COAL** Polska Grupa Górnicza: state owned LW Bogdanka SA: state owned JSW SA: state owned PG Silesia: privately owned Siltech: privately owned **BITUMINOUS COAL AND LIGNITE** Bełchatów mine (PGE Górnictwo i Energetyka Konwencjonalna (PGE GiEK)): state owned Turów mine (PGE Górnictwo i Energetyka Konwencjonalna (PGE GiEK)): state owned Konin and Adamów mines (ZESPÓŁ ELEKTROWNI PĄTNÓW-ADAMÓW-KONIN (ZE PAK Group)): state owned
Romania	**BITUMINOUS COAL AND LIGNITE** COMPLEXUL ENERGETIC OLTENIA (CEO): state owned **HARD COAL** COMPLEXUL ENERGETIC HUNEDOARA (CEH): state owned

(Continued)

Table 3.2 Continued

Country name	Mining enterprises and ownership
Serbia	**BITUMINOUS COAL AND LIGNITE** JP EPS: state owned
Turkey	**HARD COAL** Turkish Hard Coal Enterprises (TTK): state owned, systematically privatising mines **BITUMINOUS COAL AND LIGNITE** Turkish Coal Enterprises (TKI): state owned, systematically privatising mines
Hungary	**BITUMINOUS COAL AND LIGNITE** Visonta and Bükkábrány mines: large, privately owned
CIS	
Georgia	**BITUMINOUS COAL, HARD COAL** Saqnakhshiri GIG Group: privately owned
Kazakhstan	**BITUMINOUS COAL AND LIGNITE** AO Samruk-Energy, TOO Saryarka-ENERGY, TOO Karazhyra LTD, TOO Razrez Kuznetskiy, AO Gornorudnaya Company Sat Komir: large, state owned, AO Shubarkol komir: large, privately owned **HARD COAL** ArcelorMittal: privately owned
Tajikistan	**BITUMINOUS COAL AND LIGNITE, HARD COAL** Fon-Yagnob, Talo-Resource, Tajik Metallurgicheskij Kombinat, Ziddy and Angisht: state owned
Kyrgyzstan	**BITUMINOUS COAL AND LIGNITE, HARD COAL** Adylbek OsOO, Ak-Zhol-Komur OsOO, Kok-Bel-Komur LLC: state owned
Uzbekistan	**BITUMINOUS COAL AND LIGNITE** SPC Yerostigaz: privately owned AO Shargunkumir, OAO Uzbekkumir, AO Uzbekugol: state owned
Russia	**BITUMINOUS COAL AND LIGNITE, HARD COAL** SUEK AO, UK Kuzbassrazrezugol AO, EVRAZ Group S.A., Mechel Mining OAO, En+ Group, Kuzbasskaya Toplivnaya Kompaniya PAO, Russian Coal AO, SDS-Ugol, Stroyservis ZAO, EVRAZ, Mezhdurechensk OOO: large, privately owned
Ukraine	**BITUMINOUS COAL AND LIGNITE** Lvovugol, Volynugol, Selidovugol, DUEK, Krasnoarmeyskugol, Pervomaiskugol, Lisichanskugol: state owned Krasnodonugol, Rovenkyanthracite, Sverdlovskanthracite: privately owned **BITUMINOUS COAL AND LIGNITE, HARD COAL** DTEK: large, privately owned

Source: own work on the basis of data from Euracoal and Plakitkina (2013)

- costs of mine decommissioning, including covering their financial losses, provided that they have stopped operations by 31 December 2018 and the process of their physical decommissioning will be completed by 31 December 2023,
- additional costs of social (remuneration, compensation and severance pay for dismissed employees) and/or technical nature (costs of underground and surface infrastructure maintenance necessary to secure dog headings and surfaces).

The above regulations forced the state to take company action in relation to the usually unprofitable mining sector (Apostolov, 2013), which generally came down to the implementation of the following scenarios:

- mine decommissioning through the use of budget funds,
- privatisation of mines to maintain energy security and places of work,
- consolidation of mines with the state or private energy sector, ensuring energy security and the market for consolidated mining enterprises.

The direct effect of the implementation of these scenarios is the ownership structure of European mining enterprises presented in Table 3.2.

It is also worth mentioning in this context that the largest beneficiaries of state support in the period preceding the introduction of the directive were Germany, Poland and Spain. The following also benefited from state aid: Bulgaria, Czech Republic, France, Greece, Hungary, Romania, Slovakia, Slovenia and the United Kingdom, i.e. virtually all countries, in which coal mining operated (Jonek-Kowalska, 2015).

The analysis of the ownership structure and legal forms of coal companies in Russia and the CIS countries indicates the differences in coal industry operation. In Russia, the coal industry is a market segment of the economy both in the energy and coking coal sectors with almost 100% of private ownership. In the Republic of Kazakhstan, the state is one of the owners of large energy coal companies (steam coal), but most companies are private (80% of the steam coal market). The market is highly concentrated, with several major producers operating in it. The coal industry of the Republic of Uzbekistan has various forms of ownership, but state-owned companies dominate in terms of the output. There are companies with collective ownership, a minority interest (5%) belongs to the workers. In Russia, this form existed in the form of employee-owned enterprises, as well as companies with minority shares of foreign owners. In the Republic of Tajikistan, coal enterprises have both state and private ownership.

The privatisation of mining assets in the countries of the former Soviet Union was almost completed, and only few production capacities remained under state control. Restructuring in the mining industry of these countries was very painful. Thus far, various ownership structures have developed in the CIS countries in the fuel and energy complex.

To date, the coal industry in Russia is a market segment of the economy: all coal companies are private. The crisis of the state system and the transition to a market economy caused the restructuring of the coal industry in Russia in 1994. By the beginning of the restructuring, the production potential of the industry had mainly included obsolete mining facilities (more than half of the mines had operated over 40 years), the most unprofitable mines had worked with substandard coal reserves in difficult geological conditions. The mining equipment, with rare exceptions, required updating. The accident rate and industrial injuries was high (Rozhkov, 2016). The financial situation of the industry was highly unfavourable due to the unprofitability of many enterprises, the lingering indebtedness of consumers for supplied coal, and a number of other reasons of an internal and external nature.

The International Bank for Reconstruction and Development (IBRD) supported the reforming of the coal industry in the Russian Federation with development policy loans for restructuring, solving social problems, and implementing measures to privatise coal companies (Nikitin and Boyko, 2010).

The main objectives of the restructuring were:

- formation of competitive coal companies;
- social security for workers in the industry;
- reduction in government support to the industry enterprises;
- improvement of the socio-economic and environmental situation in coal mining regions.

Restructuring included the change of ownership and the creation of new types of legal structures. Corporatisation was the main method of changing ownership in the industry (Kilimnik and Radionovskij, 2003). At the beginning of 1994, 251 mines and 80 open pits were operating with a total production capacity of 371.1 million tons.

The restructuring of the coal industry in Russia was carried out in several stages. The first stage of the restructuring (1994–1997) included the optimisation of the mining facilities, their division into cost-effective and non-commercial mines and sections. The closure of unprofitable organisations allowed a reduction in the cost of coal mining, an increase in the labour efficiency and a reduction in the injury rate.

The main goal of the second stage of restructuring (1998–2004) was the cash privatisation of commercially viable mines and open pits, and coal companies. At the same time, the number of mines involved in the decommissioning process continued to grow.

In the period 1994–2004, the structure of federal financing changed dramatically: previously, the first priority was state support (subsidising) of loss-making production; then, the priorities were changed to restructuring processes, including social protection, technical work on the elimination of coal mines and open pits, local development programmes, ensuring work safety, etc. The allocation of subsidies to cover losses of the current activities was completely stopped in 2001 (Nikitin and Boyko, 2010; Rozhkov, 2016). By the end of the second stage of restructuring, the decommissioning of 203 particularly unprofitable enterprises (with high labour intensity and difficult mining and geological conditions) resulted in the reduction of employees from 859.6 thousand to 269.0 thousand people (at the beginning of 2004).

The third stage (2005–2015) featured the implementation of a sector-based corporate social policy with elements of state regulation (Krasnyansky et al., 2017). Some $13.1 billion was spent on the restructuring of the coal industry over 20 years (1994–2014), while revenues to treasuries at all levels amounted to $15.6 billion.

The consequences of the restructuring include both positive and negative results. The main positive consequence of the restructuring of the coal industry at the macroeconomic level is a reduction in federal financing of the coal industry as a percentage of GDP. The most significant result of the restructuring at the macroeconomic and regional levels of the coal industry was the achievement of the *demonopolisation–commercialisation–privatisation* goal. The industry management structures with government control were abolished.

Among the positive consequences for the industry and negative consequences for the territory, in particular, was the transfer of social infrastructure to municipal jurisdiction (Nikitin and Boyko, 2010; Rozhkov, 2016). The most negative social consequence of the restructuring was a sharp decrease in the number of employees in the coal industry. In mining towns, unemployment rose immensely due to the liquidation of particularly unprofitable coal enterprises with a completely insufficient demand for mining specialties in local labour markets; arrears of salaries and increased social transfers; socio-economic uncertainty grew sharply in the life of a large part of the population of coal-mining territories, for whom work in the coal industry was the main source of income and social support. These and other social problems (long delays in the payment of salaries, severance pay, etc.) provoked strike activity among miners, the peak of which occurred in the period 1996–1998 (Rozhkov, 2016; Korchak, 2002).

Since 2005, the initial structuring of coal industry assets has continued in the following areas:

- the establishing of coal and energy holding companies,
- metallurgical companies acquiring coal assets and power generation units.

Russian coal companies began to undertake an IPO (Initial Public Offering) in 2005: Evraz Group C.A. (2005, LSE), Mechel (2004, NYSE), Raspadskaya (2006, MMVB RTC), Severstal (2006, LSE). It was then that the privatisation process of mining enterprises began by offering company shares to stock exchange investors. After 2015, a systematic structuring of assets related to the redistribution of ownership in the coal industry began. Coal companies have continued to enlarge and expand their activities in the direction of diversification, horizontal and vertical integration, including port infrastructure, and development of mining in the old industrial regions and in the new ones.

The systematic structuring of assets and the growing complexity of the ownership structure in some cases were accompanied by the transition from public to non-public form. Delisting processes of Russian companies began on the Moscow Exchange in 2012 and on leading foreign exchanges in 2015. A change in corporate strategy in the near future was named as the main reason for that, while experts note that there is no plan to reduce corporate control and transfer the main shareholder to the position of financial investor, and market capitalisation is not considered as an important economic indicator (Belikov, 2019).

What do the owners want? How do they achieve it? And what is their position in implementing SD in mining enterprises? Case studies

After presenting the ownership structure of mining enterprises in Europe and the CIS, it is worth referring to the goals that the owners of mining enterprises in Europe and the CIS have been pursuing. In this context, further analysis focuses on Poland and Russia as the largest coal producers in the analysed regions, treating these countries as two leading case studies. This selection also makes it possible to trace different patterns of ownership transformation in the mining sector. In Poland, the largest mining enterprises remained state-owned, in Russia all of them were privatised, which significantly influenced the prioritisation of the owners' goals.

As previously mentioned, all coal companies in Russia are private. At the same time, they differ in terms of their ownership structures and legal entity types depending on the sector in which they operate (coal mining, energy generation, metal production). This is due to differences in organisational processes, owners' strategic goals, and their ability to attract financial resources. It is worth mentioning that in Russia there are also ten large important coal companies that account for 75% of the total coal production in Russia (Tarazanov, 2019), which additionally complicates the ownership structures and their goals.

In Russia, most coal companies, even those that are big in terms of their capital, size, range of activity, and share in the coal industry, are not public. They are either joint-stock companies (AOs in Russia) or private limited companies (OOOs in Russia), which determines their owners' interests and powers, the corporate management structure, the functions of governing bodies, and corporate development strategies.[2]

As noted in the previous section, Russian companies are currently changing in terms of their ownership structures. According to the Russian Federal State Statistics Service, the number of Russian commercial corporations decreased by 21.8% in the period from 2016 to 2019. Moreover, the number of public joint-stock companies fell by half, and the number of public companies increased by 39.9%.

The attitude towards IPOs and SPOs (Secondary Public Offering) demonstrated by Russian companies provides a lot of useful information for understanding their majority shareholders' interests. According to Deloitte, 73% of Russian companies have majority stakes (those exceeding 50%, which makes them controlling stakes). Of the companies in the sample 95% had at least one stake accounting for at least 25% of the total number of shares. On average, 25% of a company's shares are in free float. All of the above indicates, as researchers believe, that there has been an increase in equity concentration over the past four to five years and that the capital structure typical of joint-stock companies, which implies that there are several majority shareholders and a number of minority shareholders, has become more popular.

An analysis of the current structure of the equity capital in coal companies also showed that they do not prefer a wide distribution of equity. Equity concentration in the Russian coal industry is high, with shares being distributed among a small circle of owners. Coal companies either have one shareholder with a controlling stake (SUEK AO), two controlling shareholders (a senior one and a junior one, as in SDS-Ugol), or several major shareholders. Major shareholders are usually individuals. A common practice among Russian companies is the desire demonstrated by one shareholder to be the only owner of a controlling stake for a long period (Belikov, 2019).

OECD experts (Kostyleva and Leuede, 2012) also note that the real concentration level is higher because it can be obscured and there can be shareholder agreements involving a greater degree of influence, i.e. the co-owners of a joint-stock company can be affiliated (Faleev, 2008).

In addition, there may be strategic alliances between significant minority shareholders, i.e. those whose stakes, when put together, can guarantee that they will manage the joint-stock company. They can sign agreements on the synchronisation of corporate actions, according to which they undertake to consult each other before shareholders' meetings and take a common stand on voting; if this is not possible, they refuse to vote. If such an alliance is strong due to its members' views on economic issues and it relies on effective corporate institutions, such minority shareholders may become the collective owner of a controlling stake, and the remaining shareholders in the company will be minority shareholders. This is sure to influence the owners' behaviour, interests, and actions.

The traditional approach to strategic owners' goals assumes that their goals are long-term and aimed at increasing the company's market capitalisation or maximising its value. Therefore, the owners' strategic decisions should be aimed at improving the company's performance and ensuring sustainable development in the key areas, including economics, ecology, social development, and effective corporate management which covers all these aspects.

Currently, these traditional goals are greatly affected by changes in the functioning of big companies, including those operating in the coal industry. They include: the fact that their shares have become significantly less attractive for Western portfolio investors and a high probability the situation will stay the same (for public companies), the influence of institutional and market factors, the uncertainty of the future, and stricter requirements concerning responsible business practices that can negatively affect the company's market value (for all companies). This is why for most controlling owners, the company's market value (capitalisation) has ceased to be the most important strategic goal and the main way to earn money from owning stocks.

Since 2013, controlling shareholders' interests has gradually been shifting towards the payment of dividends as the main way to obtain economic benefits (Belikov, 2019). Growth in dividend payments reduces net profit; as a result, sustainable development is financed with whatever funds remain. For example, in 2017, metal manufacturers directed almost all of their free cash flow to shareholders (Belikov, 2019) while cutting down on investment programmes. If the outlays for investments in sustainable development increase, the net cash flow in mining enterprises will be negative, which means a shortage of financial resources.

An important feature of Russian big companies is that the owners of controlling stakes are usually over 50 years old. As a result, one of the strategic owners' goals can be to increase the future value of the company for selling the whole company or a large stake or, which is less likely, for handing it down to their heirs. According to the experts, it is not common for big companies to be inherited in Russia. The transfer of management to the second generation is extremely rare (Zagieva and Matveeva, 2017). This is due to the fact that businesses are often tied by informal agreements. Experts predict intensification in the struggle for equity control due to a decrease in corporate profits, weak macroeconomic growth, inefficient business models, and retirement of the founding owners from business due to age.

Major owners' commitment to such models will mean that they will strive to maximise the value of the company using different levers. In this case, an increase in the future value will take into account various stakeholders' interests and the company's sustainable development indicators. With regard to private companies and limited liability companies, similar conclusions about major owners and their interests can be drawn.

The goal of major shareholders is to make decisions and take part in managing the company. They, rather than the corporate governing body (the board of directors), hold the real power. The goal of minority shareholders[3] is to receive dividends (if possible, high and regular) and see an increase in the market value of their shares.

Minority shareholders in coal companies have, as a rule, small stakes, which deprives them of participating in management. At the same time, there are many corporate conflicts related to setting buyback prices, violating minority shareholders' rights, etc.

Not all Russian coal companies associate corporate social responsibility (CSR) with strategic development and the positive effects of turning social responsibility into economic opportunities. Among all coal companies and metal manufacturers, only two big companies (SUEK and Severstal PAO) regularly publish sustainable development reports, and they are leaders in various sustainable development rankings. Evraz Group S.A. published reports on social responsibility and sustainability in 2017 and 2018.

A closer look at coal companies' official reports which disclose information on a number of important aspects, including CSR indicators, reveals that most of the analytical data covers occupational safety and health issues along with environmental ones. Second place is taken by social problems related to the staff and management relations. The next aspect is interaction and relations with the society which are declared in the form of programmes and projects. However, social investment performance is not analysed or evaluated. The results of activities in social responsibility areas are not considered in the context of a unified strategy and are loosely linked to either previous periods or future targets. As there is little or no CSR reporting and the information on social and environmental aspects is superficially disclosed, it indicates that coal companies are either not or little involved in the CSR area or are trying to save on corporate accountability costs.

Many researchers (Adams, 2017, p. 4; Solomon et al., 2013; Kalabikhina and Krikunov, 2018) note that insufficient risk identification and risk management regarding negative environmental and social consequences can lead to inefficient management (CPA Australia et al., 2014). For example, for a mining company, the lack of information on social and environmental responsibility only complicates the interaction with strategic partners and limits their investment sources which could contribute to achieving sustainable development goals. According to EY (Ernst & Young), which annually conducts surveys among institutional investors regarding their interest in non-financial reporting, the share of investors who decide against investment in a company due to risks associated with various ESG factors (Environmental, Social and Governance factors) increased significantly in 2018 (Feoktistova et al., 2019).

In Poland, the largest mining enterprises (JSW SA, Polska Grupa Górnicza SA, LW Bogdanka SA) have been state-owned right from the beginning. There are only a few very small mining companies that have been privatised. This ownership structure differently shapes the system of priorities in the field of sustainable development (Paszcza, 2010). In the case of state-owned enterprises, economic goals have been clashing with social goals for many years, with the latter seeming to be the predominant winners. Since the beginning of the 1990s, Polish hard coal mining has been systematically restructured due to economic ineffectiveness. However, such a process, as is also clearly shown by the Russian experience, usually requires the significant restructuring of employment and the closure of mines (Karbownik and Stachowicz, 1994; Manowska et al., 2017). In Poland, such radical changes have not been agreed on by trade unions and the local community of Upper Silesia, which would be at risk of pauperisation. As a result, the decommissioning restructuring process has stretched over time and has been going on for over 30 years, which constitutes a significant burden on the state budget (Zientara, 2009; Newell and Pastore, 2006).

Polish mines – unlike Russian ones – have not been privatised for two key reasons. One of them is the aforementioned social reluctance. The other is related to the government's priority to maintain energy security. As shown in Table 3.1, electricity in Poland is mainly obtained from hard coal. In Russia, the energy balance is more diversified, with the share of coal constituting only 15%. Thus, the transfer of Polish mines into private hands would mean the transfer of control over the supply of electricity and heat to the economy. Nevertheless, it is worth adding that in recent years, significant amounts of cheaper and better-quality coal (including from Russia and Kazakhstan) have been imported to Poland, which will most likely accelerate the process of decommissioning further mines (Kulczycka, 2004). In light of the above, the postulate of maintaining energy security in the conditions of a free market turned out to be impossible to implement.

The above observations indicate the market necessity to prioritise economic goals by the owners. For many years, the Polish state has focused on social and energy security goals, which could not be fully implemented due to economic reasons. Currently, the owner of mining companies (the state) is focused on the achievement of positive financial results aimed at improving the financial condition and increasing the market value (Szczepański, 2003). This is the same in the case of Russian companies. In principle and in the long term, it may also contribute to maintaining jobs in mining and, at least partially, achieving social goals.

Ecological goals, from the perspective of the owners, they are in the last place in the hierarchy of sustainable development, behind the following goals: social, energy and economic security. Direct damage caused by mining operations – where financially possible – is only removed after it has occured. Although more recently, more comprehensive attempts have been made in the reclamation of post-mining areas, mainly with the use of EU funds. Cities where operations have ended are also trying to develop post-industrial tourism. Indirect environmental impacts of mining, in the form of carbon dioxide emissions or serious disturbances of the hydrosphere, are often ignored, and remedial actions are largely limited to eliminating the direct negative effects of mining activities. Local communities also underestimate these effects due to the economic benefits for the region (Kundzewicz et. al., 2019, pp. 366–380; Stefaniak and Twardowska, 2011).

It is worth adding, however, that all Polish mining enterprises prepare and publish reports on corporate social responsibility, taking into account environmental and social activities, with a large predominance of the latter, which is intended to build a favourable climate for mining investments. This is a very positive change in awareness, which requires further intensive practical activities on a larger scale than previously. Despite some flaws in the field of CSR, it must be emphasised that two (JSW SA and Bogdanka SA) out of the three largest Polish mining companies are listed on the Warsaw Stock Exchange and belong to the Respect Index, which includes companies that stand out in terms of implementing and adhering to the principles of corporate social responsibility.

As already mentioned, two mining companies are publicly traded in Poland. Nevertheless, due to the dominance of the state's participation, the increase in the market value of these companies is not the primary objective, despite the fact that their introduction to public trading was to ensure their full marketisation. Additionally, both their financial results and the resulting market value are strongly dependent on the economic situation on the global and domestic coal market. In turn, this has changed very often and dynamically in recent years, which results in high variability of their stock exchange rates (Figures 3.5 and 3.6).

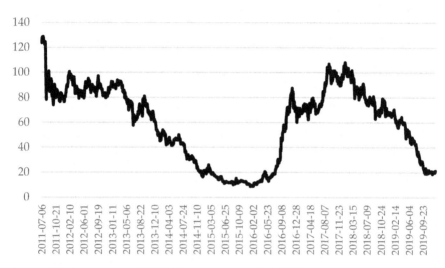

Figure 3.5 Market value of JSW SA in the years 2011–2019
Source: Money.pl

Figure 3.6 Market value of Bogdanka SA in the years 2011–2019
Source: Money.pl

During periods of growth in value, both companies achieve very good financial results due to high coal prices. Then, the realised profits may be added to the budget of the owner, being the state. The dividend for minority shareholders is paid very rarely as companies try to invest and protect savings during periods of downturn. It is also worth adding that the third unlisted mining company (Polska Grupa Górnicza SA) has been in a very difficult financial situation for years and rarely achieves a positive financial result, despite the fact that in recent years the Polish government has attached more and more importance to economic priorities.

As a summary, Table 3.3. presents the answers to the questions posed in the title of this subsection relating to the analysed cases of Russia and Poland.

The data in Table 3.3. shows that ecological priorities are the least important for owners both in Russia and Poland. In Russia, mining enterprises have been privatised, which has made economic goals stand out. In Poland, the entire industry practically remained state-owned and for a very long time the social and energy security goals were the most important. Only in recent years have economic profitability and adaptation to the requirements of decarbonisation of EU economies gained more importance.

Characteristics of strengths and weaknesses of private and state ownership in mining enterprises

The public sector plays a prominent role in any modern national economy (Adams, 2017). When analysing the role of the public sector in mining, two concepts are usually used: ownership and control (Solomon et al., 2013). Ownership is determined by company shareholdings. This indicator is relatively easy to measure by the register of shareholders.

Table 3.3 Questions concerning the cases of Russia and Poland

Summary questions	Case studies	
	Russia	*Poland*
What do the owners want? – SD goal hierarchy	1 economic (maximising financial results and market value) 2 social 3 ecological	1 social (maintaining a job) 2 energy security (maintaining own supplies of the main energy raw material) 3 economic 4 ecological
How do they achieve it?	decommissioning restructuring + privatisation of all mining enterprises	long-term remedial restructuring + maintenance of state-owned mining enterprises
What is their position in implementing SD in mining enterprises?	leading, decisive, i.e. determining the hierarchy and directions of SD implementation	leading, decisive, i.e. determining the hierarchy and directions of SD implementation

Source: own work

To measure the concept of control is more challenging, since state control is much more difficult to determine than corporate control (Kalabikhina and Krikunov, 2018). Control implies the ability to act decisively in strategically important issues (the general policy of the company, large investments, the purchase or sale of subsidiaries), to appoint and remove management. Such strategic control does not necessarily include the impact on the company's daily decisions.

The size of the public sector in the Russian economy remains relatively high (according to Moody's, the share of the public sector in the Russian economy is estimated at 40–50), and the costs are obvious.

Firstly, this leads to a decrease in the effectiveness of market mechanisms: it violates the principle of equality of companies in relations with the state (a conflict of interests of the state as the owner and guarantor of equal rules); it replaces competitive mechanisms with an administrative resource and lobbying opportunities.

Secondly, the state (as an abstract and non-personalised concept) is a less efficient owner than private entities, primarily in competitive industries. This is determined by the features of state ownership and the "principal – agent" system.

Thirdly, one of the significant consequences of these processes is the informal nationalisation of the private sector which leads to the emergence of "public–private companies" (Abramov et al., 2018).

The generally accepted opinion is that companies with state participation are inefficient in comparison with private companies and lag behind them both in financial and market indicators (Shirley and Walsh, 2000; Estrin et al., 2009; Megginson, 2016). In their review devoted to comparing the performance of private and public companies, Boardman and Vining (1989) examined the results presented in more than 50 different studies and compared them with their own calculations. The main conclusion of the authors is that large industrial companies that are state-owned or with mixed ownership are less efficient than private ones. Another review (Bërcherding et al., 1982) showed the results of 50 empirical studies, in 40 of which private enterprises proved to be significantly more effective than public, and in 7 cases it was impossible to determine the clear advantages of one of the forms of ownership.

Studies that show the higher efficiency of public companies are not only few, but also cover a narrow circle of industries (four out of five cases are related to the production and distribution of electricity). Thus, mechanisms of market competition and state regulations (rather than the advantages of private companies) can determine greater or lesser efficiency (Cherkasova, 2014).

Researchers Ang and Ding (2006) assessed the level of corporate management in public and private companies that traded on the Singapore Stock Exchange. They found that companies with state participation have a higher value even after taking into account such specific factors as profitability, leverage, company size, industry effect, foreign ownership. They also found that, on average, companies with state participation have excess returns (both on assets and equity). The authors revealed a high correlation between state control and management structure: companies with state participation have a higher standard of corporate management (Cherkasova, 2014).

The opposite situation was observed in Russia: the increase in the state's presence in oil companies (in the 2000s, the oil assets of Yukos, Sibneft, TNK-BP and Bashneft fell under state control) was connected with a decrease in oil production and industrial effectiveness (Zubov, 2015). And at present, large state-owned energy companies are not efficient enough compared to foreign competitors: revenue per employee at Rosneft is 7.8 and 4.4 times less than that of foreign competitors (ExxonMobil or Chevron).

The high efficiency of private coal companies in Russia after the restructuring could prove that private ownership is advantageous, but even in this case there can be no unequivocal statement that the form of ownership determines the effectiveness. The effects of ownership, competition and regulation often overlap, making it difficult to separate the effects of market operations and institutional influence. The efficiency of the coal industry is determined by the following: market factors, the quality of corporate management, and government requirements for companies with state participation. Coal mining and metallurgy companies operate in competitive markets with weak government regulation, while coal energy companies operate in both regulated and competitive markets.

Studies by Shapiro and Willig (1990) showed that the performance of public companies may decline due to the high responsibility in meeting social goals. Public companies are to resolve market failures by a pricing policy. Shleifer and Vishny (1994) have noted that companies with state participation are forced to pursue a political goal, for example, to maintain excess employment, whereas private companies only aim to maximise their profits. Chhibber and Majumdar (1999) have shown that companies with state participation are influenced by trade unions, workers, and ideological considerations. Thus, most authors agree that due to the emphasis on social aspects, companies with state participation may not be effective.

The analysis of the operation of mining enterprises in Poland and other European countries leads to similar conclusions. Basically, the privatisation of these companies is focused on prioritising economic goals in the form of maximising financial results and value. This is to serve economic independence and reduce the burden on the state budget. It is true that in Poland – unlike in Russia – mining enterprises have not been privatised, but their long-term remedial restructuring and problems with the lack of profits and huge debt indicate the ineffectiveness of state ownership. In this case, the domination of social goals over economic ones is also clear, which may positively shape relations with local communities, employees and trade unions, but significantly reduces the survival chances of mining enterprises, especially in the current turbulent economic environment.

Bearing in mind the above observations, Table 3.4 presents the weaknesses and strengths of private and state ownership in the context of actions for sustainable development.

Table 3.4 Weaknesses and strengths of private and state ownership in the context of sustainable development of mining enterprises

Type of ownership	Strength	Weakness
PRIVATE	the possibility of higher financial support for SD; the need to care for the image, including CSR (in the case of public trading)	shifting environmental and social goals to the background; using CSR to create an image without clear effects for SD
STATE	greater tendency to take into account social goals	marginalisation of ecological goals in agreement with owners and local communities; no or low economic efficiency which hinders a wide range of CSR

Source: own work

In the case of private ownership, two key circumstances can serve a sustainability policy. A higher focus on financial results may facilitate actions for sustainable development implemented as part of corporate social responsibility. In addition, when a company's stock is publicly traded, private shareholders may be more concerned with a favourable image of the company and creating value for all of its shareholders. Nevertheless, it is worth noting that many such activities of listed companies are often purely PR actions aimed at satisfying certain groups of stakeholders, which in turn is a weakness of private ownership in the process of influencing the sustainable development of the mining industry(Song et al., 2020; Hoelscher and Rustad, 2019).

In turn, state ownership is conducive to the achievement of social goals, including in particular employee and trade union goals. Nevertheless, the imbalance between them and economic and ecological goals may pose a serious threat to the continued existence of mining enterprises.

It is also worth adding that in both cases of ownership, if the local community cares about the economic development offered by the mining industry (Abugre and Anlesinya, 2019), and this is often the case in less developed regions of civilisation and economic development, it may be willing to establish cooperation with mining enterprises even at the cost of giving up environmental goals. Thus, it seems that neither private nor state ownership is conducive to the implementation of environmental priorities of sustainable development. The only relatively effective form of supporting these priorities are legal standards established at the regional and national level, and in the case of the European Union, also at the Community level. Thanks to them, it is possible to enforce actions aimed at environmental protection. However, it should be noted that this in turn may contribute to the disruption and abandonment of mining production, which is known to be extremely onerous for the natural environment.

Notes

1 The Commonwealth of Independent States was founded in 1991. In the period covered by this analysis, this monograph included: Armenia, Azerbaijan, Belarus, Kazakhstan, Kyrgyzstan, Moldova, Russia, Tajikistan, Uzbekistan, Ukraine (until 2018).

2 In general, the Russian stock market is characterised by several features. It should be noted that the Russian stock market is not highly developed in terms of either capitalisation or the number of transactions, and the Moscow Exchange was not included in the top 20 exchanges in the world in 2017. The total number of Russian public joint-stock companies over the past five years has been ranging from 80 to 120. In a survey conducted by Deloitte in 2015, 120 Russian companies were ranked as public whose shares at the time were included in the first-level and second-level quotation lists of the Moscow Exchange (MICEX) and were also listed on foreign exchanges. Public companies are characterised by a low float. The exchange, as a rule, is mainly used to redistribute property rather than raise funds. For many companies, the transition from being a public company to being a private one is associated with cost optimisation. Public joint-stock companies bear significant costs associated with information disclosure and being listed. Such costs are justified when the economy is growing and the management can be sure that they will raise capital.

3 The term "minority shareholder" comes from the English word "minor", which means something insignificant and secondary. In American reference literature, a minority shareholder is understood as an "equity holder with less than 50% ownership of the firm's equity capital and having no vote in the control of the firm" and a weak player in the system of corporate relations; their rights are the first to be protected. The minimum threshold for being a majority shareholder is to possess at least 25% of the voting shares plus one. Some authors point out that a shareholder can be called a minority one if their stake does not let them block decisions on critical issues at a shareholders' meeting, i.e. such shareholders have less than 25% of the voting shares (Rudkina, 2006, p. 45). A shareholder is classified as a minority one based on the situation. It depends on how power is distributed in the joint-stock company rather than on what his or her stake in the company is. Broadly speaking, a minority shareholder owns a stake which is smaller than a controlling one. Based on the legislation regarding joint-stock companies and corporate practice, the following are distinguished (Faleev, 2008, p. 118): (1) an absolute majority stake: 100% of the company's shares (or at least voting shares) belong to one person; (2) a qualified majority stake: 75% of the shares + one voting share; (3) control by majority vote: 50% of the shares + one voting share taking up 75% of the votes; (4) control by a significant number of votes: consolidation of 25–50% of the voting shares; (5) a blocking stake of the voting shares: 25%; (6) a controlling stake of the voting shares distributed among a large number of shareholders (the so-called workers' control).

Bibliography

Abramov, A., Aksenov, I., Radygin, A., Chernova, M. (2018). Sovremennye podhody k izmereniyu gosudarstvennogo Sektora: metodologiya i empirika. *Ekonomicheskaya polityka*, 13(1).

Abugre, J.B., Anlesinya, A. (2019). Corporate Social Responsibility and Business Value of Multinational Companies: Lessons from a Sub-Saharan African Environment. *Journal of African Business*, 20(4), 435–454.

Adams, C.A. (2017). Conceptualising the Contemporary Corporate Value Creation Process. *Accounting Auditing and Accountability Journal*, 30(4), 906–931.

Ahamad, M.G., (2016). Local and Imported Coal-mix for Coal-based Power Plants in Bangladesh. *Energy Sources, Part B: Economics, Planning, and Policy*, 11, 936–945.

Apostolov, M. (2013). Governance and Enterprise Restructuring in Southeast Europe. *International Journal of Social Economics*, 40(8), 680–691.

Arora, V., Shi, S. (2016). Energy Consumption and Economic Growth in the United States. *Applied Economics*, 48(39), 3763–3773.

Artobolevskiy, S.S., (2003). Coal Mining Areas in Russia: National, Regional or Local Problem. *Mining Technology*, 112(1), 27–32.

Bai, X., Ding, H., Lian, J., Ma, D., Yang, X., Sun, N., Xue, W., Chang, Y. (2018). Coal Production in China: Past, Present, and Future Projections. *International Geology Review*, 60(5–6), 1–3.

Balat, M. (2006). Turkey's Coal Potential and Future Appearances. *Energy Sources, Part B: Economics, Planning, and Policy*, 1(2), 137–147.

Balat, M. (2009). Coal in the Global Energy Scene. *Energy Sources, Part B: Economics, Planning, and Policy*, 5(1), 50–62.

Belikov, I.V. (2019). *Sovet direktorov kompanii: novyj podhod*. De Libri.

Boardman A.E., Vining A.R. (1989). Ownership and Performance in Competitive Environments: A Comparison of the Performance of Private, Mixed and State-Owned Enterprises. *Journal of Law and Economics*, 32.

Borcherding, T., Pommerehne, W., Schneider, F. (1982). Comparing the Efficiency of Private and Public Production: The Evidence from Five Countries. *Zeitschrift für Nationaloekonomie*, 89, 127–156.

Burrell, G. (2017). The Role of Coal-mining Towns in Social Theory: Past, Present and Future. *Global Discourse*, 7(4), 451–468.

Cherkasova, V.A. (2014). Vliyanie gosudarstvennogo uchastiya v akcionernom kapitale na effektivnost' kompanij na razvivayushchihsya rynkah kapitala. *Korporativnye finansy*, 4(32).

Chhibber, P.K, Majumdar, S.K. (1999). State as Investor and State as Owner: Consequences for Firm Performance in India. *Economic Development and Cultural Change*, 3, 209–238.

CPA Australia, KPMG Australia, & Global Reporting Initiative Focal Point Australia. (2014). From Tactical to Strategic: How Australian Businesses Create Value from Sustainability. https://pdf4pro.com/view/global-reporting-initiative-focal-point-a ustralia-20e374.html [access date: 09. 05. 2020].

Estrin S., Hanousek, J., Kočenda, E., Svejnar, J. (2009). The Effects of Privatization and Ownership in Transition Economies. *Journal of Economic Literature*, 47(3), 699–728.

Faleev V.V. (2008). *Ponyatie i obshchaya harakteristika polozheniya minoritarnyh akcionerov v akcionernyh obshchestva*. Vestnik RGU im. I. Kanta. Ekonomicheskie i yuridicheskie nauki, 107–114.

Feoktistova, E.N., Alenicheva, L.V., Kopylova, G.A., Ozeryanskaya, M.N., Purtova, D.R., Honyakova, N.V. (2019). *Analiticheskij obzor korporativnyh nefinansovyh otchetov: 2017–2018*. RSPP. media.rspp.ru/document/1/7/4/743222fc4c6650093518c635d0e8ecdd. pdf [access date: 09. 05. 2020].

Ghose, M.K., Majee, S.R. (2000). Assessment of the impact on the air environment due to opencast coal mining - an Indian case study. *Atmospheric Environment*, 34(17), 2791–2796.

Greenberg, P. (2018). Coal Waste, Socioeconomic Change, and Environmental Inequality in Appalachia: Implications for a Just Transition in Coal Country. *Society & Natural Resources*, 31(9), 995–1011.

Hoelscher, K., Rustad, S.A., (2019). CSR and Social Conflict in the Brazilian Extractive Sector. *Conflict, Security & Development*, 19(1), 99–119.

Jiang, S., Yang, Ch., Guo, J., Ding, Z. (2018). ARIMA Forecasting of China's Coal Consumption, Price and Investment by 2030. *Energy Sources, Part B: Economics, Planning, and Policy*, 13(3), 190–195.

Jin, T., Kim, J. (2016). Relationship Between Coal Consumption and Economic Growth for OECD and non-OECD Countries. *Geosystem Engineering*, 9(1), 1–9.

Jonek-Kowalska, I. (2015). Challenges for Long-term Industry Restructuring in the Upper Silesian Coal Basin: What Has Polish Coal Mining Achieved and Failed from a Twenty-year Perspective? *Resources Policy*, 135–149.

Jonek-Kowalska, I. (2017). Coal Mining in Central-East Europe in Perspective of Industrial Risk. *Oeconomia Copernicana*, 8(1), 131–143.

Jonek-Kowalska, I. (2019). Transformation of Energy Balances with Dominant Coal Consumption in European Economies and Turkey in the Years 1990–2017. *Oeconomia Copernicana*, 10(4), 627–647.

Jonek-Kowalska, I., Turek, M. (2011). Possibilities of Improving the Efficiency of Mining Companies. *Equilibrium. Quarterly Journal of Economics and Economic Policy*, 6(2).

Kalabikhina, I.E., Krikunov, A.S.A. (2018). New Method of Assessing the Quality of NonFinancial Reporting (on the Example of Energy Companies). *Vestnik of Saint Petersburg University. Management*, 17(3), 297–328.

Karbownik, A., Stachowicz J., (1994). Social Aspects of Restructuring Hard Coal Mining in Poland. *Resources Policy*, 20(3), 198–201.

Kilimnik, V.G., Radionovskij, V.L. (2003). *Osnovnye rezul'taty restrukturizacii ugol'noj otrasli Rossii*. https://mining-media.ru/ru/article/ekonomic/1615-osnovnye-rezulta ty-restrukturizatsii-ugolnoj-otrasli-rossii [access date: 6. 05. 2020].

Kim, H.-M., Yoo, S.-H. (2016). Coal Consumption and Economic Growth in Indonesia. *Energy Sources, Part B: Economics, Planning, and Policy*, 11(6), 547–552.

Korchak, O.A. (2002). *Organizacionno-ekonomicheskij mekhanizm sozdaniya novyh rabochih mest v usloviyah restrukturizacii ugol'noj otrasli*. Diss. na soisk. uch. step. kand. ekon. nauk. - M.: MGGU.

Kostyleva, V., Leuede, G. (2012). *Formirovanie sovetov direktorov v stranah-chlenah OESR i Rossii*. OESR. https://www.oecd.org/daf/ca/Board%20RUS.pdf [access date: 29. 03. 2021].

Krasnyansky, G.L., Sarychev, A.E., Skryl, A.I. (2017). *Economic Crises and Coal of Russia*. House of NUST MISIS. https://www.rosugol.ru/upload/pdf/Сарычев%20block2. pdf [access data: 29. 03. 2021].

Kulczycka, J., (2004). EU New Members: Implications for the Mining Industry. *Minerals & Energy - Raw Materials Report*, 19(4), 34–44.

Kundzewicz, Z.W., Painter, J., Kundzewicz, W.J., (2019). Climate Change in the Media: Poland's Exceptionalism. *Environmental Communication*, 13(3), 366–380.

Liu, S., Li, W. (2019). Zoning and Management of Phreatic Water Resource Conservation Impacted by Underground Coal Mining: A Case Study in Arid and Semiarid Areas. *Journal of Cleaner Production*, 224, 677–685.

Liu, S., Li, W., Wang, Q. (2018). Zoning Method for Environmental Engineering Geological Patterns in Underground Coal Mining Areas. *Science of The Total Environment*, 634, 1064–1076.

Manowska, A., Tobór-Osadnik, K., Wyganowska, M. (2017). Economic and Social Aspects of Restructuring Polish Coal Mining: Focusing on Poland and the EU. *Resources Policy*, 10, 192–200.

Martus, E. (2019). Russian Industry Responses to Climate Change: The Case of the Metals and Mining Sector. *Climate Policy*, 19(1), 17–29.

Megginson, W.L. (2016). Privatization, State Capitalism, and State Ownership of Business in the 21st Century. *Foundations and Trends in Financing.* http://ssrn.com//abstract=2846784 [access date: 09. 05. 2020].

Mendelevitch, R., Hauenstein, C., Holz, F. (2019). The Death Spiral of Coal in the U.S.: Will Changes in U.S. Policy Turn the Tide? *Climate Policy*, 19(10), 1310–1324.

Meng, L., Feng, Q., Zhou, L., Lu, P., Meng, Q. (2009). Environmental Cumulative Effects of Coal Underground Mining. *Procedia Earth and Planetary Science*, 1(1), 1280–1284.

Mohanty, A., Chakladar, S., Mallick, S., Chakravarty, S. (2019). Structural Characterization of Coking Component of an Indian Coking Coal. *Fuel*, 249, 411–417.

Newell, A., Pastore, F. (2006). Regional Unemployment and Industrial Restructuring in Poland. *Eastern European Economics*, 44(3), 5–58.

Nikitin, A.N., Boyko, T.M. (2010). *Restrukturizaciya ugol'noj promyshlennosti.* http://ru-90.ru/content/никитин-ан-бёйкё-тм-реструктуризация-угёльнёй-прёмышленнёсти [access date: 6. 05. 2020].

Oei, P.-Y., Mendelevitch, R. (2019). Prospects for Steam Coal Exporters in the Era of Climate Policies: A Case Study of Colombia. *Climate Policy*, 19(1), 73–91.

Oguejiofor, G.C. (2009). Using Total Quality Management as a Tool for Re-engineering Coal Production in Nigerian Coal Corporation: An Energy Industry Case Study. *Energy Sources, Part B: Economics, Planning, and Policy*, 5(1), 29–40.

Paszcza, H. (2010). Procesy restrukturyzacyjne w polskim górnictwie węgla kamiennego w aspekcie zrealizowanych przemian i zmiany bazy zasobowej. *Górnictwo i Geoinżynieria*, 34(3), 63–82.

Plakitkina, L.S. (2013). *Sovremennoe sostoyanie i tendencii razvitiya dobychi uglya v stranah SNG.* https://mining-media.ru/ru/article/ekonomic/3889-sovremennoe-sostoyanie-i-tendentsii-razvitiya-dobychi-uglya-v-stranakh-sng [access date: 24. 04. 2020].

Rozhkov, A.A. (2016). *Regulirovanie social'no-ekonomicheskih posledstvij promyshlennoj restrukturizacii (na primere ugol'noj otrasli).* Rosinformugol'.

Rudkina, E.Y.U. (2006). Zashchita interesov minoritariev. *Bezopasnost' e-biznesa*, 1, 45–46.

Schleifer, A., Vishny, R.W. (1994). Politicians and Firms. *Quarterly Journal of Economics*, 109(4), 995–1025.

Shapiro, C., Willig, R.D. (1990). Economic Rationales for the Scope of Privatization. *The Political Economy of Private Sector*, 55–87.

Shirley, M., Walsh, P. (2000). Public versus Private Ownership. The Current State of the Debate. WB Policy Research Working Paper, 2420.

Solomon, J.F., Solomon, A., Joseph, N.L., Norton, S.D. (2013). Impression Management, Myth Creation and Fabrication in Private Social and Environmental Reporting: Insights from Erving Goffman. *Accounting, Organizations and Society*, 38(3), 195–213.

Song, B., Wen, J., Ferguson, M.A. (2020). Toward Effective CSR Communication in Controversial Industry Sectors. *Journal of Marketing Communications*, 26(3), 243–267.

Stefaniak, S., Twardowska, S. (2011). Impact of Residual Coal Extraction from Hard Coal Mining Waste Dumps on Groundwater Salinity. *Desalination and Water Treatment*, 33(1–3), 41–59.

Strangleman, T. (2018). Mining a Productive Seam? The Coal Industry, Community And Sociology. *Contemporary British History*, 32(1), 18–38.

Szczepański, M.S., (2003). Radical Reconstruction of Old Industrial Region of Upper Silesia, Poland. *Mining Technology*, 112(1), 9–16.

Tarazanov, I.G. (2019). Itogy raboty ugol'noy promishlennosty Rossii za yanvar. *Ugol' – Russian Coal Journal*, 3, 64–79.

Trigg, A.B., Dubourg, W.R. (1993). Valuing the Environmental Impacts of Opencast Coal Mining in the UK: The Case of the Trent Valley in North Staffordshire. *Energy Policy*, 21(11), 1110–1122.

Wang, J., Qin, Q., Bai, Z. (2018). Characterizing the Effects of Opencast Coal-Mining and Land Reclamation on Soil Macropore Distribution Characteristics Using 3D CT Scanning. *CATENA*, 171, 212–221.

Weisenberger, M.C., Burgess, J., Schobert, H.H., Hower, J.C. (2020). Thermal Properties of Pennsylvania Anthracite. *Fuel*, 266, Article 117101.

Yanovsky, A.B. (2019). Results of Structural Reorganization and Technological Re-equipment of the Coal Industry of the Russian Federation and Objectives for Prospective Development. *Ugol - Russian Coal Journal*, 8, 8–16.

Yılmaz, A.O. (2009). Present Coal Potential of Turkey and Coal Usage in Electricity Generation. *Energy Sources, Part B: Economics, Planning, and Policy*, 4(2), 135–144.

Zafrilla, J.E. (2014). The Mining Industry under the Thumb of politicians: The Environmental Consequences of the Spanish. *Journal of Cleaner Production*, 84.

Zagieva V., Matveeva A. (2017). General'naya liniya. *Harvard Business Review Russia*. https://hbr-russia.ru/liderstvo/lidery/a19741 [access date: 29. 03. 2021].

Zhang, M., Wang, J., Feng, Y. (2019). Temporal and Spatial Change of Land Use in a Large-Scale Opencast Coal Mine Area: A Complex Network Approach. *Land Use Policy*, 86, 375–386.

Zhang, X., Chu, H.-P., Chang, T., Inglesi-Lotz, R. (2017). Revisiting Coal Consumption and Output Nexus in China and India: A Frequency Domain Approach. *Energy Sources, Part B: Economics, Planning, and Policy*, 12(11), 1015–1021.

Zhuo, Y., Shen, Y. (2020). Three-dimensional Transient Modelling of Coal and Coke Co-combustion in the Dynamic Raceway of Ironmaking Blast Furnaces. *Applied Energy*, 261, 114456.

Zientara, P. (2009). Restructuring the Coal Mining Industry: Unionism, Conflict, and Cooperation: Evidence from Poland. *Eastern European Economics*, 47(1), 41–59.

Zubov, V., Inozemcev, V. (2015). Ekonomika «chudes»: pochemu gosudarstvennye kompanii tak neeffektivny. https://www.rbc.ru/opinions/economics/28/09/2015/560923639a79472a14442d47 [access date: 29. 03. 2021].

4 Aims and attitudes of the management board in coal mining enterprise development

Interdisciplinary problems of management in extractive industries

The management boards of mining enterprises face many difficult tasks because their members must have knowledge and experience in both social sciences and technical sciences. Knowledge and experience in the field of social sciences are necessary for effective management, for solving financial and employee problems. In the case of social conflicts – and those in the hard coal mining industry are very common – the ability to negotiate and resolve group disputes is also essential.

In turn, knowledge and experience in the field of technical sciences are needed to understand the course of mining production, which affects not only its coordination and efficiency, but primarily, the safety of mining crews. In this context, the scope of responsibility of management boards in mining enterprises becomes significantly more complicated. Due to the high accident rate, including group accidents or mining disasters, the management board has above average obligations in relation to the proper conduct of investment and production processes, and ensuring compliance with the principles of occupational health and safety.

In Poland, to overcome the above challenges, two mechanisms are used in the process of appointing management boards of mining companies. The first is the creation of a fairly large number of positions in the management board, so that the scope of duties covers all possible areas of operation of mining enterprises. An example of the composition of management board positions for the three largest Polish mining companies is presented in Table 4.1.

The list in Table 4.1 shows that a typical structure of the management board's area of activity relates to financial, operational, technical, strategic and development affairs. In addition, each company has an obligation to appoint a vice president for employee affairs, who is elected and dismissed by the workforce. This emphasises the rank of employees in the company's hierarchy and confirms the prominence of social priorities in state-owned mining enterprises in Poland.

The second mechanism securing the respective competences of management board members in state-owned mining enterprises is the law, whereby positions

DOI: 10.4324/9781003091110-7

Table 4.1 List of positions on the management boards of the three largest Polish mining enterprises

Enterprise	Management board position
Polska Grupa Górnicza SA	President
	Vice-President of the Board for Production
	Vice-President of the Board for Employee Affairs
	Vice-President of the Board for Finance
Jastrzębska Spółka Węglowa SA	President
	Deputy President of the Board for Technical and Operational Affairs
	Deputy President of the Board for Development
	Deputy President of the Board for Labour and Social Policy
	Deputy President of the Board for Economic Affairs
Bogdanka SA	President
	Deputy President of the Board for Employee and Social Affairs
	Deputy President of the Board for Economic and Financial Affairs
	Deputy President of the Board for Development

Source: own work

in the management board are filled by way of a competition run by supervisory boards. In turn, members of supervisory boards must have passed a state examination or have a doctorate in economics or law. This is designed to guarantee the highest level of knowledge and experience to both management and supervisory bodies in mining enterprises.

Looking at the composition of positions of the management board and the desired competences, initially noticeable in Poland is that the issues that are priority for managers in Poland are related to the finances and safety of mining crews. Although the composition includes a member responsible for development, this development is still understood quite traditionally and mainly interpreted in the context of tangible investments. There are also no positions for sustainable development or ecological issues on the management boards, which indicates their marginalisation. These initial observations will be further verified in the context of the analysis of CSR reports and the opinions of management board members.

In the next part of this chapter, three Russian coal companies are analysed: a private joint-stock company (SUEK), a public joint-stock company (EVRAZ) and a subsidiary of a holding company (Kuzbassrazrezugol). The list of positions on the management boards of these Russian mining enterprises is presented in Table 4.2. These companies differ in terms of management policies and have many more positions on the board than Polish companies.

The quality of activities performed by Russian joint-stock companies in general – and coal companies in particular – is ensured by corporate legislation

Table 4.2 List of positions on the management boards of the Russian mining enterprises

Enterprise	Management board position
SUEK AO	**Board of Directors:** **Chairman** Chairman of the Strategy Committee Chairman of the Audit Committee Chairman of the Nomination and Compensation Committee Chief Audit Executive **The Management Board:** Chief Executive Officer Chief Operations Officer Chief Commercial Officer Chief Financial Officer and Industrial Safety Committee Risk Committee Investment Committee Procurement Committee Budget Committee Project Committee Sales Policy Committee
EVRAZ Group SA	**Board of Directors:** Chairman Chairman of Audit Committee Chairman of Nominations Committee Chairman of Remuneration Committee Chairman of HSE Committee **The Management Board:** Chief Executive Officer Senior Vice President, Business Support and Interregional Relations Senior Vice President, Commerce and Business Development Chief Financial Officer Vice President, Corporate Strategy and Performance Management Vice President, Sales Vice President, Head of the Siberia Division Vice President, Head of the Urals Division Vice President, Head of the Coal Division Vice President, Vanadium Division Chief Executive Officer, EVRAZ North America Vice President, Compliance with Business Procedures and Asset Protection Vice President, Health, Safety and Environment Vice President, Corporate Communications Vice President, Human Resources Vice President, Information Technologies Vice President, Legal

(Continued)

Table 4.2 Continued

Enterprise	Management board position
UK Kuzbassrazrezugol AO	**Director**
	Deputy Director for Production
	Deputy Director for Technology
	Deputy Director for Procurement
	Deputy Director for Resources
	Deputy Commercial Director
	Deputy Director for Construction
	Deputy Director for Economics and Finance
	Deputy Director for Human Resources and General Issues
	Deputy Director for Legal Support
	Deputy Director for Occupational Safety and Health
	Deputy Director for Environmental Issues, Process Safety, and Land Use
	Deputy Director for Underground Mining Operations

Source: own work

and management norms. In terms of corporate management quality, SUEK, the largest private joint-stock company, is the best example. Corporate management mechanisms include:

- a significant number of independent directors on the Board of Directors (50% in SUEK);
- directors' and officers' liability insurance (USD 25 million);
- considerable experience as a member of the Board of Directors (6 to 7 years on average) and in specific areas (energy, international business, finance, investments, risk management, and production).

The corporate management system includes the Board of Directors, the Management Board and management. The multi-level system provides independence in setting and achieving multiple goals in the field of company sustainability.

The Board of Directors at SUEK consists of 8 members, including 4 independent non-executive directors, 3 non-executive directors and a Chief Executive Officer. The composition is balanced in terms of work experience: each 25% of the board members has 0–3, 4–6, 7–9 or more than 9 years of experience. As for professional areas, all members of the Board of Directors have experience in the energy sector and international business; most of the top managers have experience in finance (80%), investment and risk management (70%), as well as production (60%). The Board of Directors deals with the most important issues for the development of the company from a holistic point of view, which includes improving operational efficiency in the coal and energy segments, strategic development of both the company as a whole and its segments, process safety, upgrading thermal power stations, personnel issues and the incentive system for the management.

The Board of Directors pays particular attention to the systems responsible for occupational safety and health, as well as process safety at the facilities. Its decisions are reflected in the company's HR strategy. The Board of Directors analyses the current process safety standards and the production process itself in order to develop solutions aimed at improving operational efficiency, with particular attention being paid to tunnelling operations. The report produced as a result of this analysis became a blueprint for adjustments to the budget for the year 2020.

Primary responsibility for safety rests with the Chairman of the Nomination and Compensation Committee, who focuses the Committee's activities on the improvement of labour, industrial, and environmental safety. The Committee carefully analyses the circumstances surrounding any fatal or severe occupational accident. Important aspects of the activity are ensuring compliance with industrial and environmental safety standards at the facilities, monitoring the system of key performance indicators in this area, assessing the compliance of the industrial safety system with regulatory and corporate requirements, assessing the efficiency of controls in this area, analysing the causes and consequences of accidents, as well as developing recommendations on their future prevention.

The Chairman of the Audit Committee assesses, among other audit and control issues, the effectiveness of the internal control and risk management processes. In addition to the regular preparation of the company's Annual Report, the Committee monitored the preparation status of the Sustainable Development Report for 2018–2019, which focuses on environmental protection and ecology, environmental performance, efficiency, as well as industrial and labour safety.

The Internal Audit and Compliance management system is led by the Chief Audit Executive, however, it is functionally subordinate to the Audit Committee. When planning its work, the Service applies a risk-based approach, taking into account the external environment and performance of the company, the focus areas of the Board of Directors and executives, as well as risk assessment results. In 2019, particular focus was given to the following issues: industrial and labour safety, as well as environmental protection.

Based on the recommendations of the Service, managers develop and take corrective actions aimed at improving the efficiency of the internal control system, business processes and operations. The Service monitors and analyses the efficiency of such actions.

The primary responsibilities of the Management Board are the development and implementation of the company's production, commercial and other operational plans and improvement programmes. It is also responsible for the timely and effective coordination of the resolutions of the company's executive bodies. In order to achieve its targets, under the Regulation of the Management Board, SUEK established Management Board committees and panels that enable key managers and experts from different positions to interact on the main issues affecting the company's operations, including consultations on economic, environmental and social matters.

The Board of Directors at EVRAZ Group SA consists of 9 members, including 5 independent non-executive directors, 3 non-executive directors and a Chief Executive Officer. The committees of the board differ from those at SUEK: there is no strategy committee and there is a separate HSE committee. In general, the corporate management system at EVRAZ Group SA is similar to that of the SUEK corporate governance system, with the same management models being used.

UK Kuzbassrazrezugol is a part of the UMMC Group and, in fact, a production asset, which results in a different management structure. The company pursues a policy aligned with the structure of the holding company, making independent decisions, mainly in the field of production. The management structure is linear and functional, production-oriented and headed by a director. The director and 12 deputies ensure that the company operates smoothly, primarily in terms of production. Responsibility for achieving sustainable development goals connected with ecology, social environment and CSR lies with the Director, Deputy Director for Human Resources and General Issues and Deputy Director for Environmental Issues, Process Safety and Land Use. They determine the social policy of the company, plan and keep records of personnel costs, manage the company's interaction with the authorities, determine and implement the company's environmental policy and manage the search for the best ways to solve issues in the field of environmental protection and land use, including those connected with occupational safety and health.

UK Kuzbassrazrezugol has developed several documents, including the Quality, Environment, as well as Occupational Safety and Health Policy, Process Safety Policy Statement and Human Rights Policy, environmental safety and protection documents, as well as process safety action plans.

How does the management board reach its aims, while trying to be socially responsible? Is CSR reporting fake or responsible news? Case studies

From the point of view of the operation of the Polish hard coal mining industry in the European Union, it is important for the management board that the mines engage in social business activities and sustainable development. One of the ways to ascertain whether and to what extent a given organisation implements the principles of sustainable development is their submission of annual reports on activities in the field of corporate social responsibility (CSR).

A directive has been in force in the European Union since 2014 that obliges the largest companies to disclose non-financial information annually. In Poland, such reports have to be submitted by large mining enterprises employing at least 500 people and declaring revenues of at least EUR 40 million. So far, no uniform template has been developed for the submitted reports, therefore the scope of information contained therein in practice is very different. It may only include basic information that guarantees the fulfilment of the reporting obligation (often giving the appearance of CSR activities). It can also contain very detailed financial and non-financial (descriptive) data about the functioning of the organisation and its activities for sustainable development.

At present, in Poland and the European Union, no consequences are foreseen in a situation where the CSR report is unreliable and contains false data and information. However, there are collections of good practices in the world which contain the most important guidelines for correct and comprehensive CSR reports. Therefore, it is possible to verify each of the reports of mining enterprises in terms of meeting these requirements.

The most popular and most frequently used CSR reporting model in the world are the guidelines contained in the documents developed by GRI – Global Reporting Initiative – a foundation in Boston. The information that should be included in the report prepared in accordance with the GRI principles is divided into several categories and relates to such issues as the characteristics of the enterprise and its activities for employees, the environment, local communities and other aspects relevant to sustainable development (e.g. principles of fundraising for CSR or industry benchmarking).

For the management boards of Polish mining companies, the industry document *G4 Sector Disclosures in Mining and Metals 2013* is the most important in terms of CSR reporting (GRI, 2013). The guidelines therein should be used as a reference to the requirements for reporting in the area of sustainable development by enterprises operating in the mining industry. The main issues contained in the document concern:

- monitoring, using and managing land property,
- participation/contribution to the development of the national economy and community,
- local communities and stakeholder involvement,
- employment, employment relations (employee/employer relations),
- environmental management,
- small-scale traditional mining,
- an integrated approach to the use of mineral resources.

Below, using the example of Polish mining enterprises, an analysis has been carried out to determine whether and to what extent the management boards of mining enterprises submit CSR reports, how accessible they are, and what scope of information is contained in them.

LW Bogdanka SA seems the best among Polish mining enterprises. There is a tab on the company's website entitled 'our responsibility', where you can find all the most important information on the involvement of the organisation in CSR. All integrated CSR reports submitted by the company since 2012 are also published there. In addition to CSR reports, the company also presents a policy of social involvement. This document contains structured information related to donating and joining initiatives in the field of socio-cultural sponsorship. All documentation is prepared very clearly and thoroughly. The Management Board describes in detail the purpose of spending funds geographically and by type. It also presents the rules of applying for support and exhaustively defines its priorities and principles of cooperation.

LW Bogdanka SA submits a CSR report in accordance with the GRI guidelines and the sixth integrated report, combining financial results and non-financial information. The report is prepared according to the Core version using the Mining industry supplement. The document consists of five parts. The first chapter – a developed and safe region – describes the company's operation in the region. The second chapter is on an environmentally efficient mine, presenting data on the enterprise's commitment to sustainable development. The third chapter – a safe mine – focuses on occupational safety and health issues. The fourth chapter is devoted to effective and innovative business and contains data on the financial results of the organisation and its innovativeness. Chapter five provides information on responsible management, ethics and anti-corruption. The report also contains information on the regional consequences of the cessation of mining activities in the region, which can be treated as a marketing element, but does not lessen the informative value of this document.

In the report of LW Bogdanka SA, in order to increase credibility, the management board also decided to present many practical initiatives. For example, the authors of the report indicate that in 2019 the company engaged in a partnership for urban aesthetics and sustainable development in cooperation with the local government. The enterprise also runs sponsorship activities as part of the Akademia Bogdanki programme. Activities conducted in this area concern:

- sports education for children and youth,
- supporting talents from the region,
- supporting initiatives to prevent social exclusion,
- participation in educational projects initiated by educational centres,
- participation in projects related to the improvement of safety.

The report of LW Bogdanka SA – in the part devoted to ecology – presents detailed information on the management of resources and waste, and the impact of activities on climate change and biodiversity. Interestingly, the enterprise did not just provide positive information about its sustainable development activities. The company has also conducted a thorough analysis of environmental threats, pointing out that mining activities are associated with the risk of:

- mining damage and the need for remediation,
- tightening of standards and legal regulations in the field of environmental protection law and the obligation to obtain permits for the use of the environment,
- management of waste generated after the expansion of the mining area,
- investment projects related to the presence of protected areas, where exploitation will not be possible.

In the case of Jastrzębska Spółka Węglowa SA – the second of the three largest mining companies – the website also includes a 'responsible business' tab, where you can find information on the involvement of the organisation in CSR. Reports have been made public since 2017. The Management Board instructs that the report be prepared in accordance with the GRI requirements. It contains the most important information on the company's social and environmental activities and numerous indicators documenting this activity. The JSW SA report is also detailed and extensive. However, it seems less clear than the LW Bogdanka SA document described earlier. In particular, it lacks information to indicate which version of the GRI it was prepared in accordance with and whether it also includes industry requirements for mining.

The structure of the report is based on the goals and the analysis of their implementation. In the report, these goals were formulated into the statements below:

- We respect science and use innovation so we can develop in a more sustainable way.
- We respect life and health and do not compromise on safety.
- We respect every human being, our community, taking joint responsibility for JSW and its property.
- We respect non-renewable resources through their efficient use.
- We respect the natural environment and the immediate natural and social surroundings of the areas in which JSW conducts its activities.
- We respect the needs and expectations of our customers.
- We respect transparency and honesty in management.

JSW SA refers in the report to many practical initiatives in the field of CSR and sustainable development. It describes, among other things, their participation in the Joint Social Initiatives Group – Górnictwo O.K. This is a project carried out with external partners, the aim of which is to create space and environment for the development of joint initiatives as part of broadly understood corporate social responsibility in the mining industry in Poland. The report also presents cyclical social programmes to support culture and tradition, leisure and recreation, science and education as well as health and safety. JSW SA implements them through a foundation established for this purpose.

The report also takes into account, although to a lesser extent, ecological aspects, presenting the impact of mining on the immediate natural environment of the enterprise, water management and areas of natural value. In this case, the management board did not hesitate to present the weaknesses of the activity, as testified for example in the chapter on the negative impact of mining activities, including, in particular, mining damage caused by the company and the initiatives it took to repair it.

Polska Grupa Górnicza SA (PGG SA), the third largest Polish state-owned mining company, does much worse compared to the enterprises presented above. Currently, there is no tab on the company's website devoted to corporate social activity. Before PGG SA was established, part of it operated as Katowicki Holding Węglowy SA and from that period you can find selected, individual annual CSR reports of this company, prepared in accordance with GRI standards. The second part of PGG SA – Kompania Węglowa SA – did not prepare CSR reports at all. Therefore, the consolidated PGG SA does not have any well-established information traditions regarding the implementation of the sustainable development policy, and the enterprise, which is currently focused on serious financial problems, facing bankruptcy, does not find time for topics not directly related to the economic aspects that determine the company's further operations. It is also worth recalling that PGG SA is not listed on the stock exchange, so it does not need to strive to meet the standards typical of modern public companies. In this context, however, a question arises whether LW Bogdanka SA and JSW SA would act and report on sustainable development if it was not about caring for the image among shareholders?

A synthetic assessment of the management board's reporting on the sustainable development policy for the three Polish enterprises described above is presented in Table 4.3.

It is worth comparing the results of the analysis of the reports with the results of previous Polish research on the use of the CSR concept in coal mining, which was carried out in 2017 by Jarosławska-Sobór (Jarosławska-Sobór, 2017). These studies confirm our analysis of CSR reports. They show that Bogdanka SA and JSW SA are more strongly committed to sustainable development and that they use CSR tools better than PGG SA. The reports prepared by these mining enterprises – as long as they are prepared in accordance with international standards and contain credible data – do not constitute fake news, but valuable information about the company's activities, reflecting its understanding and implementation of the SD concept.

In the Russian Federation, among large mining companies and metal manufacturers, only two companies – SUEK and Severstal, which hold top positions in various rankings – regularly disclose sustainable development information voluntarily (see Table 4.4). EVRAZ PLC issued one integrated report in 2017 and a sustainable development report in 2018.

It should be noted that most coal companies (SDS-Ugol, Kuzbassrazrezugol, EVRAZ, Mechel, Sibanthracite, Russian Coal, Kolmar and VostSibUgol), that

Table 4.3 Assessment of the content of CSR reports of mining enterprises in Poland (based on data from 2019)

Enterprise	Integrated report	GRI guidelines	G4 Mining and minerals
Polska Grupa Górnicza SA	-	-	-
Jastrzębska Spółka Węglowa SA	+	+	-
Bogdanka SA	+	+	+

Source: own work

Table 4.4 CSR performance indicators at SUEK and Severstal (Russian Federation)

Enterprise	Rankings	Years and reports
SUEK	Leader in RSPP Sustainable Development Rankings issued by the Russian Union of Industrialists and Entrepreneurs (2014–2019). 4th place in the 2018 Sustainable Development Ranking (Expert Magazine) Leader in Corporate Philanthropy (2018). Winner in the following categories: Efficient Charity Program Management, Best Social Investment Disclosure Program, and Charity Transparency (2016–2018).	2000–2018 (CSR and SD reports)
Severstal	Leader in sustainable development (the first position among Russian metal manufacturers); Expert Magazine (2019). Corporate Human Rights Benchmark (CHRB) in human rights compliance (2019). Ranks among 500 world's best employers according to Forbes (2019). place in the Social Efficiency in the Mining and Metals Industry Ranking issued by AK&M (2018). 1st place in the Mentoring in Manufacturing category of the 1st All-Russian Best Mentoring Practices Competition organized by the Agency for Strategic Initiatives (2018).	2004–2006, 2010–2018 (CSR and SD reports)

Source: own work based on Feoktistova, et al. (2020)

do not publish SD reports in accordance with international standards, have expanded information on social and environmental aspects of their activities in annual reports. Their annual reports are very similar in essence to integrated reports. It would be fair to classify both these and other documents as combined (as they are called in international reviews and the trade press).

The annual reports produced by coal companies contain information on financial performance, production, as well as environmental and social aspects. Sometimes, these sections can be quite extensive, becoming almost as comprehensive as SD reports. Most often, the sections on social and environmental aspects give information on staff numbers and structure, occupational safety and health, as well as process safety, charity and also contain environmental indicators reflecting the main areas of impact (emissions, waste and energy consumption). Many companies report having policies and corporate programmes in these spheres.

In Russia, there is a regulation for assuring integrated reports that was developed by the Council for Non-Financial Reporting of the Russian Union of Industrialists and Entrepreneurs (RSPP). The regulation defines the subject of analysis and assessment, which is the completeness and significance of the information presented in the report from the point of socially responsible business practices (as stated in the Social Charter of Russian Business and reflected in the UN Global Compact, as well as in the GOST R ISO 26000:2012 standard). It is emphasised that the company's goals, actions and performance should comply with the UN's sustainable development goals, according to the 2030 Agenda.

Based on the results of assurance, the company is given an assurance statement and a certificate of verification. The company, at its discretion, can make this assurance statement public, by including it in a report or uploading it on its website, or using it for internal purposes. This helps stakeholders compare their own point of view with the position taken by the Council's experts, which is an additional source of information.

RSPP Sustainable Development Rankings is the first and, so far, the only system in Russia for independent assessment of companies' performance in this area. It is included in the international database of ratings, rankings and sustainability indices at reportingexchange.com. This system contains a set of tools for independent assessment of contributions made by organisations to sustainable development of society, corporate responsibility and transparency.

The set of indicators for compiling indices in the system was formed based on an analysis of information requests from a wide range of stakeholders that are reflected in international SD and CSR reporting standards, the main global rankings and analytical assessments of the stock market.

For mining companies, environmental responsibility indices are calculated in addition to other indices, in order to mitigate their impact on the environment and improve the efficiency of using natural resources. The environmental responsibility ranking is based on the criteria formulated in the General Provisions for the Environmental and Social Responsibility of Mining Companies and international documents, including the Initiative for Responsible Mining Assurance (IRMA), GRI Sustainability Reporting Guidelines and the EBRD's Extractive Mining Industries Strategy. In 2019, such companies as SDS-Ugol, Severstal, Kuzbassrazrezugol, EVRAZ, SUEK, Mechel, Sibanthracite, Russian Coal, Kolmar and VostSibUgol were included in the environmental responsibility ranking (*The 2019 Environmental Responsibility Transparency Ranking of Russian Mining Companies and Metal Manufacturers*).

Fundamental aims and principles of the management board functioning in mining enterprises and its place in sustainable development – expert survey

This last section focuses on the perception and implementation of corporate social responsibility by the management of mining enterprises by looking at a survey that was conducted in Poland and Russia. The goal is to directly identify the management board's priorities in the context of implementing the concept of sustainable development. In this regard, respondents were asked about the following 15 statements:

1 I know what documents of corporate social responsibility (CSR) are regulated in my company and I can use them in practice with the principles of CSR.
2 My company discloses CSR results in corporate reporting.
3 In my experience, there were cases of CSR being applied.
4 Mining enterprises should apply CSR principles in their business activities.
5 CSR principles for mining enterprises should be more restrictive than for other industries.
6 Economic goals are a priority in the mining enterprise, in which I co-manage.
7 Social goals are a priority in the mining enterprise, in which I co-manage.
8 Safety of mining crews is a priority in the mining enterprise, in which I co-manage.
9 Environmental goals are a priority in the mining enterprise, in which I co-manage.
10 CSR issues in my company are resolved at the board level.
11 The application of CSR principles in mining enterprises has a positive effect on the financial result.
12 The application of CSR principles in mining enterprises has a positive effect on the value for all stakeholders.
13 The application of CSR principles in mining enterprises improves their image and contributes to an increase in the acceptance of mining production.
14 The application of CSR principles in mining enterprises has a positive effect on the attitude of employees to work.
15 The application of CSR principles in mining enterprises has a positive effect on health and reduction of industrial injuries.

Statements 1 to 5 allowed to identify the attitude of the managers to the idea and scope of CSR implementation in mining enterprises. Statements 6 to 10 made it possible to identify the hierarchy of importance of individual priorities. Statements 7 to 15 provided information on the assessment of the impact of CSR on: financial results, value, image, as well as the motivation and safety of mining crews.

The respondents rated the statements contained in the survey using a five-point Likert scale, where 1 means completely agree and 5 completely disagree. The assessment of the agreement in their views was carried out using the Kendall's coefficient of concordance:

$$w = 12 \times \frac{\left(\sum_{i=1}^{N} T_i^2\right) - \frac{\left(\sum_{i=1}^{N} T_i\right)^2}{N}}{m^2 \times (N^3 - N) - m \times \sum_{j=1}^{m} \sum_{k=1}^{s_j} (t_{jk}^3 - t_{jk})}$$

where:

N – sample size
m – number of different sets of (experts') assessments,
T_i – the sum of the ranks of all i observation assessments,
s_j – number of different tied ranks,
t_{jk} – number of observations in the k-th linked rank by the j-th expert.

The statistical significance of the obtained result was checked using the X^2 test at the significance level p=0.05.

In Poland, 18 experts, who are current or past members of management boards of mining enterprises, participated in the survey. The assessment of the individual statements is shown in Figure 4.1. And so, in the first group of questions, most of the experts definitely confirmed their knowledge of CSR principles, as well as their reporting and implementation as part of the mining enterprise's operations (the ratings for questions 1 to 3 ranged from 1.17 to 1.83). However, managers were less decisive in the assessment of the need to apply CSR in mining enterprises (2.39) and the application of more restrictive reporting requirements to the mining industry (2.94). Such distribution of answers proves the lack of full conviction to the practical importance of sustainable development and a certain, though minor, reluctance to emphasise the diversity of mining enterprises in the context of CSR and SD.

In the hierarchy of priorities, work safety of mining crews was rated the highest (1.22). Economic goals (1.72) were rated second, followed by environmental goals (3.56) and social goals (3.72), which were both rated much lower. This outcome confirms the conclusions from the previous considerations on the functioning of Polish mining enterprises, where the health and life of underground workers and the achievement of positive financial results guaranteeing the survival of the extraction industry in Poland are of the utmost importance. Social objectives have been marginalised to a certain extent in the assessment, which can be considered a fairly

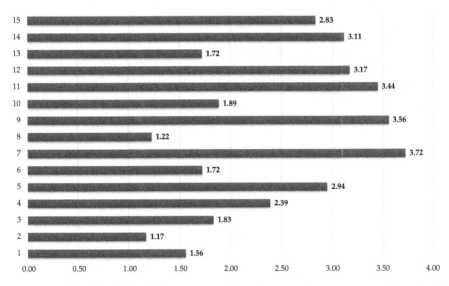

Figure 4.1 Results of the CSR survey conducted among the management boards of Polish mining companies (1–15 – questions asked in the survey)
Source: own research

significant mental change, all the more so as, in the presented assessment, they were placed behind ecological goals. Such an outcome could be assessed positively, if it were not for the low rank ultimately awarded to both social and environmental goals.

The managers of Polish mining enterprises did not notice a significant impact of the implementation of CSR on the financial results, value of mining enterprises and employees' attitudes (ratings above 3). In their opinion, the use of CSR had the best effect on the image of mining enterprises and increased the level of acceptance for running mining activities. It also had an average impact on health and the reduction in accident rates, which can be attributed to the implementation of additional accident prevention measures and training of employees in the field of OSH as part of CSR.

The agreement factor of the surveyed experts is statistically significant and its value is $W=0.4522$, which allows us to reject the null hypothesis that there is a lack of agreement between the surveyed members of the management board. Their agreement is at an average level, which makes it possible to adopt and generalise the survey results.

Summarising the obtained results, it can be stated that Polish enterprises apply CSR principles, but are not entirely convinced of their significance and impact on the functioning of mining enterprises. In their opinion, the activities undertaken in this area mainly have an image-building effect and allow the environment to look more kindly upon mining operations. However, such an approach and understanding of CSR may lead to simulating activities in this area and not achieving real benefits related to the sustainable development of the extraction industry. As part of remedial actions, education and research on the actual benefits of CSR and their real impact on the finances of enterprises should, therefore, be deepened.

Forty active functional and top-level managers of the largest coal companies took part in the expert survey in Russia. Figure 4.2. shows the graphical assessment of the survey results. The reference group included three economic departments managers, three managers of human resources and industrial safety departments, three executive managers, a public affairs manager, a manager of legal service department, 19 managers of production departments.

The first group of statements covering the general level of awareness of CSR received the highest ratings from the respondents. In particular, the first three statements were rated at 1.63–1.90. This indicates that the respondents confirm their competence in the company's CSR issues: knowledge of the principles, quality of reports, implementation projects. As for the practical application of CSR (statement 4), the assessments are more cautious and are at an average level (2.28). Interestingly, Russian experts in the coal industry are not inclined to believe that CSR requirements for coal enterprises should be more stringent than in other industries (also at an average level of 3.03).

In the hierarchy of CSR priorities, workplace safety was rated as the most significant task (1.88). At the same time, from the point of view of CSR, social and environmental goals have approximately the same significance (2.43–2.50), economic goals are in last place (3.10).

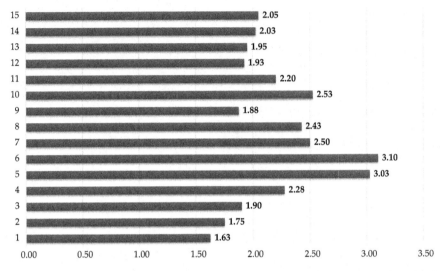

Figure 4.2 Results of the CSR survey conducted among the management boards of
Russian mining companies (1–15 – questions asked in the survey)
Source: own research

Judging by the answers to the question about who is to carry out CSR in coal companies (question 10), many respondents believe that CSR is not only the level of the company's top management, but also the competence of line managers. It is interesting to note that there is the greatest rating spread on this issue: 1 point (complete agreement) was given by 10 respondents, 5 points (complete disagreement) were given by 5 experts, i.e. the opinions of almost half of the respondents are opposite.

The last group of statements reflects the impact of CSR on the financial, environmental and social performance of coal companies. Russian respondents hold a moderately centrist position (1.93–2.20). At the same time, CSR has the greatest impact on the general environment of the company and its reputation (1.93–1.95). Statements 14 and 15 received slightly lower ratings (the impact of CSR on employee attitudes and workplace safety). It is also interesting to note that, according to Russian experts, CSR has a less positive effect on financial performance (score 2.20 to statements 11).

The agreement factor of the surveyed experts is statistically significant and its value is W=0.34, which allows us to reject the null hypothesis that there is a lack of agreement between the surveyed members of the management board. Their agreement is at very low level, which makes it possible to adopt and generalise the survey results.

Diametrically opposed views on the priority of social and economic tasks – according to Russian and Polish managers – can be explained by the difference in the respondents' sampling pattern, as well as by the form of ownership.

In terms of ownership, as noted in Chapter 2, in Poland coal enterprises are state-owned, while in the CIS countries, and especially in Russia, they are private. To some extent this explains the priorities in goal selection. In terms of the survey sampling pattern, in Poland the participants are mainly board members, in Russia they are managers of various levels, including those who directly work with staff.

Board members and top-level managers take an interest in improving the economic performance of coal companies, as this correlates with their bonuses and emoluments, depending on the company pay system. Managers at the production site, especially those employed in the field of industrial safety, are largely focused on the comfort of the work process: stability and satisfaction of personnel, social protection, conflict settling, motivation for better performance, responsibility of employees, quality of production processes.

The analysis of the results of the survey also indicates a divergence of opinions of Russian and Polish colleagues on issues 11, 12, 14. Russian experts are more inclined to believe that the application of CSR principles at coal enterprises has a positive effect on financial performance, on company stakeholders and on the attitude of employees to work. Polish respondents consider it more important to achieve environmental and economic goals, paying less attention to social goals and workplace safety. This might also be related to the form of ownership and the need to comply with all legislative norms within certain strict frameworks. Recognising the importance of social goals in Russian coal companies, the respondents emphasize the impact of CSR on employees and workplace safety, believing that the situation with industrial accidents and occupational diseases will improve.

Bibliography

Feoktistova, E.N., Kopylova, G.A., Moskvina, M.V., Ozeryanskaya, M.N., Purtova, D. R. (2020). *Decent Work – Sustainable Business*. Corporate Practices. RSPP: Moscow.

GRI (2013). Reporting with the Sector Standards. G4 Sector Disclosures in Mining and Metals. https://www.globalreporting.org/standards/sector-program/ [access date: 24. 04. 2020].

Jarosławska-Sobór, S. (2017). CSR w polskim górnictwie. Uwarunkowania funkcjonowania i rozwoju. *Scientific Papers of Silesian University of Technology. Organization and Management Series*, 112, 167–178.

The 2019 Environmental Responsibility Transparency Ranking of Russian Mining Companies and Metal Manufacturers (2019). http://media.rspp.ru/document/1/f/c/fc4fda483e6c6d162021adb4665d3edf.pdf [access date: 29. 03. 2020].

5 Employees and their position in negotiating processes

Employees of mining enterprises from an international perspective

Hard coal mining – according to the data and considerations presented in Chapter 3 – exists practically on all continents (Rafaty et al., 2020). In Europe, it is in decline, but in Asia a dynamic development of this industry can be observed (Lahiri-Dutt, 2017; Li et al., 2019). The production of coal also increases in the CIS countries, which are discussed in this monograph. There are also mining enterprises in North America, South America and Australia. Due to the scale and scope of its conducted activities, the mining industry is a significant regional and national employer, which is important for economic development, unemployment and the income of residents (Svobodova et al., 2020; Williams and Nikijuluw, 2020). Nevertheless, employment in the mining industry in the world largely depends on whether it concerns countries that significantly reduced mining production in the twentieth century, or countries that now continue to increase it, becoming leaders in mining.

For example, in the case of Poland, the number of people employed in mining has significantly decreased over the last 25 years due to the progressing mechanisation of work (Bołoz and Biały, 2020) and the deep restructuring of the industry (Kaczorowski and Gajewski, 2008). The decline in employment caused by these phenomena is illustrated in Figure 5.1, which shows that, over 25 years, the number of people employed in the Polish hard coal mining industry decreased by almost 70%.

However, such rapid changes in employment do not apply to all regions where mining enterprises operate. In Australia and the USA, which are the world's leading coal producers, a slow downward trend in the number of employees could be observed in recent years, but it was not as constant and radical as in the case of Europe (Figures 5.2 and 5.3).

This is mainly due to the restrictive decarbonisation policy in European Union countries, which is not carried out on such a large scale in other regions of the world. Moreover, the level of civilisation and economic development in Europe makes it possible to replace traditional energy and heat fuels with renewable or nuclear sources, while in less prosperous

DOI: 10.4324/9781003091110-8

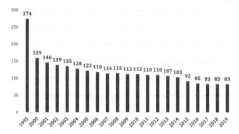

Figure 5.1 Employment in the Polish mining industry in the years 1995–2019 [in thousands of people]
Source: study based on Bluszcz (2014) and Derski (2020)

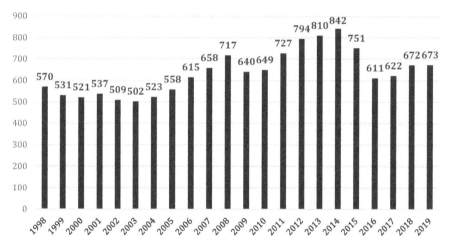

Figure 5.2 Employment in mining in the USA in the years 1998–2019 [in thousands of people]
Source: Statista (2020)

regions (Asia, Africa, South America) such a substitution is impossible or difficult for economic and/or technological reasons. Mining still remains an attractive workplace there and a source of income for many local communities. In turn, in regions such as the USA and Australia, mining is largely earmarked for exports, and the low costs due to the open-pit mining system are an additional source of competitiveness, allowing for the continuation of mining and maintaining jobs.

Despite a significant reduction in mining in the European Union, hard coal and lignite mining remains an important industry. In 2019, the countries extracting this raw material created a total of over 151 million jobs in the EU economy (Oei and Mendelevitch, 2019). Detailed data on employment in coal mining in the European Union is presented in Figure 5.4.

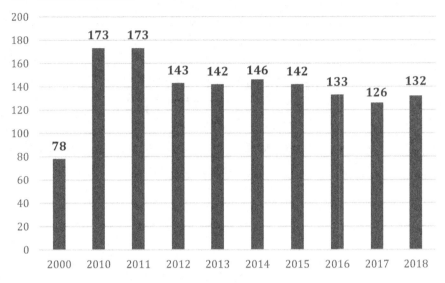

Figure 5.3 Employment in mining in Australia in the years 2000–2018 [in thousands of people]
Source: Conolly and Orsmond (2011) and Statista (2019)

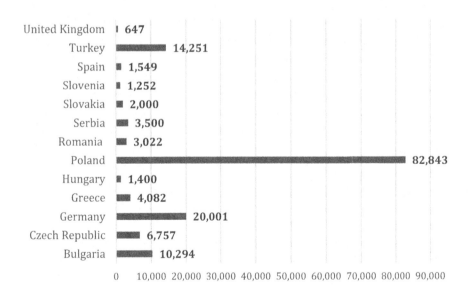

Figure 5.4 Employment in mining in the European Union [in thousands of people]
Source: Euracoal (2020)

Countries with the highest production levels employed the most people in Poland, Germany and Turkey. In other economies, employment ranged from 0.6 to 10.3 million, which indicates that mining enterprises are still of great importance in these regions.

According to Rosstat at the end of 2019 the share of people employed in coal mining in Russia was 14.4% (in total employment in mining) or 150.1 thousand people in numbers. An important trend of the last 20 years (2000–2019) is a sharp decrease in the average number of employees in coal mining and coal processing by almost 59.4% from 370.3 to 150.1 thousand people (Figure 5.5).

The decrease in the number reflects two main factors: 1) an increase in labour productivity due to the use of high-performance equipment and modernization of production, and 2) the closure of a number of coal enterprises.

The productivity increase was achieved by the following factors: production concentration, load buildup on the breakage face (in mines), on mining and conveyor equipment (in open-pit mines), the introduction of advanced technologies for the development of deposits (mine-longwall, mine-seam), and replacement of obsolete technological equipment by high-performance new generation equipment (Savon, 2018).

When writing about employment in the hard coal mining industry, one cannot ignore the issue of work safety. A mine is a very specific workplace, in which there are many natural and technical hazards that affect the difficulty and danger associated with the profession of a miner. In deep mines, these include:

- increased temperature,
- reduced oxygen content in the atmosphere,
- the presence of harmful gases,

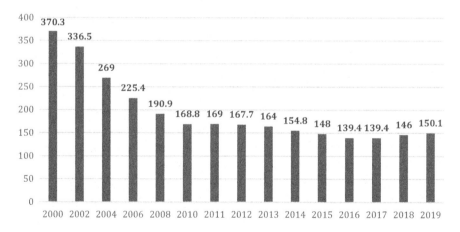

Figure 5.5 Average number of employees in coal mining companies [in thousands of people]
Source: Tarazanov and Gubanov (2020)

- heavy dust,
- the presence of high humidity,
- constant air flow,
- no daylight,
- high pressure,
- narrowness of rooms and passages,
- noise,
- vibrations,
- sudden changes in conditions in the pit,
- the presence of microbiological and radiation hazards.

(Szlązak and Szlązak, 2010; Turek et al., 2013;
Matuszewska-Majcher, 2017)

In open-pit mines, work is carried out above ground. In such a situation, the most important safety issues include the right protection of pit excavations in such a way that neither landslides and strikes nor flooding of the mine with groundwater occur (Yedla et al., 2020).

Therefore, the work of a miner is very often performed in extremely difficult conditions, which is confirmed by the industry's above-average accident rates, including those related to fatal accidents and mining disasters (Gunningham, 2006). It is associated with the occurrence of high psycho-physical load, which is manifested by employee fatigue, the occurrence of occupational stress related to the awareness of the existing risks, as well as responsibility for colleagues in the pit at that time (Shooks, et al., 2014; Matuszewska-Majcher, 2016).

Due to difficult mining conditions in underground hard coal mines, it is very difficult to reduce the accident rate, which is confirmed by Polish statistics for the hard coal mining industry (Figures 5.6 and 5.7). Despite the significant reduction in mining and employment, it was not possible to reduce the total number of accidents or the number of fatal and serious accidents to an equal extent, which is illustrated by the level of risks associated with working in mining, primarily in underground mining.

In Russia, the share of open pit mining in 2019 was 75.7% (334.1 thousand tons), underground 24.3% (107.3 thousand tons) (Yanovsky, 2019). This largely determines the causes of accidents and industrial injuries in the coal industry. At present, the state of safety measures and the level of anti-accidental stability of coal mines and open-pit mines in Russia are insufficient.

The number of fatal injuries in the coal industry in Russia is significantly higher than that of the leading coal-mining countries, and the level of occu-pational morbidity among workers is much higher than in other sectors of the domestic economy (Zholobova et al., 2016; Savon, 2018). Specific indicators of fatal injuries per 1 million tons of coal mined are as follows: in the USA 0.02 people/million tons; Australia 0.03 people/million tons; South Africa 0.035 people/million tons; Russia 0.16 people/million tons; in China 0.25 people/ million tons. At the same time, in general, since 2000, there has been a

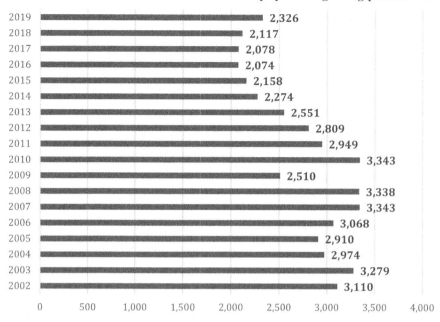

Figure 5.6 Total number of accidents in the Polish mining industry in the years 2002–2019
Source: State Mining Authority

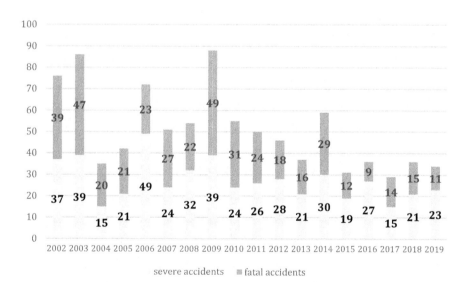

Figure 5.7 Total number of fatal and serious accidents in the Polish mining industry in
the years 2002–2019
Source: State Mining Authority

tendency towards a decrease in fatal injuries in the coal industry of the Russian Federation in terms of specific indicators (Figure 5.8).

Fires and explosions are the most frequent causes of accidents. The majority of coal mines (except for 12 mines in the Rostov region) are hazardous because of coal-dust explosions. Some 12 mines out of 101 are non-hazardous in relation to methane gas, 21 are gas-hazardous class I, 9 are class II, 16 are class III, 24 are extra-hazardous mines and 19 are prone to sudden emissions. At 10 mines, mining is carried out on seams hazardous to rock bursts (Ermak et al., 2015). Hazardous conditions can occur due to sudden outbursts of coal, rock, dust or gas; water and/or pulp breakthrough into underground mines; rock slides; the factor of human error.

The subject closely related to working conditions are the principles of employment, including, in particular, the form of employment and the level of remuneration, which, in principle, should reflect the hardship of this work and the level of risks associated with it. Meanwhile, in practice, working conditions in the mining industry largely depend on the legal regulations that exist in a given country. It is primarily influenced by the level of growth in civilisation and the level of prosperity. In developed countries, miners' wages and general working conditions are good (Peets et al., 2012). In the case of countries at a lower level of economic development, they may be at a much worse level, both in terms of the level of pay and the conditions of work safety in the mine (Malema, 2017). Nevertheless, it should be added that the level of pay in mining in these countries is generally higher than in other sectors of the economy. In turn, in the case of developed countries, such as the USA, the

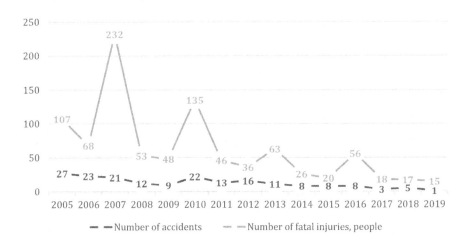

Figure 5.8 Number of accidents and number of fatal injuries in the coal industry of the Russian Federation (people)
Source: Annual Report (2020, p.100)

wages in the profession of a miner, as well as the prestige of this profession, are lower, with better working conditions and safety compared to developing countries (Itkin, 2015).

Apart from working conditions and pay, other factors that affect the quality of life of mining families are additional benefits related to employment in mining enterprises. In many countries, including Poland, miners receive various privileges related to the work of a miner, such as: allowances, awards, compensation for unused leave, benefits in kind and special conditions for retirement (Przybyłka, 2014; Kubicka, 2018; Matuszewska-Majcher, 2019). A similar situation exists, for example, in Zambia, where, despite not having the best working conditions for miners in general, workers receive privileges not found in other sectors of the economy (Grayson, 2020).

The high sectoral level of pay in mining, combined with the benefits that miners are entitled to, means the profession of miner is perceived as prestigious (Hongxia et al., 2014; Malema, 2017). In the past, it was also associated with stable employment, which resulted in great interest in working in the mines. After 2000, this situation radically changed, due to the closure of many mines for economic and environmental reasons.

What are the employee patterns of influence on mining enterprises? How does SD fulfil the requirements of employees – with facts and in reports? Case studies and observations

As already mentioned, employees of mining enterprises play a diversified role in their functioning, which largely depends on the location of the mining industry and, in particular, on the level of economic development and growth of civilisation of the region where the mining plants are located. This level seems to determine the negotiating power of employees, and thus their importance in the group of all stakeholders of mining enterprises. At the same time, it is worth emphasising that employees in the mining industry are the main link in creating value, because it is a traditional industry, in which the amount of physical work is still important for the production volume, and thus for the amount of revenues and financial profits (Meade et al., 2017; Batrancea et al., 2019).

Previous studies and publications show that the patterns of influence of mining enterprises' employees on their functioning can be sorted into three groups:

1   employees, for whom economic goals are the most important,
2   employees, who want to pursue economic goals on an equal footing with social goals,
3   employees who expect a balance of economic, social and environmental goals.

The **first** (Level 1) of these groups can – most often – be found in regions less developed economically and in terms of civilisational growth. The low level of satisfaction of living needs in these areas makes the key life priority to support oneself and the family, as well as meet existential needs. Mine employees are treated as an easily replaceable workforce. Very often, the technical and economic working conditions in the mines are very bad, and the employees themselves are deprived of legal protection or trade unions (Dong and Xu, 2016; McDuie-Ra and Kikon, 2016; Ariza et al., 2020; Cole and Broadhurst, 2020; Delina, 2020). Due to the described conditions, their impact on the functioning of mining enterprises, whether they are domestic or international corporations, is negligible. Their role is limited to performing poorly paid work, without being able to share their opinion on working conditions or the functioning of a mining enterprise in the region.

The **second** group (Level 2) includes more aware employees of mining enterprises, who want to pursue economic goals on an equal footing with social goals. In addition to decent working conditions, what is important to them is to belong to a specific professional group, operating in a defined geographical area, in a specific local community. This need to belong to a group is fulfilled by them by creating trade unions and industry organisations. This is very often additionally strengthened by many years of cultivating mining traditions and customs. At the same time, it is worth adding that higher awareness and the level of fulfilment of needs in this case is – most often – associated with a much better satisfaction of existential needs and those related to occupational safety and health in mining plants. Employees included in this group have a much greater impact on the functioning of the mining enterprise. Their opinions are voiced primarily through the trade unions, that are able to negotiate pay and working conditions. These employees are also supported by the local community, very often local self-government authorities (Zientara, 2009; Gunningham and Sinclair, 2014; Müller, 2018; Brauers and Oei, 2020). The collective nature of this influence gives them great negotiating power and the possibility of fulfilling many employee priorities.

The **third** group (Level 3) of employees sets the highest possible expectations for mining enterprises and is most aware of the benefits and risks related to the functioning of the mining industry. These employees not only think about satisfying economic and social needs, but also expect the fulfilment of ecological tasks, including, in particular, the prevention of the negative effects of mining operations and care for the quality of the natural environment. A characteristic feature of this group is the high level of satisfaction of material needs resulting from the functioning in highly developed economies, where the well-being of future generations is also important (Bosca and Gillespie, 2018; Strangleman, 2018; Bosca and Gillespie, 2019). This group has a very strong impact on the activities of mining enterprises through the combined influence of employees, the community and environmental organisations. This force is manifested – in many cases – in the possibility of suspending or liquidating mining investments in a given region or even a country.

The described categorisation clearly shows the evolutionary nature of employee goals, which is a direct reference to the concept of sustainable development. Therefore, it can be concluded that the third group of employees has the greatest impact on the implementation of SD principles, as this group is aware of the importance of sustainability, but also has material and civilisation conditions to create such equivalence.

Bearing in mind the large differentiation of the role of employees forming particular groups, the literature and economic practice postulate a constant effort to balance the position of employees in the mining industry, regardless of the level of economic development and growth in civilisation of the region, in which they provide work for mining enterprises. It is one of the conditions for effective implementation of the principles of sustainable development.

The formal and material expression of efforts in this area is the development of additional reporting standards in the field of corporate social responsibility for mining enterprises under the *Global Reporting Initiative* (GRI). In this case, the oil, gas and coal extraction sector was covered by special, more restrictive requirements (Moneva et al., 2006; Weber and Banks, 2012; Stammler and Ivanova, 2016; Boiral and Heras-Saizarbitoria, 2017). Among the detailed guidelines in the GRI sector list, there is also a group of data and indicators related to employment. The task of reporting in this area is primarily to prevent such industry failures as:

- violation of fundamental human rights,
- employment of minors,
- racial discrimination,
- restriction of the freedom of association,
- forced employment,
- non-compliance with the rules of occupational health and safety,
- low level of remuneration,
- overtime.

These phenomena primarily concern the first of the above-mentioned groups of employees, but they also occur in the second. In order to prevent them, the authors of the GRI sector standard propose reporting in several key employment groups, which are presented with the required indicators in Table 5.1.

The scope of reporting defined in Table 5.1 is very extensive, but it is intended to increase the transparency of mining enterprises' activities towards employees and lead to sustainable employment in the mining industry in all areas of the world.

Bearing in mind the above observations and guidelines, two case studies on the role of employees in shaping the sustainable development of enterprises are referred to in the next part of this section. The first one concerns Poland as a representative of the European Union, and the second concerns Russia as a representative of the Commonwealth of Independent States.

In Poland – from the point of view of the classification presented in the introduction – in mining enterprises, there is the second group of employees, who have a strong awareness of economic and social needs and goals. This attitude is manifested in frequent and intense strike actions, supported by

Table 5.1 The areas and indicators covered by GRI sector reporting aimed at preventing employment failures in mining enterprises

Area of employment	Reporting requirements
Employment practices	GRI 103: Management Approach GRI 401: Employment disclosure: New employee hires and employee turnover; Benefits provided to full-time employees that are not provided to temporary or part-time employees; Parental leave GRI 402: Labour/Management Relations disclosure: Minimum notice periods and consultation regarding operational changes GRI 404: Training and Education disclosure: Average hours of training per year per employee; Programs for upgrading employee skills, as well as for transition, worker transfer and redeployment assistance GRI 414: Supplier Social Assessment disclosure: New suppliers that were screened using social criteria; Negative social impacts in the supply chain and actions taken
Forced labour and modern slavery	GRI 103: Management Approach GRI 408: Child Labour disclosure: Operations and suppliers at significant risk for incidents of child labour GRI 409: Forced or Compulsory Labour disclosure: Operations and suppliers at significant risk for incidents of forced or compulsory labour GRI 412: Human Rights Assessment disclosure: Operations that have been subject to human rights reviews or impact assessments GRI 414: Supplier Social Assessment disclosure: New suppliers that were screened using social criteria
Diversity and non-discrimination	GRI 103: Management Approach GRI 202: Market Presence disclosure: Ratios of standard entry-level wage by gender compared to local minimum wage; Proportion of senior management hired from the local community GRI 401: Employment disclosure: Total number and rate of new employee hires during the reporting period, by age group, gender, and region GRI 404: Training and Education disclosure: Average hours of training per year per employee by gender and employment category GRI 405: Diversity and Equal Opportunity disclosure: Diversity of governance bodies and employees; Ratio of basic salary and remuneration of women to that of men GRI 406: Non-discrimination disclosure: Incidents of discrimination and corrective actions taken
Freedom of association and collective bargaining	GRI 103: Management Approach GRI 407: Freedom of Association and Collective Bargaining disclosure: Operations and suppliers in which the right to freedom of association and collective bargaining might be at risk

Source: GRI Sector Standard Draft: oil, gas and coal. https://www.globalreporting.org/

mining trade unions and local communities, which strongly identify local development with the development of the mining industry (Rybak and Rybak, 2016; Jonek-Kowalska, 2015). Ecological goals exist in the minds of these employees, but they are not a priority and do not have to be implemented completely (Pactwa et al., 2020; Kuchler and Bridge, 2018), which is undoubtedly a key disadvantage of such an approach and proves that the idea of sustainable development is not fully understood, and most important is that current needs are met in the first place. Such an attitude may be partially justified by the incomplete economic development of Poland and its short functioning in the period of the free market economy (Kamiński, 2009). This results in the pursuit of satisfying economic needs in conditions of full availability of goods and services, after years of functioning in the economy of scarcity.

The macro perspective of the Polish mining industry presented above is also reflected at the individual level. Reports on the social responsibility of mining enterprises are dominated by a social approach, focused on exposing the employee and their relationship with the management board, colleagues, as well as social and economic environment. For example, in Jastrzębska Spółka Węglowa SA, two of the seven key sustainable development goals relate to human resources:

1   We respect life and health, and we do not compromise on safety.
2   We respect every individual, our community, taking joint responsibility for JSW and its property.

As part of the first of them, the enterprise's activities focus on:

• maintenance of PN-N-18001 certified management systems in the field of coal mining, processing and sale;
• engaging employees in improving the OHS Occupational Health and Safety (OHO) management system, including developing solutions that would be focused on the specificity of particular work stations;
• maintaining high-quality OHS training, with particular emphasis on the topicality and practicality of the discussed issues.

The second includes:

• diagnosing the current situation, i.e., directly asking employees how they feel about working in the company;
• creating, among other things, a coherent policy on objective employee assessment, promotion, training and development planning and protection against discrimination;
• providing practical tools to eliminate any such undesirable behaviour at every level of the organisation.

In this company, a number of risks typical of the industry and the region are also noticed, including:

- recruitment of employees from relatively small communities, causing an increased risk of connections between specific employees, other than business ones, which may result in typical conflicts of interest (in terms of increased risk of nepotism, related to the fact that family members and relatives might work in the same company, but also the risk of, e.g., animosities between specific people etc.);
- traditional domination of mining by men, while the perception of women present in the minds of many people, marginalising their professional roles, is maintained.

Nevertheless, in the employment group, descriptive reporting methods in the field of corporate social responsibility are mainly used, and the GRI specific indicators are used to report:

- total number and rates of new hires and employee turnover by age group, gender and region;
- return to work and retention rates after maternity/paternity leave, in terms of gender.

Additionally, in the area related to occupational safety, the following data is given:

- percentage of the total number of employees represented on formal health and safety committees (made up of management and employees) that advise and monitor occupational health and safety programs;
- injury, occupational disease, lost days and absence rates, as well as work-related fatalities by region;
- employment in conditions of increased risk of occupational diseases.

Based on the presented considerations and data, it should, therefore, be concluded that, both from the employee and managerial point of view, the approach to the issue of sustainability requires some supplements. Nevertheless, SD is noticed, described, exposed and made visible, which is important for its implementation and popularisation.

Jobs that are traditionally associated with mining in Russia and the CIS countries include shaft workers, explosives technicians, operators of coal-mining machines and electric trains, and wiremen. Despite the fact that most of the work is mechanised and automated, there is still a lot of manual and hard work in adverse conditions.

The level of miners' wages is determined by many factors: the quality and volume of coal mined, the region of production, the qualifications and length of service of the miner, the level of job complexity and harmful and/or dangerous working conditions. This leads to significant differentiation of wages in different enterprises. Differentiation of wages in Russia by production regions is due to the wide geography of the fields and the current system of incentive allowances in the form of regional coefficients in the range from 1.2–2 and coefficients to wages for workers in the Far North regions, as well as regions equated to them, in the range from 10 to 100%. However, wage growth in coal mining remains the lowest among mining companies. The wages in the industry are two times lower than in oil and gas enterprises, and also lower than the average value for the extractive industries (Table 5.2).

As mentioned, the volume of production is the main indicator that affects the level of wages of workers. In coal companies, a piece-work bonus wage system prevails, which stimulates workers to increase the intensity of labour but provokes violation of safety requirements.

In Russia, the share of workers operating in harmful and/or dangerous working conditions (at the end of 2019) in the extractive industry was 55.4% compared to other industries. In coal mining the share was 80.3%, in the extraction of metal ores it was 71.9%, and in the extraction of oil and natural gas 33.2%. The greatest influence on the labour process in coal mining is exerted by the following factors: hard labour (57%), noise, ultrasound (47.1%); aerosols (37.8%), vibrations (23.3%) (*Labuor and Employment in Russia*, 2019). The impact of these factors surpasses similar factors in other mining industries.

Thus, under more difficult, harmful or dangerous working conditions in the coal industry, wages are significantly lower than in other extractive industries. This fact causes dissatisfaction of workers in the industry.

The workers' satisfaction at coal enterprises is not limited only to the level of wages, social status, and employment guarantees. Their interests and expectations are also associated with the possibility of career growth, advanced professional training and requalification, the possibility of getting higher education, satisfaction with working conditions and work performed, compliance with the terms of an employment contract by the enterprise, payment of a corporate pension, ensuring industrial safety and labour protection, social protection of workers and their families.

A multilevel system of social partnership has been developed in Russia, which largely protects the rights and insurance arrangements of workers. The system involves collective bargaining at various levels: the federal, regional and

Table 5.2 Ratio of the average monthly nominal wages of workers in the extractive industries to the average Russian level

Nature of business (in extractive industries)	2010	2015	2016	2017	2018
Mining operations, %, including:	190	187	191	190	190
coal mining, %	131	133	134	135	136
oil and natural gas extraction, time	2.9 times	2.8 times	2.8 times	2.7 times	2.9 times
metal mining, %	154	160	165	156	162

Source: Labour and Employment in Russia (2019, p.111)

municipal authorities with work unions of Russia, industry work unions, territorial trade unions and representatives of employers and employees at the enterprise level.

The Federal Sectoral Agreement on the Coal Industry of the Russian Federation (*Federal Sectoral Agreement,* 2019) is in force for coal enterprises. The Agreement is updated every three years and contains rules and principles governing social and labour relations in accordance with the Constitution of the Russian Federation, federal legislation, and ILO Conventions. The agreement includes the following sections: social partnership, employer–employee relationship, safety and health management, social benefits.

Among SUEK's SD goals, four goals were selected to interact with the company's employees. The company emphasises that it is focused on sustainable growth while ensuring safe working conditions. Two points were identified as staff development priorities:

1   A high level of OSH culture;
2   Professional development and social well-being of the company's staff.

To develop in the first area, the following measures were proposed:

- continuous improvement of OSH methods;
- improving the OSH parameters of the company's coal-producing, energy, and logistics assets;
- introducing modern security systems and control devices;
- improving discipline in the workplace and developing OSH culture;
- providing workplace health programs.

To help the staff with their professional development, the company has developed measures and is working in the following areas:

- human capital development;
- fair remuneration and social welfare payments.

It should be noted that professional development measures are supported by solving the problems of developing the social environment in the region where the company operates through the development of human capital and the use of the best social practices and tools.

Employees' interests in relation to the company include fair and decent remuneration, social responsibility commitment, the development of professional and personal competencies, OSH improvement, and social welfare programs for employees and their family members. An analysis of the employees' goals and interests that was carried out using SUEK's SD report showed that the company's employees can be classified as standing at Level 2. At the moment, the employees are focusing on achieving their own well-being, including such an aspect as the social environment. Level 3, which is characterised by employees' responsible attitude to the environment, has not yet been achieved by coal industry workers. The predominant interaction formats are agreements with trade unions and collective agreements, joint committees and commissions, corporate training and development systems, social welfare programs, meetings with managers, corporate media, and employee opinion surveys.

With regard to these aspects, several steps have been taken. First, an effective remuneration and motivation system has been developed and is consistently used. This system includes wages and salaries, benefits, and intangible rewards. The pay scale itself is based on such parameters as the quantity and quality of labour and it takes into account the achievement of key performance indicators, including OSH and environmental ones, which balances out the interests at play. In the field of employee motivation, there is currently a trend towards using the project-based approach that improves the quality of interactions between employees and the company's corporate culture. As for providing benefits, the company adheres to the best practices in the mining industry.

Second, social welfare includes both fringe benefits and measures to improve the living standards of the company's employees and their families. Fringe benefits include a wide range of basic and additional benefits. When developing the system of fringe benefits, the company interacts with trade unions. Cooperation with trade unions, as well as with SUEK's employees, is based on the principle of social partnership, which includes collective bargaining, employee participation in management, and joint resolution of labour disputes. It should be noted that there are the Russian Independent Trade Union of Coal Industry Workers and the Russian Independent Trade Union of Miners that cooperate with Russian coal companies. Social partnership agreements are signed at the industrial, territorial, and local levels.

Third, the personnel training and development system in the company has several functions and uses a number of tools. The main functions are the provision of professional training programs to the company's workers and managers, human resource development, and also attracting and retaining young employees. Professional training programs include reskilling, training in a related field, advanced training, and OSH training. The training system for the older generation being developed at SUEK can be recognized as a socially innovative instrument. This program has been implemented since 2019 as part of the Older Generation Federal Program, which, in turn, is part of the Demography National Project. The program is focused on developing mentoring skills for transferring experience and knowledge to young employees.

Differentiating the role of employees, depending on economic and civilisation development in world regions

The considerations presented in this chapter show that, both in the EU and CIS countries, employees are guaranteed full employment rights, including an appropriate level of remuneration and other social benefits, also in the event of liquidation of a mining enterprise. The full employment rights allow employees to participate and shape the social conditions of sustainable development. Both groups of countries are also at the second level of impact on the sustainable development of mining enterprises. They are aware of their rights and are able to guarantee them. They also function in economies, where the levels of economic and civilization development guarantee the observance of the rights of mining crews. Nevertheless, they do not fully understand and accept the environmental goals of sustainable development, preferring them to the socio-economic goals, which prevents them from achieving full environmental awareness and the third degree of impact on sustainable development.

The results of the study bear out the need to continue developing issues of coal industry perception by employees. It is possible to increase the involvement of employees in corporate responsibility by increasing their real earnings, incentives, social guarantees, and providing in-company development and training.

Employees dissatisfied with wages and social guarantees constrict the possibilities for sustainable development. A large proportion of responsibility for the problem lies with the state and the regions. An effectively developed national economic policy aimed at the state interests in the sphere of labour and employment, and a regional personnel policy guarantee the basis for the implementation of socio-economic contractual relationships.

Given the significant changes in the technological and digital support of production activities, mining companies should pay more attention to professional training of workers, education in the field of environmental safety, and sustainable development. Management should accept current circumstances and take into account that only real concern for the physical and psychological health of the employee can guarantee staff loyalty and commitment to the objectives of the company.

Bibliography

Ariza, J., Vargas-Prieto, J., García-Estévez, A. (2020). The Effects of the Mining-energy Boom on Inclusive Development in Colombia. *The Extractive Industries and Society*, 22, 1597–1606.

Annual Report on the Activities of the Federal Service for Environmental, Technological and Nuclear Supervision in 2020. (2020) http://www.gosnadzor.ru/public/a nnual_reports/Гёдёвёй%20ётчет%20ё%20деятельнёсти%20Рёстехнадзёра%20в% 202019%20гёду.pdf [access date: 29. 03. 2021].

Batrancea, I., Batrancea, L., Nichita, A., Gaban, L., Masca, E., Morar, I.-D., Fatacean, G., Moscviciov, A. (2019). An Econometric Approach on Production, Costs and Profit in Romanian Coal Mining Enterprises. *Economic Research - Ekonomska Istraži-vanja*, 32(1), 1019–1036.

Bluszcz, A. (2014). Proces przemian struktury zatrudnienia w górnictwie węgla kamiennego. Zeszyty Naukowe Wydziałowe Uniwersytetu Ekonomicznego w Katowicach. Studia Ekonomiczne: Uwarunkowania współczesnego rynku pracy i ich skutki w sferze społeczno-ekonomicznej, 196.

Boiral, O., Heras-Saizarbitoria, I. (2017). Corporate Commitment to Biodiversity in Mining and Forestry: Identifying Drivers from GRI Reports. *Journal of Cleaner Production*, 10, 153–161.

Bołoz, Ł., Biały, W. (2020). Automation and Robotization of Underground Mining in Poland. *Applied Sciences*, 10, 7221.

Bosca, H.D., Gillespie, J. (2018). The Coal Story: Generational Coal Mining Communities and Strategies of Energy Transition in Australia. *Energy Policy*, 26, 734–740.

Bosca, H.D., Gillespie, J. (2019). The Construction of 'Local' Interest in New South Wales Environmental Planning Processes. *Australian Geographer*, 50(1), 49–68.

Brauers H., Oei, P.-Y., (2020). The Political Economy of Coal in Poland: Drivers and Barriers for a Shift Away from Fossil Fuels. *Energy Policy*, 144, 111621.

Cole, M. J., Broadhurst, J.L. (2020). Mapping and Classification of Mining Host Communities: A Case Study of South Africa. *The Extractive Industries and Society*, 6, 954–964.

Conolly, E., Orsmond, D. (2011). The Mining industry From Bust to Boom. Research Discussion Paper. Economic Analysis Department Reserve Bank of Australia.

Delina, L.L., (2020). Topographies of Coal Mining Dissent: Power, Politics, and Protests in Southern Philippines. *World Development*, 5, 105194.

Derski, B. (2020). Zatrudnienie w górnictwie rośnie, choć wydobycie spada. https://forsal.pl/artykuly/1407981,zatrudnienie-w-gornictwie-rosnie-choc-wydobycie-spada.html [access date: 05. 12. 2020].

Dong, S., Xu, Lei. (2016). The Impact of Explicit CSR Regulation: Evidence from China's Mining Firms. *Journal of Applied Accounting Research, 17(2)*, 237–258.

Ermak, G.P., Myasnikov, S.V., Skatov, V.V., Gendler, S. G. (2015). The Main Directions of Rostechnadzor's Work on Monitoring the State of Industrial Safety and Reducing Accidents in the Coal Mining Industry in Russia. GIAB https://cyberleninka.ru/article/n/osnovnye-napravleniya-raboty-rostehnadzora-po-kontrolyu-nad-sostoyaniem-promyshlennoy-bezopasnosti-i-snizheniyu-avariynosti-v [accessed date: 30. 08. 2020].

Euracoal (2020). https://euracoal.eu/info/coal-industry-across-europe/ [access date: 5. 12. 2020].

Federal Sectoral Agreement on the Coal Industry of the Russian Federation for 2019–2021 (2021). https://mintrud.gov.ru/docs/agreements/1298 [access date: 30. 03. 2021].

Grayson, K. (2020). Working and Living Conditions of Workers in the Mining Sector in Zambia. https://alrei.org/education/working-and-living-conditions-of-workers-in-the-mining-sector-in-zambia-by-grayson-koyi [access date: 05. 12. 2020].

Gunningham, N. (2006). Safety, Regulation and the Mining Industry. *Australian Journal of Labour Law*, 1, 30–58.

Gunningham, N., Sinclair, D. (2014). Building Trust: Work Health and Safety Management in the Mining Industry. *Policy and Practice in Health and Safety*, 12(1), 35–51.

Hongxia, L., Yongbin, F., Shuicheng, T., Fen, L., Huan, L. (2014). Study on the Joint Stress of Miners. *Procedia Engineering*, 84, 239–246.

Itkin, D. (2015). Wage and Employment Patterns in the Mining Sector. https://www.bls.gov/oes/mining.pdf [access date: 05. 12. 2020].

Jonek-Kowalska, I. (2015). Challenges for Long-term Industry Restructuring in the Upper Silesian Coal Basin: What Has Polish Coal Mining Achieved and Failed from a Twenty-year Perspective? *Resources Policy*, 135–149.

Kaczorowski, P., Gajewski P. (2008). Górnictwo węgla kamiennego w Polsce w okresie transformacji. Acta Universitatis Lodziensis, *Folia Oeconomica*, 219, 201–227.

Kamiński, J. (2009). The Impact of Liberalisation of the Electricity Market on the Hard Coal Mining Sector in Poland. *Energy Policy*, 925–939.

Kubicka, J. (2018). *Human Capital of the Polish Mining and Energy Sector*. https://www.google.pl/url?sa=t&rct=j&q=&esrc=s&source=web&cd=&cad=rja&uact=8&ved=2ahUKEwiHzZbAwrftAhWrmIsKHQLpA6kQFjADegQIAxAC&url=http%3A%2F%

2Feko-unia.org.pl%2Fwp-content%2Fuploads%2F2018%2F06%2Fmini-report-2_ HR_PL.pdf&usg=AOvVaw0o7TJ1BxlYcPbf6IY8UFrW [access date: 05. 12. 2020].

Kuchler, M., Bridge, G. (2018). Down the Black Hole: Sustaining National Socio-technical Imaginaries of Coal in Poland. *Energy Research & Social Science*, 23, 136–147.

Labour and Employment in Russia (2019). https://rosstat.gov.ru/storage/mediabank/ Trud_2019.pdf [access date: 29. 03. 2021].

Lahiri-Dutt, K. (2017). Resources and the Politics of Sovereignty: The Moral and Immoral Economies of Coal Mining in India, South Asia. *Journal of South Asian Studies*, 40(4), 792–809.

Li, Y., Chiu, Y., Lin, T.-Y. (2019). Coal Production Efficiency and Land Destruction in China's Coal Mining Industry. *Resources Policy*, 63, 101449.

Malema K.M. (2017). The Working Conditions in the Mining Sector: The Case of Mchenga and Kaziwiziwi Coal Mines in Malawi. *Open Science Journal*, 2(1), 1–30.

Matuszewska-Majcher, E. (2016). Relacja wieku emerytów górniczych do ogółu emerytów w kontekście warunków wykonywania pracy górniczej. Moderni matematicke metody v inzenyrstvi. Cesko-polsky seminar, sbornik z 25. seminare, Horni Lomna, 1–6.

Matuszewska-Majcher, E. (2017). Wpływ warunków wykonywania pracy górniczej na stan zdrowia pracowników kopalń. *Systemy Wspomagania w Inżynierii Produkcji*, 6(2), 197–204.

Matuszewska-Majcher, E. (2019). Working Conditions and Retirement Privileges on the Example of Mining. *IOP Conference Series: Earth and Environmental Science*, 261, 012031.

McDuie-Ra, D., Kikon, D. (2016). Tribal Communities and Coal in Northeast India: The Politics of Imposing and Resisting Mining Bans. *Energy Policy*, 20, 261–269.

Meade, M.R. (2017). In the Shadow of the Coal Breaker: Cultural Extraction and Participatory Communication in the Anthracite Mining Region. *Cultural Studies*, 31 (2–3), 376–399.

Moneva, J.M., Archel, P. (2006). Carmen Correa GRI and the Camouflaging of Corporate Unsustainability. *Accounting Forum*, 121–137.

Müller, K. (2018). Mining, Time and Protest: Dealing with Waiting in German Coal Mine Planning. *The Extractive Industries and Society*, 11, 1–7.

Oei, P.-Y., Mendelevitch, R. (2019). Prospects for Steam Coal Exporters in the Era of Climate Policies: A Case Study of Colombia. *Climate Policy*, 19(1), 73–91.

Pactwa, K., Woźniak, J., Dudek, M. (2020). Coal Mining Waste in Poland in Reference to Circular Economy Principles. *Fuel*, 6, 117493.

Peets, D., Murray, G., Muurlink, O. (2012). Work and Hours Amongst Mining and Energy Worker. *Australian Coal and Energy Survey*, Centre of Work, Organizational and Wellbeing, Griffith University.

Przybyłka, A. (2014). Przywileje związane z pracą w górnictwie na tle innych grup zawodowych. *Studia Ekonomiczne Uniwersytetu Ekonomicznego w Katowicach*, 196, 196–207.

Rafaty, R., Srivastav. S., Hoops, B. (2020). Revoking Coal Mining Permits: An Economic and Legal Analysis. *Climate Policy*, 20(8), 980–996.

Rybak, A., Rybak, A. (2016). Possible Strategies for Hard Coal Mining in Poland as a Result of Production Function Analysis. *Resources Policy*, 30, 27–33.

Savon D.Y. (2018). Modern Approaches to Production Safety in Coal Mining. *Gornyy informatsionno-analiticheskiy byulleten*, 11, 227–235.

Shooks, M, Johansson, B., Andersson, E., Lööw, J. (2014). *Safety and Health in European Mining*. Division of Human Work Science, Luleå.

Stammler, F., Ivanova, A. (2016). Resources, Rights and Communities: Extractive Mega-Projects and Local People in the Russian Arctic. *Europe-Asia Studies, 68(7)*, 1220–1244.

State Mining Authority (2021). Accident statisticshttps://www.wug.gov.pl/bhp/statys tyki_wypadkow [access date: 05. 12. 2021].

Statista (2019). Number of Employees in the Mining Industry in Australia from the Financial Year 2012 to 2019. https://www.statista.com/statistics/682989/australia -employment-in-mining-industry/ [access date: 05. 12. 2020].

Statista (2020). United States Employment in Support Activities for Mining from 1998 to 2019. https://www.statista.com/statistics/193228/employment-in-support-activi ties-for-mining-in-the-us-since-1998/ [access date: 05. 12. 2020].

Strangleman, T. (2018). 'Mining a Productive Seam?' The Coal Industry, Community and Sociology. *Contemporary British History*, 32(1), 18–38.

Svobodova, K., Owen, J.R., Harris, J. (2020). The Global Energy Transition and Place Attachment in Coal Mining Communities: Implications for Heavily Industrialized Landscapes. *Energy Research & Social Science*, 3, 101831.

Szlązak, J., Szlązak N. (2010). *Bezpieczeństwo i higiena pracy*. Kraków: Wydawnictwo AGH.

Tarazanov, I.G., Gubanov, D.A. (2020). Results of the Work of the Coal Industry in Russia for January–December 2020. *Coal*, 3, 54–69. doi:10.18796/0041-5790-2020-3-54-69.

Turek, M., Prusek, S., Rosmus, P. (2013). Specyfika środowiska pracy podziemnej kopalni węgla kamiennego. In W. Konopko (Ed.), *Bezpieczeństwo pracy w kopalniach węgla kamiennego, Górnictwo i Środowisko*. Katowice: Główny, Instytut Górnictwa.

Weber, O., Banks, Y. (2012). Corporate Sustainability Assessment in Financing the Extractive Sector. *Journal of Sustainable Finance & Investment*, 2(1), 64–81.

Williams, G., Nikijuluw, R. (2020). Economic and Social Indicators Between Coal Mining LGAs and Non-coal Mining LGAs in Regional Queensland, Australia. *Resources Policy*, 17, 101688.

Yanovsky, A.B. (2019). Results of Structural Reorganization and Technological Re-equipment of the Coal Industry of the Russian Federation and Objectives for Prospective Development. *Ugol–Russian Coal Journal*, 8, 8–16.

Yedla, A., Kakhki, F.D., Jannesari, A. (2020). Predictive Modeling for Occupational Safety Outcomes and Days Away From Work Analysis in Mining Operations. *International Journal of Environmental Research and Public Health*, 17(19), 7054, 1–17.

Zholobova, Y.S., Safronov A.E., Kushchiy N.A., Savon, D.Y. (2016). Minimizatsiya vozdeystviya na okruzhayushchuyu sredu pri primenenii novykh tekhnologiy obogashcheniya ugley i utilizatsii otkhodov dobychi. *Gornyy zhurnal*, 5, 109–112.

Zientara, P. (2009). Restructuring the Coal Mining Industry: Unionism, Conflict, and Cooperation: Evidence from Poland. *Eastern European Economics*, 47(1), 41–59.

6 The role and functioning of trade unions in coal mining enterprises

Trade unions' rules and the scale of operating in extractive industries

Trade unions in Europe began to emerge as early as the 18th century in the form of organisations associated with the pursuit of a craft or the practice of a particular profession. The pioneer in this regard was Great Britain, where the first national trade union organisation was established in 1833 (Crowley, 2016). Subsequently, trade unions were formed in other Western European countries and in the USA. The development of trade unions was slower in Central and Eastern Europe because of the region's weaker socio-economic progress. Nowadays, trade unions represent the interests of workers around the world, with more than 300 million people in their ranks (Jończyk, 2017; Kryszczuk and Wenzel, 2017; Galgoczi, 2014).

Unions in the mining industry play an important role due to several key factors. First and foremost, this is an industry that employs hundreds, thousands, or even millions of people. Without their employment, mineral extraction would not be possible. The number of employees largely determines the strength of their impact on the operations of mining companies. Moreover, it is also an industry where the work is not only very hard but also dangerous. For this reason, workers, fearing for their rights and safety, are eager to establish and work for union organisations (Homer, 2009; Gunningham and Sinclair, 2014).

In the European Union, there are many pieces of legislation that guarantee workers' protection and freedom of association, including, most importantly, decent pay for work and health and safety at work. This stems from European traditions of respect for democracy and workers' rights. However, in other countries where hard coal mining operates, trade unions may not enjoy such good conditions for development. This is partly related to civilisation conditions, and partly results from political conditions.

In the third-world countries the presence of trade unions is a rare privilege. Violations of not only workers' rights, but also elementary human rights are much more frequent (Cunningham, 1985). Thus, when compared to the European Union, these are countries at the opposite pole in terms of freedom to establish trade union organisations.

DOI: 10.4324/9781003091110-9

Meanwhile, in the concept of sustainable development, workers' freedom of association is one of the key determinants of social sustainability. The *Global Reporting Initiative* devotes a separate Standard No. 407 to this issue. It refers to guaranteeing the right of employers and workers to form, to join, and to run their own organisations without prior authorisation or interference by the state or any other entity. Under this standard, it is also necessary to report on the possibility of collective bargaining and the conclusion of collective agreements between workers and employers that regulate working conditions, employment, and the relationship between worker and employer.

The freedom to form trade unions is reflected in their number and the level of employee unionisation, which is defined as the percentage of employees who are members.

Table 6.1 presents general union characteristics for European coal mining countries in the past or present. This provides a starting point for the narrowing consideration of trade unions active in hard coal mining that will follow later in this chapter.

Analysing data on collective bargaining coverage and proportion of employees in unions, it can be concluded that the countries with the highest levels of unionisation are Greece, Germany, Romania, and the Czech Republic (Myant, 2007). The level of collective bargaining varies. This is conducted at the company level and at the industry level. In the countries with the highest unionisation, it is mainly the industry level, which on the one hand indicates a high concentration, but on the other hand confirms the high power of influence and role in the conduct of negotiations on working conditions. Workplace representation is absent only in Bulgaria, and board representation does not exist only in Romania.

In Poland, the focus of this monograph, the level of unionisation is low, due in large part to the need to pay a contribution rate of 1% of wages and the wide dispersion of industries. In the past, union membership was more common, especially during the centrally planned economy (Kloc, 2007; Somogyi, 1995; Mason, 1987).

Today, trade unionists are both women and men. Trade union membership rate is higher than average among older workers aged 45 to 54 and especially 55 to 64, living in cities with a population of up to 20,000, employed in state-owned enterprises and public institutions, representatives of middle staff and technicians, as well as managers and professionals with higher education (CEBOS, 2016). Such a characterisation of the average trade unionist refers directly to people who are sentimental about and accustomed to trade union organisations dating back to the times of the centrally planned economy. Notably, the evaluation of trade union activity in Poland has clearly deteriorated over time (see Figure 6.1). At the beginning of the 1990s, 45% of respondents positively assessed the activity of trade union organisations for the benefit of the national economy, while in the second decade of the 21st century, that percentage decreased to 39%. This trend has persisted over time and indicates the decreasing role of trade unions in the socio-economic life of Poland (Lis, 2014).

Table 6.1 Information on the functioning of trade unions in coal mining countries in Europe

Country name	Collective bargaining coverage	Proportion of employees in unions	Principal level of collective bargaining	Workplace representation	Board-level representation
Bulgaria	30%	20%	company	no	union – but law also provides for the election of other representatives
Czech Republic	38%	17%	company	union – but works council can be set up as well	yes: state-owned and private companies
Greece	65%	25%	industry – but crisis and consequent legal changes have given greater role to company negotiations	union – works councils exist in theory but not often in practice	yes: state-owned companies
Germany	62%	18%	industry	work council	yes: state-owned and private companies
Poland	15%	15%	company	union (or works council)	yes: (formerly) state-owned companies
Romania	36%	33%	industry and company	union – another employee representation possible but rare	no
Hungary	33%	12%	company	union and works council	yes: state-owned and private companies

Source: https://www.worker-participation.eu

Interestingly, the decreasing popularity of trade unions in Poland was to a large extent caused by strikes of mining crews and their demands for further wage increases and industry privileges. Unionisation was and still is increasingly negatively perceived because it hinders effective restructuring of the mining industry and moving away from coal in Polish power and heating industries.

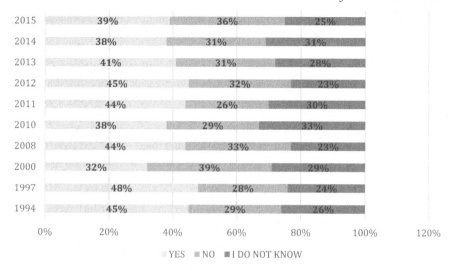

2015	39%	36%	25%	
2014	38%	31%	31%	
2013	41%	31%	28%	
2012	45%	32%	23%	
2011	44%	26%	30%	
2010	38%	29%	33%	
2008	44%	33%	23%	
2000	32%	39%	29%	
1997	48%	28%	24%	
1994	45%	29%	26%	

0%   20%   40%   60%   80%   100%   120%

YES NO I DO NOT KNOW

Figure 6.1 Does union activity benefit the country?
Source: CEBOS, 2016

This is confirmed by the lowest support for trade union activities during periods of intense protests and strikes, i.e. in 2000 and in 2014–2015 (Zientara, 2014).

The functioning of Polish trade unions is regulated by the *Act on Trade Unions of May 23, 1991*, which also directly applies to trade union organisations established in mining enterprises.

According to the provisions of this Act, a trade union is a voluntary and self-governing organisation of working people, established to represent and defend their rights, professional and social interests. It is independent in its statutory activities from employers, state, and local administration and from other organisations, and the right to form and join trade unions is granted to persons performing paid work. Interestingly, however, retirement or disability pension does not deprive former employees of the right to belong to and join trade unions. One can also belong to more than one trade union (Borkowski, 2019).

A trade union is formed by virtue of a resolution on its establishment, passed by at least 10 persons authorized to form trade unions. Those who have passed a resolution to form a trade union adopt a constitution and elect a founding committee of 3 to 7 persons. Notably, trade union authorities are protected from termination of employment. This is because the employer cannot terminate or dissolve the employment relationship with a member of the trade union board. In addition, members of the board are entitled to exemption from the obligation to provide work for the term of office (Petelczyc and Matuszczyk, 2019; Baran, 2018). The above-quoted provisions bestow great privilege and are often the reason for numerous abuses, including the establishment of more unions only to protect the jobs of board members and exempt them from work obligations. Unfortunately, it happens very often in the Polish coal mining industry.

Due to the possibility of establishing practically unlimited number of trade unions in one workplace, the law establishes the so-called representative trade union organisations, which are entitled to direct contact with the company and to conduct negotiations.

Thus, a representative supra-company trade union organisation is a union that unites at least 15% of all persons performing paid work covered by the scope of the statute, but not less than 10,000 persons performing paid work, or that unites the largest number of persons performing paid work for whom a specific supra-company collective agreement is to be concluded (Baran, 2019).

Trade union activities in Poland are financed by membership fees. Trade union organisations may apply for an earmarked grant from the state budget to pay institutional dues in international trade union associations. Given the fairly high wage levels in the mining industry, paying 1% dues in exchange for unlimited union protection is not a major problem. Many workers even choose to belong to several unions at the same time, reflecting their strength and effectiveness in defending workers' rights.

The trade union was a significant institutional structure in enterprises in the USSR when all the 15 republics were a part of it (Kazakhstan, Uzbekistan, Kyrgyzstan, Ukraine, etc.). The enterprises had three levels of control. The first one was of the political party. At this level, the top managers and the top workers were supervised by the party. The second level was of the Komsomol. Almost all young workers were members of the Komsomol, but not all passed into the category of party workers. The third level was for non-partisan workers and they were under the control of the trade union (Bizyukov, 2020).

The union was mainly concerned with the distribution of goods, namely, apartments, large household appliances, and package holidays. In the process of the transition from socialism to post-socialism, self-organised groups of workers (workers' clubs) began to emerge. The 1989 miners' strike gave a powerful impetus to such initiatives.

The scale of this strike was gigantic, unprecedented in the history of the country. It began in Kuzbass on July 11. A week later, according to various estimates, from 400 to 600 thousand people from Sakhalin to the Ukrainian Donbass went on strike. The miners put forward mainly economic demands for higher wages, social benefits and improved labour safety. However, the leaders of the trade union at that moment took the position of the authorities. This led to the creation of new trade union organisations.

The first independent and most powerful trade union (the miners' union) came into being in 1991. It grew out of workers' committees. The trade union put forward new approaches to the regulation of labour relations. The union contract began to include obligations and sanctions for the breach of it. In 1991, this was an innovation. The strength of the trade union was great, but it did not last long.

Gradually, trade unions ceased to be a significant institutional structure. In the late 1990s, they were excluded from the political process. Later, guarantees for union leaders were seriously weakened. It was decided that trade union leaders could be dismissed on a general basis, that is, the people who organised the activity below were left defenseless. The positions of trade unions in collective bargaining became vulnerable. Since the 2000s, restrictions on strikes have been introduced and the unions have had to switch from shaping an agenda in the interests of workers to adapting to the conditions offered by the employer.

At present, there are several large trade union associations in Russia. The first and largest is the Federation of Independent Trade Unions of Russia. It unites 122 organisations and more than 20 million people. Trade union organisations represent 82 territorial associations and 40 branch trade unions. The percentage of trade union membership in the districts of Russia varies from 51.2% of the working population of the Northwestern Federal District to 87.3% of the North Caucasians (Trade Unions Today, 2019).

The second trade union association is the Confederation of Labour of Russia. This includes the former alternative trade unions, dispatchers, dockers, the interregional trade union of workers in the automotive industry, such unions as the Action, the Teacher, and University Solidarity. Their numbers are much smaller and they are weaker. Both the first and the second have a voice, they can speak out, but they cannot carry out real actions.

At the level of the Eurasian Economic Union (EEU) the General Confederation of Trade Unions consolidates the largest national trade union centers of Armenia, Belarus, Kazakhstan, Kyrgyzstan and Russia. The VKP has many years of experience in business interaction with interstate entities in the post-Soviet space, in particular, with the Interparliamentary Assemblies of the CIS and, until recently, the EurAsEC (Lastochkina, 2018; VKP, 2021).

Trade unions have been granted the right to participate in rule-making (creation of regulatory legal acts) in all member countries of the Eurasian Economic Union. These rights also include the right to participate in the preparation of draft regulatory legal acts and to receive them for approval. This is because the states, as the successors of the Soviet legal system, have adopted some of its provisions.

In 2014, as a result of the adoption of the new Act "On Trade Unions" in the Republic of Kazakhstan, trade unions received more powers to participate in rule-making activities. They were given the right to take part in the development of regulatory legal acts affecting the labour and social rights and interests of citizens (About Trade Unions, 2014). Independently they develop draft plans and programs for the social protection of their members and submit them as proposals to the relevant state bodies. These programs and plans include programs to struggle against unemployment, ensure job security, protect laid-off workers, establish a subsistence level and follow it, adjust annual inflation, increase the minimum wage, pensions, scholarships, benefits, etc.

In the Kyrgyz Republic, trade unions have the right to rule-making initiatives as well, which allows them to submit proposals to state authorities on the adoption, amendment or abolition of legislative and other normative acts on labour and socio-economic issues. Trade unions, according to the laws of the Kyrgyz Republic, have the right to participate in the conclusion of interstate agreements on migration, employment, labour, pricing and social security (On Trade Unions, 1998).

In Belarus, trade unions' rights are much more limited and embrace only such issues as worker safety and health, prevention of occupational diseases and environmental safety.

In Russia, trade unions are given the right to take part in the development and amendment of laws, which are passed only by the trade unions themselves.

There are no significant differences when it comes to contract jurisdiction, carried out by the signing of union contracts and agreements of various levels (Nekrasova, 2003) (general, sectoral tariff and local agreements). Trade unions of all EEU member states have such rights. In the countries of Western Europe, preference is given to the conclusion of sector agreements. In Italy, France, Spain local agreements are more frequent (Lastochkina, 2018). For the EU member states agreements of all types are equally common.

The structure of trade unions in the CIS countries is approximately the same, there are branch unions everywhere. The structure of participation in trade unions is different (Table 6.2.).

Analysing the data on the share of workers in trade unions, it can be concluded that the countries with the highest level of trade unions are Russia, Ukraine and Uzbekistan.

How do the trade unions co-create and destroy SD in coal mining enterprises? Case studies

In this section, the activity of trade unions and their impact on sustainable development will be described based on case studies from Poland and Russia – the key representatives of hard coal mining in the EU and CIS regions, respectively.

In Poland, trade unions are currently active in all of the largest mining companies, namely Polska Grupa Górnicza SA, Jastrzębska Spółka Węglowa SA, and LW Bogdanka SA. However, the data on trade unions operating in hard coal mining differ significantly from the national data presented in the previous section. The level of unionisation in PGG SA and LW Bogdanka SA is 100% and in JSW SA periodically even over 120%, because employees belong to more than one trade union. There are also more than 24 trade union organisations in the mining industry, which is probably a world-wide phenomenon. Under legal conditions, the boards of these unions do not work and are protected from termination. It is estimated that the budget of companies and the state budget loses more than 110 million zlotys per year on these privileges (Baca-Pogorzelska and Surdej, 2016; Fedorowycz et al., 2020).

Mining trade unions in Poland are also privileged regarding collective disputes. Under the current legislation, even an illegal collective dispute can

Table 6.2 Trade unions' activity in the coal-mining countries of the CIS

Countries	Types of trade unions, number of organisations and members	Principal level of collective bargaining	Proportion of employees in unions
Russia	Federation of Independent Trade Unions of Russia (FNPR) 122 organisations and more than 20 million people	industry and company	69.2%
Ukraine	The Confederation of Free Trade Unions of Ukraine (KVPU) – a member of the International Confederation of Trade Unions The Federation of Trade Unions of Ukraine is a trade union association of Ukraine The total number of trade union members in Ukraine is about 12 million people	industry and company	46.2%
Kazakhstan	The Federation of Trade Unions of the Republic of Kazakhstan (FPRK) is a public organisation that unites most of the large trade unions of Kazakhstan 1,725,000 trade union members, 17,474 primary trade union organisations, 23 branch trade unions, 17 territorial trade union associations	industry and company	19%
Georgia	The union has 41 thousand members, united in 766 primary organisations (450 in agricultural and 316 in processing enterprises)	industry and company	26%
Kyrgyzstan	28 trade union organisations	industry and company	16%
Uzbekistan	14 branch trade unions, 12 regional associations of trade union organisations, more than 6.1 million people	industry and company	46.9%
Tajikistan	a successor to the Council of Trade Unions of the Republic of Tajikistan (Tajiksov-prof), more than 800 thousand people	industry and company	16%

Source: designed by authors using VKP, 2021

become a reason for a legal strike, which for an individual mine means financial losses of several millions. Moreover, not only mine unions, but also central unions, located at the level of the whole company, may act on behalf of individual mines that are part of mining companies. This leads to absurd collective disputes. For example, the central trade unions of JSW SA did not agree to the liquidation of the Krupiński mine, even though the changes were agreed to by the mines' trade unions, which recognized the need for changes and the unprofitability of mining. On the other hand, at LW Bogdanka mine, the company trade unions agreed to make the company's shares public, but were opposed by their headquarters located in Silesia, a completely different region of Poland (Baca-Pogorzelska and Surdej, 2016).

It is also important to note that under Poland's current trade union laws, an industrial dispute with an employer can go on virtually indefinitely if the trade union organisation is unwilling to come to an agreement, which gives it unique empowerment and power to influence the mining company. Trade union organisations can also carry out sit-down strikes on the premises of a mining company, including underground, which leads to very dangerous situations and constitutes an instrument of aggressive coercion, where the lives and health of striking miners are at stake. However, the approval of an occupational strike requires only 25% of the votes in favor of its implementation, with a 50% referendum turnout. All this makes strikes in the Polish coal mining industry way too frequent and disrupts not only the production process but also the social peace (Baca-Pogorzelska and Surdej, 2016).

Social dialogue in the circumstances described above is very difficult. Miners defend their traditions, jobs, and economic livelihood. Many of them come from multi-generational mining families and cannot imagine working outside the industry. It should also be added that in the Upper Silesian and Lublin Coal Basins, mining companies remain the key link in the local economy, and their liquidation may cause a slowdown in development and pauperisation of the region. Nevertheless, trade unions rarely see the need for change, including employment restructuring or the introduction of a flexible remuneration system immune to changes in the economic climate. This leads to a stalemate in which mining is unprofitable, yet ways are still being sought to maintain the entire industry at the expense of the state and taxpayers, which in recent years has given rise to growing social opposition and public resentment towards the activities of mining companies.

Research conducted after the recent mining protests in Poland[1] shows that 36% of those surveyed did not support the protests of miners and only 26% of respondents declared strong support for such initiatives (Figure 6.2 and Figure 6.3).

Additionally, it should be noted that non-union members were more radical in their negative assessment of the protesters than union members (Table 6.3). The latter supported the striking miners by 69%. However, as many as 29% found the mining industry's protests unjustified, highlighting a general dislike of the protesting miners even among those actively working for workers' rights.

Even fewer respondents identify with the demands of striking miners. Asked whether the trade unions represent the interests of people like the respondent by organising these protests, 40% of respondents said definitely yes or probably yes, and more than half felt that the protesting miners did not represent their interests.

The circumstances described above lead to the conclusion that in Poland, in the mining sector, the actual decision-making power is held by trade unions. This is also reflected in the fact that very often negotiations concerning restructuring of the mining sector are conducted between the government and trade unions without the participation of company managements or with their illusory participation.

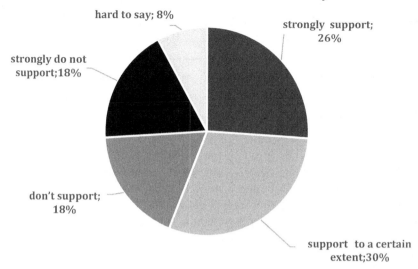

Figure 6.2 Do you personally support protest action organised by trade unions?
Source: CEBOS, 2016

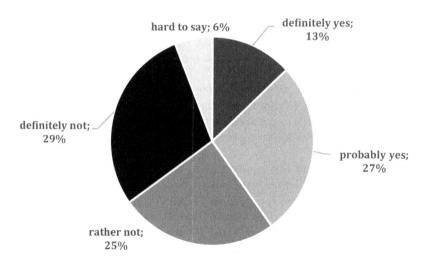

Figure 6.3 By organising these protests, are the trade unions expressing the interests of
people like you?
Source: CEBOS, 2016

During the period of reorganisation (1994–1997), some social problems occurred and their solutions were inconsistent at times. The results were: long delays in the payment of wages and compensation payments to dismissed miners, a lag in providing employment, a sharp deterioration in social

Table 6.3 Information on the functioning of trade unions in coal mining countries in Europe

Do you support the protests organised by trade unions?	Overall	Workers	Members of trade unions
YES	56%	56%	69%
NO	36%	38%	29%
HARD TO SAY	8%	6%	2%

Source: CEBOS, 2016

conditions in mining municipalities, etc. These shortcomings led to a surge in social tension in the coal-mining regions. Thus, the number of coal industry enterprises on strike increased from 329 in 1995 to 613 in 1996. The protests of miners, their wives and children heated up in the form of hunger strikes, refusal to leave mining sites, blocking highways, etc. The financial performance of the industry remained one of the most urgent concerns. Measures that were taken during this period and subsequent years to stabilise the socio-economic situation in the industry and in the country as a whole ensured a significant decrease in the intensity of the strike movement and its decline to the state of local industrial disputes (Grun, 2008).

The protests significantly impacted the restructuring process of the industry. The main areas of improvement are the following:

- social protection (support) of employees of closed and operating enterprises;
- employment of laid-off workers;
- organised migration (resettlement) of miners' families, pensioners and disabled people from northern and unpromising coal-mining areas;
- financial support for coal mining municipalities in connection with the municipalisation of social infrastructure facilities.

At present, the Russian Independent Trade Union of Coal Industry Workers (Rosugleprof) works to protect the rights of miners. It consists of 26 territorial organisations uniting 276 primary trade union organisations. Rosugleprof operates in 19 constituent entities of the Russian Federation: Republics (Buryatia, Komi, Sakha-Yakutia, and Khakassia), Territories (Krasnoyarsk, Primorsky, and Khabarovsk), Regions (Amur, Irkutsk, Kemerovo, Magadan, Moscow, Novosibirsk, Rostov, Tula, Sakhalin, Chelyabinsk, and Chita) and the city of Moscow. Rosugleprof has more than 147,000 members, of which more than 113,000 are employed (Rosugleprof, 2021).

Rosugleprof is a member organisation of the Federation of Independent Trade Unions of Russia (FNPR), the Global Federation of Industrial Trade Unions (IndustriAll), the Association of Trade Unions of the Basic Industries and Construction of the Russian Federation, and is engaged in international activities.

Rosugleprof, together with IndustriAll and other Russian trade unions, is participating in the development of strategies and tactics and coordinated actions to mitigate the social consequences of the global crisis for workers. To solve emerging problems, Rosugleprof cooperates with the International Labour Organization (ILO), the Foundation named in honour of Friedrich Ebert and other international organizers.

The foundations of social partnership are laid down in the Law of the Russian Federation "On Collective Agreements and Agreements" and other regulatory legal acts. Social partnership is implemented through a system of agreements at the federal level, at the sectoral, territorial, professional levels and the conclusion of union contracts at enterprises, organisations and institutions.

Based on national conditions and practice, under the Federal Law "On the Fundamentals of Labour Protection in the Russian Federation", joint committees (commissions) on safety and labour protection were organised at mining enterprises. Representatives of employers, professional unions or other representative bodies authorised by employees are their members.

The main tasks of the committees are:

- protection of the legal rights and interests of employees;
- organisation of public control over working conditions and compliance with labour protection legislation at workplaces, over the implementation of measures provided for in the union contract to prevent accidents and occupational diseases;
- analytical treatment of the state of occupational safety and health at the enterprise and preparation on its basis of recommendations for the prevention of industrial injuries and diseases.

The state-level regulation of social, labour and economic relations in the coal industry provides only minimum rights and guarantees for workers. Conversely, a union contract at the enterprise is the most specific legal act that can provide a higher level of rights and guarantees.

In 2019, the Russian Public Opinion Research Center (VTsIOM) presented data from a study on the topic of trade unions (Figure 6.4.). Violation of labour rights leads to a job change (7%) or negotiations with bosses on the problem (6%). Only 2% of respondents applied to a trade union or work council. Russians are rather sceptical about the work of trade unions: 53% believe that they do not help protect labour rights (Trade Unions Today, 2019).

Some 82% of the respondents believe that trade unions do not play a significant role in their country. However, trade unions pay little attention to the real protection of workers' rights. Statistics show that trade union lawyers take part in litigation on labour law issues in 14–15 cases a year. Whereas, in 2014, 507,000 labour disputes were considered in the court of first instance. It can be concluded that trade union lawyers are involved in only 3% of labour disputes (Banks Today, 2019).

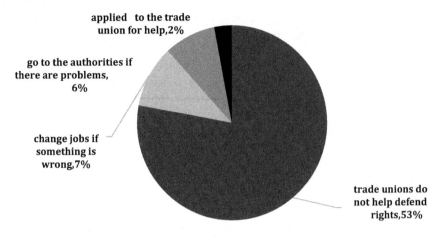

Figure 6.4 Statistics of applications to trade unions
Source: Banks Today, 2019

Trade unions' influence on coal mining enterprises

The idea of the existence of trade unions and the roles assigned to them are by definition desirable, appropriate, and allow for the protection of workers from a more powerful employer and often from an influential multinational corporation that does not always act in an ethical and moral manner. In theory, therefore, their activities benefit the dissemination and implementation of the concept of sustainable development (Thomas, 2021; Felli, 2014). This is because it supports the social dimension and counterbalances economic priorities in mining companies. Fundamental human rights, decent wages, and safe working conditions become important in this context. All this, including trade union activity itself, should be legally sanctioned, controlled, and improved.

However, in practice, trade union activity does not always meet these standards, and distortions in this area are a serious barrier to sustainable development.

On the one hand, there are practices of banning trade unions in less civilised countries, and on the other hand, as in Poland or Spain, trade unions abuse their position and power to systematically destroy the values and image of the entire extractive industry (Herrero and Lemkow, 2015). So, the internal unsustainability of trade union activities hinders the practical implementation of the concept of sustainable development.

Notably, in both said cases, the consequences of such extreme situations are quite severe for mining companies. Lack of respect for workers' freedoms contributes to the deterioration of mining companies' image, which in times of common access to immediate information has not only PR effects, but often translates into concrete decisions on refusal to grant a mining permit or to stop mining. In turn, excessive privileging of professional mining unions leads to economically irrational decisions, which in the long-term perspective results in permanent loss of profitability of production and liquidation of mines. Therefore, general and internal balancing within the framework of particular priorities of sustainable development should be in the interest of all entities connected with a mining company. Practice clearly shows that any deviation from the accepted norms causes negative consequences for the existence and survival of the mining industry.

The protest movements of Russian miners played a decisive role in matters of social protection only in the period 1989–2003 while the country's political life was turbulent. During this period, regulatory mechanisms and measures were developed to mitigate the negative consequences by changing the priorities of the social policy of restructuring and improving the mechanisms of state support for the restructuring of the coal industry. At present, the activity of trade unions is manifested in the organisation of rallies and other mass events (as a rule, they are not considered as protests). For example, every year it is the trade unions that organise the procession of workers to the demonstration on May 1.

The work of trade unions in Russia, for the most part, is assessed as ineffective. They have little influence and they are forced not so much to form an agenda in the interests of workers as to adapt to the conditions that the employer offers them (Bizyukov, 2020). This violates the basic principle of their organisation – independence and adherence to the protection of workers' rights.

The ineffective work of "official" trade unions and their close relationship with employers contribute to the fact that the number of workers in them is constantly decreasing. For those who do not want to pay their earned 1% of income, it is enough to submit an application to the head of the trade union organisation and the chief accountant and stop contributing. The employee does not lose support and legal assistance and can turn to the State Labour Inspectorate or the prosecutor's office.

Trade unions that protect and represent the rights and interests of workers in the field of labour and related socio-economic relations are directly interested in the unification and harmonisation of the legislation of the EEU member states in the field of labour migration, since this allows ensuring equal social and labour rights of workers and their guarantees (Lastochkina, 2018).

Note

1 The survey was conducted using computer-assisted face-to-face interviews (CAPI) on March 11–18, 2015 with a representative random sample of 1,052 Polish adults (CEBOS, 2016).

Bibliography

About Trade Unions. Law of the Republic of Kazakhstan. (2014). https://kasipodaq.kz/ё-прёфессиёнальных-сёюзах/ [access date: 30. 06. 2021].

Baca-Pogorzelska, K., Surdej A. (2016). *Przyszłość czy bankructwo? Nowoczesne górnictwo made in Poland*. Raport Centrum im. Adama Smitha: Warszawa.

Banks Today (2019). Trade Unions in Russia: Imitation of Work or Real Protection of Labor Rights?https://bankstoday.net/last-articles/profsoyuzy-v-rossii-imitatsiya-ra boty-ili-realnaya-zashhita-trudovyh-prav [access date: 29. 03. 2021].

Baran, B.K. (2019). Model of Collective Labour Agreements in the Polish Legal System. *Praca i Zabezpieczenie Społeczne*, 2, 6–8.

Baran, K.W. (2018). Refleksje o ochronie stosunku zatrudnienia działaczy związkowych na poziomie zakładowym po nowelizacji ustawy związkowej z 5 lipca 2018 r. *Praca i Zabezpieczenie Społeczne*, 10, 21–26.

Bizyukov, P. (2020). Today any Trade Union Leader Knows That There is no Need to Run Up and Go to Conflict. Why Are Trade Unions Helpless in Russia? *Realnoe Vremya*. https://realnoevremya.ru/articles/175603-pochemu-bespomoschny-profsoyu zy-v-rossii [access date: 29. 03. 2021].

Borkowski, A. (2019). (Prawie) każdy może być związkowcem: czyli jakie zmiany wprowadza nowelizacja ustawy o związkach zawodowych. *Personel i Zarządzanie*, 3, 74–78.

CEBOS (2016). *Opinie o związkach zawodowych i protestach górników* (Opinions on Trade Unions and Miners' Protests), https://cbos.pl/SPISKOM.POL/2015/K_066_15.PDF [access date: 06. 05. 2020].

Crowley, M.J. (2016). Compensation, Retraining and Respiratory Diseases: British Coal Miners, 1918–1939. *Labor History*, 58(4), 432–449.

Cunningham, P.W. (1985). Trade Unions and Politics in South Africa. *South African Journal of Sociology*, 16(2), 43–48.

Fedorowycz, D., Malu, A.C. Gatto, Maydom, B. (2020). State-sponsored Trade Unions after Democratic Transitions. *Democratization*, 27, 142–1161.

Felli R. (2014). An Alternative Socio-Ecological Strategy? International Trade Unions' Engagement with Climate Change. *Review of International Political Economy*, 21(2), 372–398.

Galgoczi, B. (2014). The Changing Role of Trade Unions in the Sustainable Development Agenda. *International Review of Sociology/Revue Internationale de Sociologie*, 24(1).

Grun, V.D. (2008). Activities of the State Institution "Sotsugol" at the Stages of Restructuring of the Coal Industry in Russia – Pages of History. *Coal*, 8, 12–16.

Gunningham, N., Sinclair, D. (2014). Building Trust: Work Health and Safety Management in the Mining Industry. *Policy and Practice in Health and Safety*, 12(1), 35–51.

Herrero, A., Lemkow, L. (2015). Environmentally Blind Discourses on Coal Extraction and the Idealization of the Miner in Spain. *Capitalism Nature Socialism*, 26(4), 215–235.

Homer, A.W. (2009). Coal Mine Safety Regulation in China and the USA. *Journal of Contemporary Asia*, 39(3), 424–439.

Jończyk, J. (2017). O związkach zawodowych. *Praca i Zabezpieczenie Społeczne*, 11, 8–12.

Kloc, K. (2007). Trade Unions and Economic Transformation in Poland. *Journal of Communist Studies*, 125–132.

Kryszczuk, M.D., Wenzel, M. (2017). Związki zawodowe w świetle przemian cywilizacyjnych: możliwości, wyzwania i zagrożenia. *Zarządzanie Publiczne*, 3(41), 34.

Lastochkina, K.A. (2018). The Participation of Public Organizations in Law-making for Harmonization of Legislation of the Member Countries of the EEU (on the example of trade unions). *Vestnik of the Mari State University. Chapter "History. Law"*, 4(1), 63–69.

Lis, A. (2014). Strategies of Interest Representation: Polish Trade Unions in EU Governance. *Europe-Asia Studies*, 66(3), 444–466.

Mason, D.S. (1987). Poland's New Trade Unions. *Soviet Studies*, 39(3), 489–508.

Myant, M. (2007). Czech and Slovak Trade Unions, *Journal of Communist Studies*, 59–84.

Nekrasova, M.E.K (2003). Voprosu o roli normativnogo dogovora v pravovoi sisteme Rossii [On the role of the normative treaty in the Russian legal system]. Gosu-darstvennost' i gosudar-stvennaya sluzhba Rossii: puti razvitiya: materialy sovmest. mezhdistsiplinar. aspirant. konf. RAGS – SZAGS [Statehood and public service of Russia: ways of development: materials of combined interdisciplinary postgraduate's conf. RAPA – NWAPA], Saint Petersburg, 3, 280–282.

On Trade Unions: Law of the Kyrgyz Republic, October 16. (1998). No. 130. Gov-ernment of the Kyrgyz Republic. http://www.gov.kg [access date: 30. 06. 2021].

Petelczyc, J., Matuszczyk, K. (2019). Zaangażowanie związków zawodowych w Polsce w prawa okołopracownicze - perspektywa związkowców. *Polityka Społeczna*, 3, 20–24.

Rosugleprof (Russian Independent Trade Union of Coal Workers) (2021). http://rosu gleprof.ru/ [access date: 30. 06. 2021].

Somogyi, P.J. (1995). Assisting Independent Trade Unions in Post-Communist Countries. *Problems of Post-Communism*, 42(2), 3–7.

Thomas A. (2021). 'Heart of Steel': How Trade Unions Lobby the European Union over Emissions Trading. *Environmental Politics*.

Trade Unions Today (2019). https://wciom.ru/analytical-reviews/analiticheskii-ob zor/profsoyuzy-segodnya [access date: 30. 06. 2021].

VKP (2021). VKP Yesterday and Today: Interaction with the Bodies of the CIS. EurAsEC, EAEU: General Confederation of Trade Unions. http://www.vkp.ru/about.html [access date: 30. 06. 2021].

Zientara, P. (2014). *Human Resource Management in Emerging Economies*. London, New York: Routledge.

Part III

External stakeholders in SD of coal mining enterprises

7 Suppliers and recipients as main links in a value chain of a coal mining enterprise

The role of recipients in a value chain of a coal mining enterprise

In the mining industry, the value chain ranges from the supply of mining machinery, devices and equipment to the sale of coal or other fossil fuels to the end consumer (Sekar et al., 2019; Wuest and Thoben, 2015). Value chain management in the mining industry involves the process of planning, implementing and monitoring day-to-day operations, from raw material procurement, through management and production availability, to the distribution of finished products. This type of value chain consists of several elements connected by the flow of products and services. From the global view of the value chain of the mining sector, the mine itself is only one of its links (see Figure 7.1), which consists of:

- Mine suppliers – manufacturers of mining machinery and equipment, producers of material equipment for mining excavations and external service providers;
- Mines – coal mining in the mine;
- Recipients – energy production in a power plant, Combined Heat and Power (CHP) or steel production using coking coal;
- End customers – supplying energy through the distribution network to customers or supplying steel to end customers, primarily the automotive industry.

Directly in the mine itself, the value chain consists of seven elements (Görner et al., 2020):

Figure 7.1 Value chain in the mining industry
Source: own research based on (Mineral Industry, 2020)

DOI: 10.4324/9781003091110-11

1   Mine – extracting materials;
2   Processing plant – processing raw materials;
3   Inventory – managing inventory levels and quality;
4   Rail – moving materials to the port;
5   Port – stockpiling, loading and managing ships;
6   Ship – shipping materials to destination;
7   Market – delivering materials to the customer.

Mining enterprises are very much dependent on the end customers, which – for steam coal – are power plants and CHPs and – in the case of coking coal – coking plants and/or the metallurgical industry. In Poland, the most common recipients of mine products are companies from the energy sector. This is confirmed by the data presented in Figure 7.2, which shows that, in 2018, 93.3% of coal was sold on the domestic market and only 6.2% was exported. On the domestic market, 53% of recipients involved commercial power engineering, 2.8% industrial power, 7.6% non-professional and professional heating plants, 0.7% other industrial customers, 15.3% coking plants and 14.4% other domestic customers. The analysis of the sales structure of mining enterprises confirms the clear dependence of the level of their production and sales possibilities on the demand in the commercial and industrial power engineering, as well as in the coke and metallurgical industries. This implies a very strong influence of recipients on the price and quality conditions. The latter, due to the growing environmental requirements, have recently been of great importance and, in fact, are associated with a strong pressure to reduce the sulphur content and increase the calorific value of the raw material extracted in Polish mines.

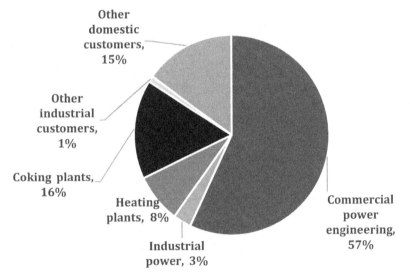

Figure 7.2 The structure of hard coal sales in Poland
Source: Laskowski and Stępiński, 2019

Similarly, recipients, i.e. the power industry, must adapt to the growing requirements in terms of social responsibility, especially in terms of environmental protection. These requirements result from many documents, among which the decarbonisation policy currently implemented in the world and in the European Union is an important one. As part of the European Green Deal, in 2020, the European Commission proposed increasing the target level of reduction of greenhouse gas emissions to at least 55% by 2030, compared to 1990 levels (EU Climate Action, 2020). The implementation of these goals has a very large impact on the energy sector and indirectly on its mining companies and the mines operating in them.

In the case of the European Union countries, decarbonisation is one of the pillars of the implementation of EU goals. It is assumed that its achievement should take place through the use of activities, such as:

- increasing the share of renewable sources of electricity production;
- reduction of greenhouse gas emissions to the atmosphere;
- creating a favourable framework for projects using zero-emission fuel technologies for electricity production.

The pressure of consumers in the European Union countries to supply clean energy leads to a situation of a continuous decline in energy production from non-renewable fuels and an increase in production from renewable sources. The effects of this pressure can be seen in Figure 7.3, which shows the volume

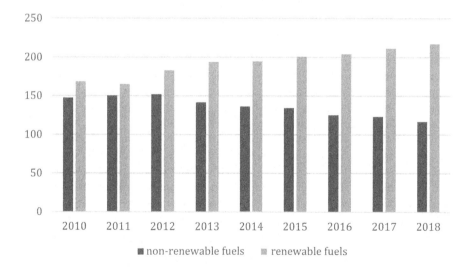

Figure 7.3 Production of energy from non-renewable and renewable sources in the European Union countries in 2010–2018 [Mtoe]
Source: European Commission, 2020

of energy production from non-renewable and renewable sources in the European Union countries in 2010–2018.

Already almost 10 years ago, it was noted in Poland that the decarbonisation policy pursued by the European Union could endanger Poland's energy security. It can also disrupt its sustainable socio-economic development (Bednorz, 2012). The liquidation of the mining industry may contribute to an increase in the level of unemployment, as well as to the dependence of the economy on unstable supplies of energy resources (Kasztalewicz, 2018).

Poland's situation is additionally complicated by the fact that the hard coal mining industry is currently excluded in the European Union from the right to receive sectoral state aid. State support may be directed only to state-owned, restructured and liquidated mines. The European Commission agreed that, in Poland, due to the large role of the mining industry in the economy, support for the restructured state-owned mines should be granted until 2023. Nevertheless, with over 70% share of coal in the energy balance, it is a very short period, insufficient for a complete energy transformation.

It is worth noting that, also in countries outside the European Union, legal acts are issued, that affect coal producers and recipients by exerting pressure on decarbonisation, which – in turn – contributes to the creation of regulations imposing even greater environmental requirements for the mining industry. The increasingly stringent requirements for sustainable development in the mining sector have been reflected, for example, in the RECLAIM Act, introduced in 2017 in the USA, under which public funds generated by enterprises involved in coal mining can be used to improve the living conditions of communities that have suffered greatly from the cessation of coal mining in their vicinity.

The considerations presented in this chapter show that energy companies, under the influence of the need to adapt to European Union and Polish law, put pressure on the use and development of more and more advanced and environmentally friendly mining technologies. The aim of this type of approach is to lead to an increase in production efficiency, while limiting its negative impact on the environment. This way, mining companies can better adapt to the requirements of sustainable development.

The most important activities that mining companies must take under the influence of their suppliers include – in particular – the production of the so-called low-emission coal, also known as smokeless coal. It is a fuel product, that has been degassed in a controlled manner in the technological process, meaning that the volatile parts polluting the original raw material were removed. The fuel produced in this way shows a large decrease in particulate matter, including PM2.5 and PM10, and an almost complete decrease in Benzo[a]pyrene emissions during combustion.

Another technology, with which there is the greatest hope that mines will be able to provide suppliers with the required, environmentally friendly product, is the coal gasification process. The process is based on gasification, in which a solid fuel, largely composed of coal, is converted into gas. The products of this process can be used to produce electricity, as well as various fuels, e.g. transport fuels. However, it should be emphasised that the currently described technologies are experimental and are carried out on a relatively small scale.

Due to the specificity of mining activities and the high dependence of mining companies on customers, this industry often experiences vertical or horizontal consolidation within international machine or material corporations, as well as within energy groups.

An example of vertical consolidation in the mine industry and energy companies is the consolidation that took place in Poland in the Tauron Group. This group operates in all basic areas of the energy market. Thanks to this, it maintains control over the process of generating and supplying energy. The Tauron Group focuses on the energy value chain, from coal mining in a mine, through energy production in a power plant or combined heat and power plant, to delivering it through the distribution network to customers. The structure of the Group corresponds to the next links in the energy chain. It is a fully integrated energy group, made up of autonomous commercial companies. The Group is headed by TAURON Polska Energia S.A. as the parent company. Individual companies of the Tauron Group watch over the security of the entire energy chain. Tauron is one of the largest energy companies in Poland.

Tauron Group's operations are based on seven Business Areas, defined in accordance with the individual links of the value chain: mining, production, heating, renewable energy sources, trade, distribution and sales. Particular links of the energy chain of the Tauron Group are shown in Table 7.1.

Similar consolidation processes were carried out in other European Union countries, which focused on the extraction of hard coal and lignite, including, among others, on a large scale in Germany. The purpose of these consolidations is to ensure a market for mining enterprises, while also ensuring national energy security. Then, the recipient in the form of the energy sector and the supplier, i.e. the mining company, are fully integrated.

All the federal subjects of Russia consume coal. The major coal consumers on the domestic market are power plants and coke plants. According to corporate reports, coal-mining companies supplied 181.3 million tons of coal to the domestic market in 2019 to meet the needs of:

- power plants: 84.1 million tons (a decrease of 1.7 million tons, or 2%, on 2018);
- coke plants: 31.5 million tons (a decrease of 0.1 million tons, or 0.3%, on 2018);
- households and the agricultural sector: 26.3 million tons (an increase of 1.4 million tons, or 5.6%, on 2018);
- other consumers (metal manufacturers, energy producers, Russian Railways, the Ministry of Defense, the Ministry of Justice, the Ministry of Internal Affairs, the Ministry of Transport, the Federal Border Service, the nuclear industry, The Federal Agency for State Reserves, cement manufacturers, etc.): 39.4 million tons (an increase of 1.2 million tons, or 3.1%, on 2018). The major coking coal consumers in Russia are large holding companies producing metal.

(Tarazanov, 2019)

Table 7.1 Energy value chain in the Tauron Group

Links in the energy chain	A company in the Tauron Group	Range of activities
Mining	TAURON Sprzedaż TAURON Sprzedaż GZE	Includes activities related to the extraction, enrichment and sale of hard coal for the power industry and individual clients. In addition to hard coal extraction, mining activities are also carried out, consisting in the extraction of limestone using the opencast method, as well as its processing and sale within the Group and outside it.
Production	TAURON Wytwarzanie	Includes the production of electricity from conventional sources (also in biomass combustion process). Electricity is generated in conventional units in five hard coal-fired power plants with a total capacity of approx. 4.3 GWe and 1.2 GWt. These power plants also have two biomass units installed. The power plants are located in the following cities: Łaziska Górne, Będzin, Trzebinia, Stalowa Wola and Jaworzno.
Heating	TAURON Ciepło	Covers the production, distribution and sale of heat and electricity from sources producing in cogeneration. Heat is generated in three CHP plants with a total capacity of approx. 0.3 GWe and 1.2 GWt, located in Katowice, Tychy and Bielsko-Biała, as well as in local boiler plants.
Renewable energy sources	TAURON Ekoenergia	Covers the production of electricity from renewable sources, except the combustion of biomass. Manages 34 hydropower plants with a total capacity of 133 MW, located mainly in the south of Poland, and 9 wind power plants with a total capacity of 381 MW, located mainly in the north of the country.
Distribution	TAURON Dystrybucja	Covers the distribution of electricity through a network located in southern Poland. TAURON provides electricity in the following provinces: Lesser Poland, Lower Silesia, Opole and Silesia, as well as partially Holy Cross, Subcarpathia, Łódź, Greater Poland and Lubusz.
Trade	TAURON Polska Energia S.A.	Covers wholesale electricity, trading and management of CO_2 emission allowances and property rights resulting from electricity certificates of origin and fuels.
Sale	TAURON Sprzedaż TAURON Sprzedaż GZE	Covers the sale of electricity, gas and related products to end customers. Sale is conducted throughout the country and, on a smaller scale, on the Czech and Slovak markets. In this area, also services related to street lighting and services in the field of energy efficiency and smart technology are provided mainly by TAURON Dystrybucja Serwis sp. z o.o., managing approx. 750 thousand street lights.

Source: own work based on TAURON, 2019

On average, coal costs constitute 10–15% of rolled steel production costs. Access to high-quality coking coal ensures that Russian metal manufacturers rank among the best in the world in terms of production costs. The total commercial reserves of coking coal (grades A, B, and C1) in Russia are sufficient to cover the global needs of ferrous metallurgy for the next 100 years at the current consumption rate. Kuzbass coal accounts for 73% of the reserves and 80% of the production volume. There are also large coking coal reserves in Siberia (namely in South Yakutia and the Tyva Republic). These reserves include the most valuable grades of coking coal – K, KZh, KO, OS, and KS – which, together with grades Zh and GZh, are the main feed materials in coke production in the Russian Federation.

Local coal production is a competitive advantage for Russian metal producers for three reasons. The fall of the ruble that started in 2014 and continued in 2017–2018 made the Russian coal industry one of the most efficient in the global market. After the devaluation of the ruble, the cost of Russian coal before shipping from ports ranged from 70 to 90 USD per ton at the end of 2019, which is still profitable for Russian companies even though global coal prices dropped to a range of 140 to 150 USD per ton. It should be noted that almost all metallurgical holdings have in-house coal production, which allows them to compensate for the costs of their metal manufacturing operations with profits earned by coal-mining companies.

The major thermal coal consumers in Russia are holding companies producing energy, whose subsidiaries include thermal power plants. About 1/5 (200 billion kWh) of all electricity produced in Russia is generated using coal. The ongoing growth in energy consumption in Russia is mainly covered by gas-fired power plants. After 2010, thermal coal exports first equaled coal supplies to domestic power plants and then exceeded them. The share of supplies to Russian thermal power plants fell to 21.14% (2019).

Low-quality coal grades account for 90% of the total annual coal consumption at coal-fired power plants in Russia. High-quality grades are exported (Marinicheva, 2012). Despite the growth in thermal coal refining in Russia, refined coal is not supplied to Russian power plants. There is a shortage of high-quality coal on the domestic market; power plants cannot purchase the coal they need in sufficient quantity, or suppliers offer it at prices that are too high for electricity production. As a result, power plants started to use non-standard coal grades and even coal mining and preparation waste, which increases the equipment failure rate. The existing coal-fired power plants (with some minor exceptions) were designed to use specific grades of coal from particular deposits, while high-quality coal is needed by modern coal-fired power plants using clean coal technologies which are not used in the electric power industry of Russia. To create demand for high-quality thermal coal, the country's coal-fired power generation facilities need to be upgraded.

The increase in the consumption of low-quality coal grades and waste from coal production should be turned into an advantage. Facilities using solid fuels could use environmentally friendly technologies to become "factories" for the disposal of substandard raw materials as well as industrial and household waste, meeting European environmental standards in the future. It is necessary to switch to cogeneration technologies to ensure waste-free production of heat and energy and high-value coal-derived products and chemicals, such as coking coal products, carbon adsorbents, briquettes, coal liquefaction products, methanol, fertilizers, complex metal concentrates, building materials, associated gas (nitrogen, liquid argon, oxygen), etc.

More than half of Russian coal (51% as of 2019) is exported (Figure 7.4).

Thermal coal accounts for the major share of total coal exports (173.3 million tons, or 90%). The share of coking coal is 10% (19 million tons). Some 13 million tons (7% of the total exports) were shipped to CIS countries and 179.3 million tons were shipped to other countries (93% of the total exports). In 2019, there was a pronounced downward trend in coal prices in the global market. They fell by 10–40% compared to previous years (Yanovsky, 2019; Tarazanov, 2019).

In the future, the role of Russia in the global coal market will become more important. Contrary to global trends, coal production in the Russian Federation is constantly growing. To boost sales, the country seeks to increase its share in the markets of the Asia-Pacific region, where coal consumption is increasing by 140 million tons per year. The share of Russia in this market is only 8.6%, and the immediate goal is to bring this figure to 15%. With a favorable commodity pricing environment, the share of Asia-Pacific countries in the total coal exports may reach 53%. However, there are also several constraints, such as insufficient railway and port capacities in the Far East of Russia. According to optimistic estimates, Russian coal exports may reach 240 to 250 million tons by 2030 (taking into account the needs of the key consumers in the Asia-Pacific region). If the growth in this region is moderate, total coal exports will not

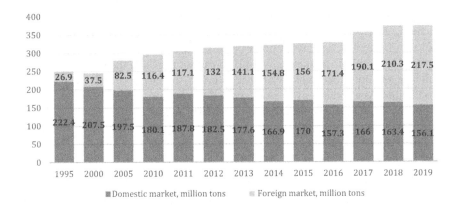

Figure 7.4 Supply of Russian coals including export, million tons
Source: designed by authors using Yanovsky, 2019

exceed 215 or 220 million tons. It is interesting to note that despite the general decrease in the production and consumption of coal in European countries, the export of Russian coal to this region is growing.

In general, the prospects for the development of the domestic coal industry in the foreseeable future look promising. Factors that make it possible to give such an assessment include:

- availability of sufficient coal reserves;
- the fact that Russian coal companies are attractive to investors, which is evidenced by the growth in investments in their fixed assets over the past few years;
- a steady upward trend in coal production capacity;
- promising international coal markets, primarily those in the Asia-Pacific region.

The role of recipients in a value chain of a coal mining enterprise

For the mining industry, suppliers play a very important role, not only in the mining value chain itself, but also for the region, in which the mining company and its mines operate. This is confirmed by the data presented in Figure 7.5,

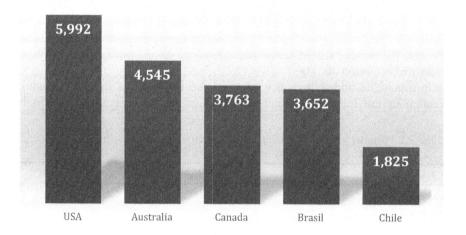

Figure 7.5 Number of mining suppliers in the leading mining countries worldwide in 2018
Source: https://www.statista.com/statistics/550994/number-of-mining-suppliers-in-leading-mining-countries-worldwide/#statisticContainer [access date: 08.01.2021]

referring to the number of mining-related companies operating in countries with the most developed mining industry. It is usually a few thousand companies that generate hundreds of thousands of jobs (Ejdemo, 2013; Fleming and Measham, 2014; Radetzki, 1982; Rolfe et al., 2007). Due to the specificity of the mining industry, diversification or complete change of the business profile in these companies is possible to a small extent, which means that the suppliers of mining enterprises and the jobs they offer to local communities are highly dependent on the existence and development of the mining industry.

The coefficient of multiplication of jobs by a mining enterprise depends on many factors, including, first of all, the extent to which the local community and local suppliers use the opportunities offered to them as a result of the mining industry in the region. The main factors affecting the size of the job multiplier include: the size of the mine, the extent of the mining region, geographic location, as well as the presence of mining clusters located in the area (Archibald and Ritter, 2001). For example, the results of research conducted in Ghana indicate at least five jobs are created in mining-related companies per one job in a mine (Kusi-Sarpong and Sarkis, 2016; Baah-Boateng, 2018). On the other hand, econometric studies conducted in Sweden (Moritz et al., 2017) showed that for every 10 new jobs created directly in the mining sector, there were about 8.5 jobs in other industries, not directly related to mining.

The number of jobs generated in EU economies extracting hard coal or lignite in mining-related enterprises is presented in Table 7.2.

The data in Table 7.2 clearly illustrates the diminished role of coal mining in the analysed countries. Nevertheless, those of them that are still largely dependent on coal, still employ large numbers of people in the mining-related sector.

It is estimated that in Poland – the largest producer of hard coal in the EU – one job in the mining industry generates three or four jobs in its environment, in companies that are suppliers and co-operators of mining enterprises. In the case of Poland, the mining-related sector also employs a huge number of employees, estimated at around 400,000.

It should be added here that, due to the processes of decommissioning mining in the European Union, described in the previous chapters, Polish

Table 7.2 Number of jobs in mining-related enterprises in European Union countries extracting hard coal and/or lignite

Country	Employment numbers
Bulgaria	45,000
Germany	20,000
Greece	2,000
Slovenia	2,400
Hungary	800
Slovakia	400

Source: own work based on Euracoal, 2020

suppliers of mining machinery, equipment and mining services have become European monopolists, and their activities also cover non-European mining markets. Interestingly, however, the expansion into foreign markets by Polish manufacturers of mining machinery and equipment happened mainly in 2010–2015 (Dudała, 2012). In 2016, manufacturers of mining machinery were one of the main driving forces of Polish export, but in 2020, as a result of the collapse of mining production, they found themselves in a very difficult economic situation (Oksińska and Kacprzak, 2020). The decarbonisation policy implemented in more and more countries in the world has caused – and still causes – that the global market is shrinking at a very fast pace and it is more and more difficult to place mining products and services on it.

The most important groups of suppliers of the mining industry, that generate jobs and contribute to better regional development, include:

- manufacturers of mining machinery and equipment;
- manufacturers of material equipment for excavation works;
- outsourcing of preparatory works;
- companies handling the distribution and sales of mining products;
- companies handling the service and repair of mining machinery and equipment;
- outsourcing of catering services.

A very important group of mining-related enterprises is the mining machinery and equipment industry. The structure of this industry varies depending on the products and services offered. It can be divided into a core composed of manufacturers of machines and equipment, supplied primarily for the mining industry, and enterprises of a more universal nature, i.e. suppliers of machines, equipment and materials, that can be used in a wider range (Jonek-Kowalska and Michalak, 2013). The statistics show that there are about 200 enterprises in Poland that manufacture only mining machinery and equipment (Oksińska and Kacprzak, 2020). In total, the entire mining machinery and equipment industry has about 1,000 commercial and institutional partners, where approximately 40 companies manufacture basic equipment for mines (Jonek-Kowalska and Michalak, 2013). The largest Polish manufacturers of mining machinery and equipment operating on the domestic and foreign market are Famur SA and Kopex SA.

Research in Poland shows a very high dependence of mining industry suppliers on the situation in the mining industry. The poor economic situation in the mining industry has a very strong impact on mining-related enterprises. Extensive research conducted in 2017 among Polish mining-related companies by Gawlik and Pepłowska showed that over 50% of the surveyed companies generate more than 50% of their income operating for the needs of the mining industry (Gawlik and Pepłowska, 2017). In some companies, mining industry-related operations equal 80–90% and, in some extreme examples, they are as high as 100%. The presented data proves that mining-related enterprises are highly dependent on the condition of the mining industry. Therefore, the liquidation or significant limitation of the operations of mining enterprises results – for enterprises related to mining – in a decrease in sales and revenues, inhibition of the development process, mass layoffs of employees, loss of financial liquidity and, ultimately, liquidation of the enterprise.

This group of suppliers and contractors working with coal companies includes: Russian companies supplying mining equipment and mining vehicles; foreign companies supplying mining equipment and mining vehicles; suppliers of other types of fixed assets and inventories; design organisations acting as contractors; contractors providing professional services and works; Russian Railways; other transport organisations, including ports; companies providing infrastructure services (resource-supplying organisations); universities and colleges. Each subgroup is of interest as they differ by the products they produce, the works they perform, the services they provide, the frequency of interactions, and the terms regulating their business relationships.

The key suppliers of the coal industry are companies producing mining equipment and mining vehicles. In Russia, there are 44 factories producing these types of products. An analysis of equipment procurement in Russian coal companies shows that over the years, both underground and open-pit mines in Russia have become increasingly dependent on imported equipment used in their coal mining, transportation, and processing operations, with open-pit mines demonstrating this trend more prominently (Rozhko, 2017).

Among manufacturers that are not domestic, the following companies act as the key equipment suppliers for Russian open-pit and underground coal mining operations: DBT, Eickoff, Gluckauf Liebherr, Terex (Germany); Fazos, Glinik KOPEX GROUP, Huta Stalowa Wola, Dressta (Poland); OSTROJ, TAGOR, T Machinery a.s. (Czech Republic); Bucyrus, CAT, Joy, Caterpillar, P&H, Marion (USA); CODCO, ZMJ (China); Volvo (Sweden); Hitachi, Komatsu (Japan); Hyundai, Daewoo (Korea); Gorlovskiy Mashinostroitel JSC (Ukraine); BelAZ (Belarus) (Rozhko, 2017). On average, 65% of all the equipment that was used by Russian coal mining companies in 2017 had been imported, with the average indicator being 54% for underground mines and 79.6% for open-pit mines (Krasnyansky et al., 2017).

At the beginning of 2018, the shearers used at the mines of Russia predominantly originated from Poland (25.4%), Germany (23.8%), and the USA (17.7%) (JSC, 2018; Rozhkov and Karpenko, 2019).

Almost all Russian coal companies use infrastructure and transportation services provided by railways and seaports. On the territory of Russia, coal is the key cargo for the Russian Railways Joint Stock Company; by 2018, its share in the freight turnover had grown from 35% to 44% over a decade (State Report, 2018). Railway and port capacities in Russia lag behind the growing exports, which is a hindrance to the development of the coal industry. The government takes part in developing a legislative and regulatory framework for regulating natural monopolies. Some coal companies have their own infrastructure facilities (such as coal ports and terminals), which gives them more control over product pricing and allows them to plan their logistics operations independently.

Despite the fact that the government has taken numerous measures aimed at import substitution (such as research and development subsidies, loan benefits, and special investment contracts), it has not given the necessary boost to the domestic production of mining equipment.

Heavy engineering in Ukraine is one of the most developed sectors of the country. It is characterised by a large number of companies and has long-established engineering and production traditions. Mining equipment manufacturers are located in Mariupol (Azovmash), Kramatorsk (Novokramatorsk Machine-Building Plant), Donetsk (Mining Machines), Sumy (Sumy Frunze NPO), Kharkov (Electrotyazhmash, Turboatom), Kiev (Bolshevik), and Dnepropetrovsk (Dneprotyazhmash). The largest manufacturer of mining equipment in Ukraine is Mining Machines (Donetsk) (NewsRuss.ru, 2020). Ukrainian coal companies are provided with domestic mining equipment.

Since Kazakhstan holds the development of the oil and gas industry as its priority, the development of mechanical engineering to meet the needs of this particular sector has great prospects. The share of engineering products manufactured domestically amounts to only approximately 13%, with the remaining 87% of the country's needs being covered by exports (mainly from Russia) (ukrexport.gov.ua, 2008).

In Central Asia, about 2/3 of engineering products are produced in Uzbekistan (State Committee of the Republic of Uzbekistan on Statistics, 2019). At the moment, the Republic of Uzbekistan is the largest car manufacturer in Central Asia and ranks second among the CIS countries in terms of its share of domestically produced passenger cars (about 45–55%), trucks and buses (about 15–30%) (Invest.gov.uz, 2021).

In general, it should be noted that most CIS countries depend to a moderate or large extent on imports to cover their needs for heavy machinery.

Coal producers and Russian railways are each other's key stakeholders. Currently, almost all of the Russian coal that goes for export is transported to seaports by rail. The infrastructure that delivers coal to Western countries is well developed, but the demand for coal in this region is decreasing. At the same time, the Baikal–Amur Mainline and the Trans-Siberian Railway that deliver coal to Eastern countries have limited capacities. They are used by coal producers to transport coal to the ports of the Far East of Russia, from where it is transported to the markets of the Asia-Pacific region that are characterised by strong demand for coal and high prices as compared to Europe.

This problem is being solved by the government, and one of the solutions is the use of the ship-or-pay mechanism, which is a common practice of signing contracts whose provisions require that a shipper should either deliver a particular amount of cargo or pay a fine if it is not delivered. However, coal transportation is generally unprofitable for Russian Railways, which is the reason why the monopoly has no interest in long-term agreements. In 2020, shippers delivered 353.3 million tons of coal via the Russian Railways network, which is 5% less than a year earlier. It should also be noted that coal is the least profitable cargo for Russian Railways because it is transported at a reduced fare. The 44% of Russian Railways' freight turnover creates only 20% of the company's total income, the rest of which is accounted for by other goods (RBC, 2021).

For coal companies, the terms of ship-or-pay contracts can reduce the risks of uneven shipment patterns thanks to guarantees provided by Russian Railways. However, coal companies and metal manufacturers are heavily dependent on the global market changes which are difficult to predict even a month in advance; therefore, fixing significant quantities to be delivered in contracts can present a new risk for shippers.

The Russian government intends to scale up Russian coal exports eastward, which includes the possibility of allocating resources from the National Welfare Fund (NWF). In this context, the state and the private sector have matching interests. The largest coal-mining companies (for example, the Elgaugol company, which is developing the promising Elga deposit located in Yakutia) are ready to invest their own money in the development of the necessary transport infrastructure within the framework of concession agreements (RBC, 2021).

The suppliers of mining enterprises also include service providers, comprising enterprises and institutions offering innovative mining technologies. Nevertheless, according to research conducted in Latin American countries, despite the growing demand of mining companies for new, technologically advanced solutions, only a few of them can integrate them into their value chain. The analyses in this area show that only two types of organisations can take advantage of the emerging opportunities: the first type consists in organisations that have already been strongly embedded in the market and are strongly integrated with the mining sector, with the other being new innovative venture companies, such as spin-offs or start-ups just getting their feet wet (Pietrobelli et al., 2018).

In Poland, in the field of providing modern mining technologies, research and development units specialising in mining production cooperate with such enterprises as The Central Mining Institute in Katowice, the Institute of Mineral Raw Materials Management of the Polish Academy of Sciences in Kraków and KOMAG in Gliwice. State-owned universities also offer quite extensive facilities, especially: AGH University of Science and Technology in Kraków, the Silesian University of Technology in Gliwice and the Wrocław University of Technology. These are internationally recognised centres with rich experience and long years of mining tradition. Cooperation with suppliers of research services and modern technologies is a chance for the survival of mining enterprises.

Technological development of the Russian coal industry in terms of such aspects as prospecting, exploration, and mine planning, coal mining operations, coal and waste processing, and coal transportation is ensured by more than ten industry research centres, including the Skochinsky Institute of Mining (Moscow), the Central Research Institute for Economics and Technology in the Coal Industry (Moscow), the State Eastern Research Institute for Occupational Safety in the Mining Industry (Kemerovo), and others.

Russia has amassed considerable experience in the implementation of Smart Mine projects. Under the Industry 4.0 Program, research centres are currently developing a platform for the implementation of the Digital Mine of the Future projects.

How do suppliers and recipients participate in the sustainable development of coal mining enterprises? What is their indirect influence on the sustainability of extractive industries?

This chapter's analysis shows that the recipients have a much stronger influence on the sustainable development of mining enterprises, due to their dominant position in the value chain. Mining enterprises produce a homogeneous product and have few options of modifying both this product and the business profile. The aforementioned circumstances make the existence of mining enterprises almost entirely dependent on the demand in the energy and coking industries (metallurgical industry). The growing pressure towards decarbonisation leads to rapid decline of this demand and mining companies in the European Union have largely been shut down. The importance of recipients for the functioning of mining enterprises is also illustrated by the example of CIS, where the lack of decarbonisation restrictions and the proximity of eastern coal-based economies favour continued hard coal mining.

It is impossible not to notice, however, that the very idea of reducing the use of coal in the energy and metallurgical industries contributes to the achievement of the environmental goal of sustainable development. Less use means fewer environmental risks to the health and life of present and future generations. On the other hand, however, the sudden closure of mining enterprises and the abandonment of the use of coal are a risk to the achievement of economic and social goals. Renewable sources are not able to completely replace non-renewable raw materials in a short time, which poses a risk to economic development. Moreover, the end of hard coal mining means the elimination of many jobs and the pauperisation of still quite numerous mining regions.

It follows from the above that, in order to ensure the right approach to sustainable development in the value chain of mining enterprises, the following – often contradictory – issues must be taken into account:

- The mining industry has a very large, positive impact on the economy of the entire region, in which the mines operate. This is because the industry generates a lot of jobs in mining-related enterprises and contributes to the improvement of the quality of life and wealth of the inhabitants;
- Extraction of fossil resources ensures the country's energy independence and reliable, constant supplies for the energy system;
- Traditional coal technologies are harmful to the natural environment, while the sustainable development policy involving the decarbonisation process exerts pressure on recipients (CHP) to limit the use of coal in the combustion process and to implement modern, cleaner technologies.

The best solution to the dilemma, from the point of view of sustainable development, is certainly not a quick departure from coal combustion, as this would lead to the bankruptcy of many mining-related companies, impoverishment of the regions and lack of money for development, including pro-ecological activities. The mining industry should slowly switch to newer, cleaner technologies, while – at the same time – continuing to slowly switch to renewable energy. This process can be facilitated by vertical consolidation, especially of mines with energy companies, which provides mines with additional capital and forces the transition to new technologies, while allowing power plants to maintain continuity of supply. It is also worth noting that the use of modern technologies is often conditioned by the existence of suppliers, who offer such solutions, which will allow the development of alternative jobs related to the functioning of the mining industry.

Bibliography

Archibald, R, Ritter, M. (2001). Canada: From Fly-in, Fly-out to Mining Metropolis. In McMahon, G., Rémy, F. (Eds) *Large Mines and the Community. Socioeconomic and Environmental Effects in Latin America, Canada and Spain*. World Bank: Washington, DC.

Baah-Boateng, W. (2018). Job Creation in the Mining Sector: Evidence from Ghana. United Nations Conference on Trade and Development. 24–24 April, Geneva. https://unctad.org/system/files/non-official-document/GCF2018_BaahBoateng_23042018.pdf [access date: 08. 01. 2021].

Bednorz, J. (2012). Decarbonisation of the European Union as a Threat to its Energy Security and Sustainable Development. *Energy Policy Journal*, 15(3), 181–195.

Dudała, J. (2012). Polskie maszyny górnicze. *Biuletyn Górniczy*, 12, 209–210.

Ejdemo, T. (2013). Mineral Development and Regional Employment Effects in Northern Sweden: A Scenario-Based Assessment. *Mineral Economics*, 25, 55–63.

Euracoal (2020). Coal Industry Across Europe. https://euracoal.eu/info/coal-industry-across-europe/ [access date: 5.12.2021].

European Commission (2020). EU Climate Action and the European Green Deal. https://ec.europa.eu/clima/policies/eu-climate-action_en [access date: 08. 01. 2021].

European Commission (2020). EU Energy Statistical Pocketbook and Country Datasheets. https://ec.europa.eu/energy/data-analysis/energy-statistical-pocketbook_en [access date: 08. 01. 2021].

Fleming, D.A., Measham, T.G. (2014). Local Job Multipliers of Mining. *Resources Policy*, 41, 9–15.

Gawlik, L., Pepłowska M. (2017). Zależność przedsiębiorstw okołogórniczych od sytuacji w górnictwie – badania ankietowe. *Zeszyty Naukowe Instytutu Gospodarki Surowcami Mineralnymi i Energią Polskiej Akademii Nauk*, 97, 43–56.

Görner, A., Kudar, G., Mori, L., Reiter, S., Samek, R. (2020). The Mine-to-Market Value Chain: A Hidden Gem. https://www.mckinsey.com/industries/metals-and-mining/our-insights/the-mine-to-market-value-chain-a-hidden-gem# [access date: 08. 01. 2021].

Invest.gov.uz (2021). Engineering Sphere. http://invest.gov.uz/ru/investor/mashinos troitelnaya-sfera/ [access date: 29. 03. 2021].

Jonek-Kowalska, I., Michalak, A. (2013). *Prognozowanie kierunków internacjonalizacji na przykładzie maszyn i urządzeń górniczych*. CeDeWu: Warszawa.

JSC (2018). Technological Equipment of Mines and Open-pit Mines in 2017. JSC "Rosinformugol".

Kasztelewicz, Z. (2018). *Raport o stanie branży węgla brunatnego w Polsce i Niemczech wraz z diagnozą działań dla rozwoju tej branży w I połowie XXI wieku*. Akademia Górniczo-Hutnicza: Kraków.

Krasnyansky, G.L., Sarychev, A.E., Skryl, A.I. (2017). Economic Crises and Coal of Russia. House of NUST MISIS. https://www.rosugol.ru/upload/pdf/Сарычев%20block2.pdf [access date: 29. 03. 2021].

Kusi-Sarpong, S., Sarkis, J. (2016). Green Supply Chain Practices and Performance in Ghana's Mining Industry: A Comparative Evaluation Based on DEMATEL and AHP. *International Journal Business Performance and Supply Chain Modelling*, 8(4), 320–347.

Laskowski, A., Stępiński, P. (2019). *Czy węgiel ma przyszłość?*Instytut Jagielloński: Warsaw.

Marinicheva, O. (2012). Coal Returns to Generation. *Energy and Industry of Russia*, 11 (199).

Moritz, T., Söderholm, P., Wårell, L. (2016). The Local Employment Impacts of Mining: An Econometric Analysis of Job Multipliers in Northern Sweden. *Mineral Economics*, 30, 50–65.

NewRuss.ru (2020). Mechanical Engineering of Ukraine Is a Large Branch of the Manufacturing Industry in Ukraine. http://newsruss.ru/doc/index.php/Машинёстрёение_Украины#cite_note-22 [access date: 29. 03. 2021].

Oksińska, B., Kacprzak, I. (2020). Producenci maszyn górniczych w opałach. https://energia.rp.pl/surowce-i-paliwa/21620-producenci-maszyn-gorniczych-w-tarapatach [access date: 08. 01. 2021].

Pietrobelli, C., Marin, A., Olivari, J. (2018). Innovation in Mining Value Chains: New Evidence from Latin America. *Resources Policy*, 58, 1–10.

Radetzki, M. (1982). Regional Development Benefits Of Mineral Projects. *Resources Policy*, 8(3), 193–220.

RBC (2021). Russian Railways Are Driving Coal Miners into the Tariff Corner. https://www.rbc.ru/newspaper/2021/02/20/602f6e289a7947d8bd047bb0 [access date: 08. 01. 2021].

Rolfe, J., Petkova, V., Lockie, S., Ivanova, G. (2007). *Mining Impacts and the Development of the Moranbah Township*. Research report no. 7. Centre for Environmental Management. Central Queensland University: Australia.

Rozhko, A.A. (2017). Structural Analysis of Import Substitution in the Coal Industry of Russia: Reality and Forecast. *Mining Industry*, 6(136), 4–13.

Rozhkov, A.A., Karpenko, N.V. (2019). Analysis of the Use of Domestic and Foreign Technological Equipment for Coal Mining Enterprises of Russia. *Ugol' – Russian Coal Journal*, 7, 58–64.

Sekar, S., Lundin, K., Tucker, Ch., Figueiredo, J., Tordo, S., Aguilar, J. (2019). *Methodology and Value Chain Analysis. Background Paper for Building Resilience: A Green Growth Framework for Mobilizng Mining Investment*. World Bank Group: Washington.

State Committee of the Republic of Uzbekistan on Statistics (2019). Socio-economic Situation of the Republic of Uzbekistan. Tashkent: State Committee of the Republic of Uzbekistan on Statistics.

State Report (2018). State Report on the State and Use of Mineral Resources of the Russian Federation in 2018. Moscow.

Tarazanov, I.G. (2019). Itogy raboty ugol'noy promishlennosty Rossii za yanvar. *Ugol' – Russian Coal Journal*, 3, 64–79. doi:10.18796/0041-5790-2019-3-64-79.

TAURON (2019). TAURON Raport Zintegrowany. https://raport.tauron.pl/grupa-ta uron/lancuch-wartosci-dodanej-i-model-biznesowy/ [access date:08. 01. 2021].

ukrexport.gov.ua (2008). Machine-Building Industry of Kazakhstan. Almaty. http:// ukrexport.gov.ua/i/imgsupload/file/Machinery_rus.pdf [access date: 29. 03. 2021].

Wuest, T., Thoben, K.D. (2015). Comparing Mining and Manufacturing Supply Chain Processes: Challenges and Requirements. *Production Planning and Control*, 26(5), 81–96.

Yanovsky, A.B. (2019). Results of Structural Reorganization and Technological Re-equipment of the Coal Industry of the Russian Federation and Objectives for Prospective Development. *Ugol – Russian Coal Journal*, 8, 8–16. doi:10.18796/ 0041-5790-2019-8-8-16.

8 Competition for renewable and non-renewable resources in the mining sector

Extraction of renewable and non-renewable resources and their complementarity and substitutability

Since the industrial revolution, non-renewable fossil fuels have increasingly been used (Chen et al., 2017). The rapid growth of economies around the world, including countries in the European Union, requires a significant and ever-increasing demand for energy (Bhaskar et al., 2011; Escobar et al., 2009). Approximately 75% of the fossil fuels were consumed for heat and electricity production and only 20% for material production. Today, meeting these needs using only traditional fossil fuels such as coal, natural gas, or oil is not possible. The problem is not only the looming depletion of fossil resources but also environmental pollution (Ang et al., 2015). For this reason, renewable energy sources should be increasingly used to ensure an appropriate level of sustainability.

Currently, it is not yet possible to achieve the level of abandoning the use of energy from non-renewable sources (Piwowar and Dzikus, 2019). The demand for energy from the growing global economy is so high that the best option is to ensure the right mix of non-renewable and renewable energy use (Jeerson, 2006). While renewable sources cannot currently provide a sufficient alternative to non-renewable energy sources, they can complement them very well. In the future, the goal should be to increase the share of renewable energy for both demand and environmental reasons.

The most important renewable energy sources that compete with the non-renewable sources discussed in this monograph include:

- water,
- wind,
- solar radiation,
- biomass,
- radioactive decay,
- gravity.

Their properties are shown in Table 8.1. The availability and extent of use in a country of renewable energy sources are strongly dependent on the local

DOI: 10.4324/9781003091110-12

Table 8.1 Basic classification of renewable energy sources

Primary sources of energy		Natural energy transformation	Technical energy transformation	Form of generated energy
Sun	Water	Evaporation, melting of ice and snow, precipitation	Water power plants	Electricity
	Wind	Atmospheric currents	Wind farms	Thermal energy and electricity
		Energy of waves	Wave power plants	Electricity
	Solar radiation	Ocean currents	Ocean current energy plants	Electricity
		Heating of atmosphere and Earth's surface	Ocean thermal energy plants	Electricity
			Heat pumps	Thermal energy
		Solar radiation	Collectors and thermal solar plants	Thermal energy
			PV cells and solar power plants	Electricity
			Photolysis	Fuels
	Biomass	Biomass production	Heating and thermal power plants	Thermal energy and electricity
			Conversion devices	Fuels
Earth	Radioactive decay	Geothermal sources	Heating and geothermal power plants	Thermal energy and electricity
Moon	Gravity	Tidal waves	Tidal power plants	Electricity

Source: Marks-Bielska et al., 2020

topography, climatic, biological, and geographical conditions. For this reason, countries vary to a large extent in the potential and feasibility of specific types of renewable energy (Mundo-Hernández et al., 2014).

As far back as 2000, renewable energy sources produced a total of 2.8 TWh of electricity. The share of this sector continued to grow, reaching 3.8 TWh in 2008 and 6.7 TWh in 2018. According to the International Energy Agency (IEA), solar energy demonstrated the highest average annual growth rate in developed countries between 1990 and 2018 (33.1%). It was followed by wind power and biogas (20.4 and 11.3%, respectively).

Since 2012, more than half of the whole new installed capacity has been accounted for by renewable energy sources. In 2019, a record was set: according to the International Renewable Energy Agency (IRENA), 75% of all newly commissioned energy facilities produced green energy. The latest data provided by IRENA show that over one-third of the world's energy is generated using environmentally friendly energy resources.

Investments in the renewable energy sector are also growing. The IEA (2020) states that, as of 2020, investments in renewable energy amounted to $281 billion, second only to the oil and gas sector ($322 billion). Moreover, even though less money was invested in the energy sector than in the previous years, the fall seen in the renewable energy sector was less pronounced than the one witnessed in the oil and gas sector (Figure 8.1).

According to current forecasts, green energy will become the largest energy sector in terms of investments between 2025 and 2030 (IEA, 2020). Renewable energy in 2017–2019 was more effective in creating jobs in the USA than coal or oil. Globally, the renewable energy sector employs about 11 million people (Schneer and McGinn, 2019). Table 8.2 presents a summary of the share of energy from renewable sources in each country of the European Union from 2004 to 2019.

Based on the data presented in Table 8.1 it can be concluded that in all countries of the European Union the use of non-renewable energy sources is gradually increasing. In the case of the entire European Union (Fig. 8.2), the percentage of non-renewable sources in 2004 was 8.5%, in 2010 it increased to 14.4%, and in 2019 it was predicted to attain 19.7%. Over a period of 15 years, the increase was approximately 150%. The identified trend results in increasing raw material competition in the energy production market. This competition is intensifying, and producers of coal, gas or oil are forced to fight fiercely on the market, which is largely hindered by the unfriendliness of traditional energy raw materials.

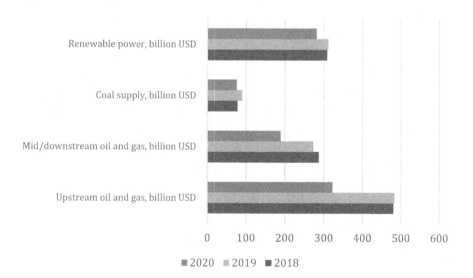

Figure 8.1 Energy investment by sector, 2018–2020
Source: IEA, 2020

Table 8.2 Percentage of energy from renewable sources in European Union countries from 2004 to 2019

Specification	Years					
	2004	2010	2014	2016	2018	2019
European Union (27 countries)	*8.5*	*14.4*	*17.4*	*18.0*	*18.0*	*19.7*
European Union 28 countries	–	13.1	16.2	16.9	18.0	18.8
Belgium	1.9	6.0	8.0	8.7	9.4	9.9
Bulgaria	9.2	13.9	18.0	18.7	20.5	21.5
Czech Republic	6.8	10.5	15.0	14.9	15.1	16.2
Denmark	14.8	21.8	29.3	32.0	36.1	37.2
Germany	6.2	11.6	14.3	14.8	16.5	17.3
Estonia	18.4	24.5	26.1	28.7	30.0	31.8
Ireland	2.4	5.7	8.5	9.1	11.1	11.9
Greece	7.2	10.0	15.6	15.3	18.0	19.6
Spain	8.3	13.8	16.1	17.4	17.4	18.3
France	9.5	12.6	14.4	15.5	16.6	17.2
Croatia	23.4	25.1	28.8	28.2	28.0	28.4
Italy	6.3	13.0	17.0	17.4	17.8	18.1
Cyprus	3.1	6.1	9.1	9.8	13.9	13.8
Latvia	32.8	30.3	38.6	37.1	40.3	40.9
Lithuania	17.2	19.6	23.5	25.6	24.4	25.4
Luxembourg	0.9	2.8	4.4	5.3	9.1	7.0
Hungary	4.4	12.7	14.6	14.3	12.5	12.6
Malta	0.1	0.9	4.7	6.2	8.0	8.4
Netherlands	2.0	3.9	5.4	5.8	7.4	8.7
Austria	22.6	31.2	33.5	33.3	33.4	33.6
Poland	6.9	9.3	11.6	11.4	11.3	12.1
Portugal	19.2	24.1	29.5	30.8	30.3	30.6
Romania	16.8	22.8	24.8	25.0	23.9	24.2
Slovenia	16.1	21.0	22.4	21.9	21.1	21.9
Slovakia	6.4	9.0	11.7	12.0	11.9	16.8
Finland	29.3	32.2	38.7	39.0	41.2	43.0
Sweden	38.7	46.5	51.8	53.3	54.6	56.3
United Kingdom	0.9	3.8	6.7	9.0	11.0	12.3

Source: Eurostat, 2020

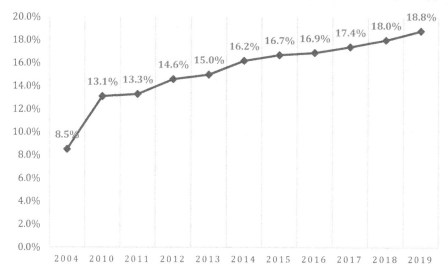

Figure 8.2 The use of energy from renewable sources in European Union countries from 2004 to 2019
Source: Eurostat, 2020

Notably, in the case of Sweden, the percentage of energy originating from non-renewable sources already exceeded 50% in 2013 and is now over 56%, a record share in the European Union. This means that the majority of energy in this country is produced from renewable sources. In the future, this amount is sure to be exceeded by other countries such as Finland which currently produces 43% of its energy from renewable sources, Latvia which uses them at over 40%, and Denmark that uses renewable sources at over 37%.

On the other hand, the countries where the rates of use of energy from non-renewable sources are at the lowest level are Belgium (9.9%), Netherlands (8.7%), Malta (8.4%) and Luxembourg (7%). Poland is in a group of countries with low use of renewable sources. Currently, only 12.1% of energy is generated from these sources. Nevertheless, also in this case, in comparison with 2004, there was an almost 100% increase in the use of such sources.

For 20 years, the energy mix in CIS has remained virtually unchanged (Table 8.3).

Since 2000, the share of hydroelectricity has decreased by 1%, that of gas has increased by 3%, and that of coal has decreased by 2%. Throughout the entire period, gas has been the most popular energy source (with a share of about 50%) in the CIS countries, with coal and oil also having substantial shares (15% and 20%, respectively).

According to BP's *Statistical Review of World Energy* (2020), Russia, Uzbekistan, and Turkmenistan have the lowest renewable energy shares in their energy mixes. However, Russia has recently seen a significant increase in investment in

Table 8.3 Energy mix in CIS by year

Year	Source of energy [%]						
	Oil	Gas	Coal	Nuclear energy	Hydroelectricity	Renewable power	Total
2000	21.26	51.35	16.63	4.19	6.57	0.00	100.00
2002	20.50	52.11	16.65	4.40	6.34	0.00	100.00
2004	20.51	52.66	16.02	4.26	6.55	0.00	100.00
2006	20.49	53.69	15.32	4.38	6.12	0.00	100.00
2008	20.66	53.06	16.24	4.45	5.57	0.02	100.00
2010	20.37	54.21	15.02	4.60	5.77	0.03	100.00
2012	21.39	52.98	15.77	4.50	5.33	0.03	100.00
2014	22.33	52.91	14.66	4.57	5.50	0.03	100.00
2016	21.94	52.80	14.47	4.91	5.83	0.05	100.00
2018	21.25	54.02	14.28	4.77	5.63	0.05	100.00

Source: BP, 2020

renewable energy facilities. In 2018, the renewable energy sector accounted for only 7.6% of the newly commissioned power generation facilities in the country. By the end of 2019, its share had grown, reaching 29.1%, Fig.8.3.

The Azerbaijani government seeks to increase the share of renewable energy in the country's total electricity production from the current 17% to 30% by 2030 (Ru.qaz.wiki, 2021).

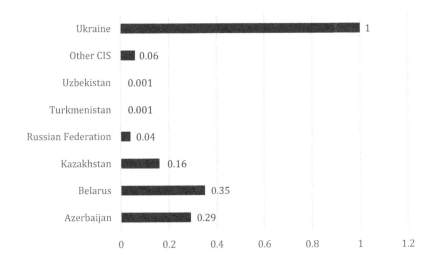

Figure 8.3 Renewable power in CIS in 2018 [%]
Source: BP, 2020

As of today, there are 89 renewable energy facilities in Kazakhstan with an installed capacity of 1,022.1 MW, including 19 wind, 30 solar, 37 hydroelectric, and 3 biofuel power plants. The country intends to continuously increase the share of renewable energy in its energy mix with the following targets: 6% in 2025, 10% by 2030, and at least 50% by 2050 (*RES*, 2019).

Among the countries under consideration, the best results in terms of renewable energy use are currently shown by Ukraine (1%) and Belarus (0.35%).

In Ukraine, more than 3,139 renewable energy facilities with a total capacity of about 500 MW were put into operation in 2018 (Shovkoplyas, 2019). However, the main problem for the development of the country's renewable energy sector is that prices for hydrocarbons are currently at a quite low level. On the domestic market, electricity prices are now several times higher than those in Europe. The country practices cross-subsidisation to reduce the price per kWh at the expense of nuclear and hydroelectric power plants (Vesti ua, 2020).

The State Cadastre of Renewable Energy Sources in Belarus includes over 300 renewable energy facilities with a total capacity of 500 MW. Annual solar irradiance in Belarus is comparable to that in Germany, Poland, and other European countries. According to the concept of energy security of Belarus, the share of primary energy production from renewable sources should reach 8% in 2030 and 9% in 2035 (Belta, 2019).

How does competition stimulate best practices in sustainable development? How do renewable resources force cleaner mining?

As stated in the previous section, the growing use of renewable energy poses a threat to organisations operating in the mining industries. They must adapt to legal and market pressure, which to a large extent stimulates actions connected with the implementation of sustainable development practices. It can be considered as a positive side effect of increasing competition on the raw materials market.

The mining industry, especially hard coal mining in the European Union, is influenced by the climate policy, whose goal is to reduce carbon dioxide emissions in the European Union countries (Sovacool et al., 2021). This type of approach makes renewable energy, since there are no carbon emissions involved, increasingly competitive with the mining industry. In order to survive in the market, mining companies must adapt to the new requirements and invest in the best possible sustainable practices to reduce carbon emissions before anything else.

Despite the unquestionable disadvantages of non-renewable raw materials, however, we cannot forget that they are still used and needed in most of the world's economies, and therefore they also have quite specific sources of competitive advantage. Table 8.4 lists the most important sources of non-renewable energy, presenting advantages and disadvantages of each of them. The table also includes a summary of the advantages and disadvantages of conventional energy sources.

Table 8.4 Advantages and disadvantages of different sources of non-renewable energy

Source	Advantages	Disadvantages
Hard coal	• of all non-renewable energy sources, hard coal has the largest reserves • low price • no risks associated with transportation, storage, and use • combustion has high energy efficiency	• high atmospheric carbon dioxide emissions from combustion • limited resources • negative environmental impacts • landscape degradation • dust emissions
Natural gas	• high efficiency • short power plant construction time • flexibility of use • low price • ease of transportation	• poisonous at high concentration • hazardous to store • carbon dioxide is emitted into the atmosphere during combustion • high volatility of energy costs due to price volatility
Crude oil	• easy, direct mining of deposits • convenient distribution through pipelines • easy to store	• risk of leakage during extraction and transportation • emissions to the atmosphere during combustion • high cost of energy generation • dependence on energy exporters
Uranium	• low failure rate of power plants • low emissions of harmful substances • low fuel consumption • high level of energy concentration • long plant life	• risk of radiation hazard • high cost of providing adequate safety measures • high cost of disposal of radioactive waste • difficulty in overcoming public opposition
Non-renewable sources together	• relatively low cost of generating energy • competitive technology • high level of energy generation per unit mass • easy access to energy sources	• air pollution due to emission of harmful substances into the atmosphere • risk of global pollution or nuclear power plant failure • problems with disposal of harmful waste • irreversible landscape changes

Source: Eurostat, 2020

The European Union strongly supports and promotes the use of renewable energy. European Union Directive 2018/2001 has set an overall renewable energy target of at least 32% in 2030, with the aim of achieving climate neutrality in all EU economies by 2050.

In Poland, the new Energy Policy 2040 was adopted on February 2, 2021, according to which the share of renewable energy sources in gross final energy consumption by 2040 is to be at least 23%. Thermal needs of all households will be covered by system heat and by zero- or low-emission individual sources. The presented plans and actions aimed at their implementation will lead to a significant reduction in the use of non-renewable energy sources, and in time perhaps to their complete elimination from the energy balances of EU countries.

In the European Union, the market pressure methods are applied to limit the costs of CO_2 emission. They consist in setting permits that authorise entities to emit a strictly specified amount of CO_2 (Radmehr et al., 2021). In case the organisation does not have enough emission rights, they can be purchased on the free market. Nevertheless, the number of emission permits is gradually reduced, which causes an increase in demand and, consequently, an increase in the price of allowances. This phenomenon has been gaining momentum over the last few years. A particularly severe increase in the price of CO_2 emission allowances occurred in the period 2017–2020. It was an increase from a level of about €5 to a level of about €40 over four years. This is a very big threat for the mining industry because burning fossil fuels, especially hard coal, causes a lot of CO_2 emissions.

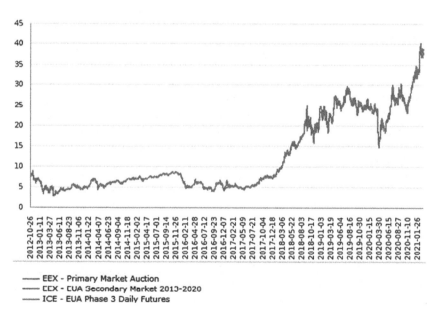

—— EEX - Primary Market Auction
—— EEX - EUA Secondary Market 2013-2020
—— ICE - EUA Phase 3 Daily Futures

Figure 8.4 CO_2 free market prices 2012–2020 (€)
Source: Emission Trading, 2020

Increasing pressure to reduce carbon emissions is driving coal-based power plants to adopt technologies that enable them to operate with fewer emissions.

To some extent, this is possible through the use of new technologies. Increasing the average efficiency of coal-fired electricity and heat generation can be achieved, among others, through the following technologies:

- popularisation of blocks working at supercritical parameters (27÷29 Mpa/ 570÷580°C) achieving 44–46% efficiency;
- application of units operating at ultra-supercritical steam parameters (35 MPa/ 720°C). These are the systems on which research works and demonstration projects are carried out at present, and their aim is to lead to a solution in which electricity will be produced with efficiency reaching 55%;
- the use of integrated gas-steam systems, which will increase the efficiency of electricity generation to around 48%, while facilitating the capture of carbon dioxide produced during combustion;
- the use and dissemination of boilers with atmospheric fluidised bed combustion, a technology which is already available and mature today and which makes it possible to generate electricity with an efficiency of around 45%;
- introduction of oxygen combustion, which significantly reduces the size of the power plant and avoids the need to extract carbon dioxide from the flue gas stream;
- the use of a chemical loop, which consists of supplying oxygen for fuel combustion through a chemical compound and to obtain concentrated carbon dioxide in the flue gas stream.

(Stańczyk and Bieniecki, 2007; Ploumen et al., 2011; Lee et al., 2020; Kamkeng et al., 2021)

The use of these types of solutions can reduce carbon dioxide emissions by approximately 30% to 50%. It is particularly important to capture and safely store carbon dioxide using technologies that efficiently separate this gas from the combustion gas stream.

Clean coal technologies are an opportunity for the mining industry. The term Clean Coal Technologies refers to the entire carbon chain from the extraction of coal to the disposal of the residues of its use (Franco and Diaz, 2009). The use of modern coal combustion and gasification technologies is especially important (Ding et al., 2021). These can include:

- oxy-combustion technologies or combustion in oxygen: Combustion in oxygen leads to a significant reduction in the amount of flue gas emitted, which reduces the cost of flue gas cleaning. The problem is that such systems require the construction of an air separation plant, which is a source of large investment costs and energy consumption.
- coal gasification technologies in polygeneration systems: The solution offers the opportunity to increase the overall efficiency of primary energy use and

significantly improve the economics of production. The technology allows for the removal of carbon dioxide from the gas before the combustion process, which results in lower losses in electricity generation efficiency compared to classic combustion technologies.

(Marcisz et al., 2017; Breault, 2020)

Rising CO_2 emission prices will lead to increased competition from renewable energy producers. In this situation, the mining industry must invest in solutions to reduce the negative impact on the environment, because only in this way will it be able to maintain a competitive position on the market allowing it to survive. Nevertheless, it should be noted that in the EU, non-renewable energy sources will be systematically eliminated due to environmental conditions by an extremely strong pressure from renewable energy producers, which is not present in other regions of the world.

While Russia ranks fifth in the world in energy generation, its installed wind-generated and solar capacity is many times lower than that of other top energy producers (Sidorovich, 2020). However, it should be noted that the Russian renewable energy sector, which was non-existent not long ago, is growing and its growth rate is increasing. For example, in 2020, despite the coronavirus pandemic and the consequent restrictive measures, Russia commissioned renewable energy facilities with a total capacity of more than 1 GW, an increase of 70% from the year 2019.

A literature review has revealed several factors that have a negative impact on the development of the renewable energy sector in Russia. Among them are:

1 The lack of production capacities for manufacturing-specialised equipment and the need for localisation. Localisation assumes that an energy-generating facility is built using a certain proportion (65 to 70%) of locally made components, which can lead to an increase in the cost of energy per unit.
2 Prices for electricity generated from renewable energy sources are not competitive enough, resulting in the need for government support.
3 Insufficient experience in such areas as the construction, maintenance, and operation of renewable energy facilities and the need for government control in these areas.

The regulatory framework of energy generation in Russia prioritises the goal of improving the energy efficiency of the electric power industry through the use of renewable energy sources. Mechanisms have been developed for the period through to 2024 that are aimed at fostering renewable energy generation. They have given a strong impetus to the development of both this new segment of the Russian economy and the energy sector in general.

Due to the existing competition in the renewable energy market, the average capital costs per 1 KW of installed capacity decreased in 2016–2019: at the end of 2019, this indicator decreased by 59.5% for solar energy compared to 2015; in the wind power industry it decreased by 58.2%.

Renewable energy equipment has been produced with a total capacity of 900 MW per year (compared to 140 MW per year in 2012), and it is claimed that it is possible to further improve this indicator to reach the figure of 1.4 GW per year.

The current program for the development of the Russian renewable energy sector was intended to work until 2024. Taking into account the positive results that the program has already produced, the government has decided to extend it as it will help to preserve the potential for the production of renewable energy equipment in Russia, follow the global trends in the development of energy systems, reduce the anthropogenic impact on the environment, and use Russia's rich natural and climate resources.

It should be noted that Russia ranks first in the world in terms of wind energy potential (Sidorovich, 2020). However, as it has large fossil fuel reserves, including those of coal, it is not planned to make a transition to renewable energy of the same scale as that seen at the global level or in European countries in particular. The plans for the development of the renewable energy sector are not grand, and the current share of renewable energy in Russia's energy mix is low. As a result, by 2024, Russia will rank only among the top 40–50 countries in terms of renewable energy generation capacity. It is forecasted that Russia's renewable energy sector will have a share of 4.5%, with the current share standing at 2%. Thus, it is impossible to consider renewable energy sources to be highly competitive in Russia.

Some of today's coal-based energy generation technologies are highly efficient, environmentally friendly, and also 1.3 times cheaper than wind power and 1.9 times cheaper than solar power. "Clean" coal power generation has significant competitive advantages over renewable energy technologies in terms of electricity and heat generation costs (Yanovskiy, 2017).

The key problem for making coal power generation greener is to reduce the emissions of such hazardous gases as sulfur and nitrogen oxides. Russia utilises only 14% of coal power generation by-products, which is not enough compared to other countries (Germany – 99%; China – 67%; the USA – 48%) (Verzhanskii, 2017).

The latest European standards limit the dust content of flue gases at 10–20 mg/Nm3. To meet these standards, dust removal efficiency must reach at least 99%. At Russian coal-fired power plants, emissions of fine suspended particles are 10 times higher. Therefore, it is important to accelerate the transition to stricter standards, improve coal preparation and combustion efficiency, and introduce advanced flue gas cleaning systems.

The most important factor in making the industry greener is improving energy conversion efficiency at thermal power plants, which currently varies from 20 to 38% (subcritical parameters). An increase of 1% reduces emissions of particulate matter by 2%. Energy conversion efficiency can be improved by increasing temperature and steam pressure. If a plant uses supercritical technologies, its energy conversion efficiency reaches 40%. Supercritical technologies help to reach a value of 43%, and ultra-supercritical technologies result in values of up to 53%. In Russia, the latter type was planned to be introduced starting from 2020 (Verzhanskii, 2017).

Upgrading the coal industry is aimed at increasing the share of clean coal power generation based on utilising combined cycle gas turbines with ultra-supercritical steam parameters along with carbon capture and storage technologies and extracting rare earth elements and valuable metals from coal ash and wastewater.

Bibliography

Ang, B.W., Choon, W.L., Ng, T.S. (2015). Energy Security: Definitions, Dimensions and Indexes. *Renewable and Sustainable Energy Reviews*, 42, 1077–1093.

Belta (2019). How Renewable Energy Develops in Belarus. https://www.belta.by/economics/view/kak-v-belarusi-razvivaetsja-vozobnovljaemaja-energetika-366492-2019/ [access date: 30. 03. 2021].

Bhaskar, T., Bhavya, B., Singh, R., Naik, D.V., Kumar, A., Goyal, H.B. (2011). Thermochemical Conversion of Biomass to Biofuels. In Pandey, A., Larroche, C., Ricke, S.C., Dussap, C.G., Gnansounou, E. (Eds), *Biofuels—Alternative Feedstocks and Conversion Processes*. Academic Press: Oxford, UK, 51–77.

BP (2020). *BP Statistical Review of World Energy*. https://www.bp.com/en/global/corporate/energy-economics/statistical-review-of-world-energy.html [access date: 30. 03. 2021].

Breault, R.W. (2020). Gasification Processes Old and New: A Basic Review of the Major Technologies, *Energies 3(2)*, 216–240.

Chen, W.-H., Budzianowski, W., Lee, K.T. (2017). Preface—Sustainable Biofuels. *Energy Conversion Management*, 141, 1.

Ding, Q., Khattak, S.I., Ahmad, M. (2021). Towards Sustainable Production and Consumption: Assessing the Impact of Energy Productivity and Eco-Innovation on Consumption-Based Carbon Dioxide Emissions (CCO_2) in G-7 Nations. *Sustainable Production and Consumption*, 27, 254–268.

Emission Trading (2020). https://unfccc.int/process/the-kyoto-protocol/mechanisms/emissions-trading [access date: 5. 12. 2020].

E2nergy (2019). RES Development in Kazakhstan: Results of 2019 and plans for 2020. https://eenergy.media/2019/12/11/razvitie-vie-v-kazahstane-itogi-2019-g-i-plany-na-2020-g/ [access date: 30. 03. 2021].

Escobar, J.A., Lora, E.E., Venturini, O.J., Yánez, E., Castillo, E.F., Almazán, O. (2009). Biofuels: Environment, Technology and Food Security. *Renewable Sustainable Energy Review*, 13, 1275–1287.

Eurostat (2020). News Release. https://ec.europa.eu/eurostat/documents/2995521/10335438/8-23012020-AP-EN.pdf/292cf2e5-8870-4525-7ad7-188864ba0c29 [access date: 7. 03. 2021].

Franco, A., Diaz, A.R. (2009). The Future Challenges for "Clean Coal Technologies": Joining Efficiency Increase and Pollutant Emission Control. *Energy*, 34, 348–354.

IEA (2020). Energy Investment by Sector 2018–2020. https://www.iea.org/data-and-statistics/charts/energy-investment-by-sector-2018-2020-2 [access date: 31. 03. 2021].

Jeerson, M. (2006). Sustainable Energy Development: Performance and Prospects. *Renewable Energy*, 31, 571–582.

Kamkeng, A.D.N., Wang, M., Hu, J., Du, W., Qian, F. (2021). Transformation Technologies for CO_2 Utilisation: Current Status, Challenges and Future Prospects. *Chemical Engineering Journal*, 409, 128–138.

Lee, B.L., Lee, J.I., Yun, S.Y., Hwang, B.G., Lim, Ch., Park, Y. (2020). Methodology to Calculate the CO_2 Emission Reduction at the Coal-Fired Power Plant: CO_2 Capture and Utilization Applying Technology of Mineral Carbonation. *Sustainability*, 12, 7402.

Marks-Bielska, R., Bielski, S., Pik, K., Kurowska, K. (2020). The Importance of Renewable Energy Sources in Poland's Energy Mix. *Energies*, 13, 4624; doi:10.3390/en13184624.

Marcisz, M., Probierz K., Chmielniak, T., Sobolewski, A. (2017). Czyste technologie węglowe – szansa rozwoju sektora górniczego. *Systemy Wspomagania w Inżynierii Produkcji*, 6(3), 121–135.

Mundo-Hernández, J., de Celis, A.B., Hernández-Álvarez, J., de Celis-Carrillo, B. (2014). An Overview of Solar Photovoltaic Energy in Mexico and Germany. *Renewable and Sustainable Energy Review*, 31, 639–649.

Piwowar, A., Dzikus, M. (2019). Development of Renewable Energy Sources in the Context of Threats Resulting from Low-Altitude Emissions in Rural Areas in Poland: A Review. *Energies*, 12, 3558.

Ploumen, P., Sitienstra, G., Kamphuis, H. (2011). Reduction of CO_2 Emissions of Coal Fired Power Plants by Optimizing Steam Water Cycle. *Energy Procedia*, 4, 2074–2081.

Radmehr, R., Henneberry, S.R., Shayanmehr, S. (2021). Renewable Energy Consumption, CO_2 Emissions, and Economic Growth Nexus: A Simultaneity Spatial Modeling Analysis of EU Countries. *Structural Change and Economic Dynamics*, 57, 13–27.

Ru.qaz.wiki (2021). Renewable Energy in Azerbaijan. https://ru.qaz.wiki/wiki/Renewable_energy_in_Azerbaijan [access date: 30. 03. 2021].

Schneer, K., McGinn, A. (2019). Fact Sheet. Jobs in Renewable Energy, Energy Efficiency and Resilience. https://www.eesi.org/papers/view/fact-sheet-jobs-in-renewable-energy-energy-efficiency-and-resilience-2019 [access date: 30. 03. 2021].

Shovkoplyas, S. (2019). *Introduction of RES – Results and Prospects in Ukraine*. https://aw-therm.com.ua/vie-2018-vnedrenie-v-ukraine-rezultaty-i-perspektivy/ [access date: 30.03.2021].

Sidorovich, V. (2020). *Rossijskaya otrasl' vie v mezhdunarodnyh sravneniyah: solnechnaya i vetrovaya energetika*. Informacionno-analiticheskij centr «NOVAYA ENERGETIKA». https://renen.ru/wp-content/uploads/2015/09/Russian-RES-Industry-international-comparisons-RenEn.pdf [access date: 30. 03. 2021].

Sovacool, B.K., Cabeza, L.F., Pisello, A.L., Dawoud, B., Martiskainen, M. (2021). Decarbonizing Household Heating: Reviewing Demographics, Geography and Low-Carbon Practices and Preferences in Five European Countries. *Renewable and Sustainable Energy Reviews*, 139, 110703.

Stańczyk, K., Bieniecki, M. (2007). Możliwości redukcji emisji CO2 i jej wpływ na efektywność i koszty wytwarzania energii z węgla. *Górnictwo i Geoinżynieria*, 32(2), 575–586.

Verzhanskii, A.P. (2017). Ekologizaciya ugol'noj generacii. *Ugol'*, 9, 11–16 [access date: 30.03.2021].

Vesti ua (2020). Why Green Energy Is Going "Sideways" to the Ukrainian Economy. https://vesti.ua/strana/pochemu-zelenaya-energetika-vyhodit-bokom-ukrainskoj-ekonomike [access date: 30. 03. 2021].

Yanovskiy, A.B. (2017) Main Trends and Prospects of Development of the Coal Industry in Russia. *Coal*, 8, 10–14.

9 Government policy in the field of natural resources and energy policy

International review of government resources and energy policy

Energy feedstock policy depends on two key considerations, which are feedstock availability and energy security (Christmann et al., 2007; Warden-Fernandez, 2005).

Having said that, the high availability of energy resources, whether renewable or non-renewable, will promote the maintenance of energy security. However, such an arrangement of resource policy determinants does not include social and environmental aspects. It abstracts from environmental issues and quality of life issues for future generations (Güney, 2019). Therefore, it can be argued that deciding on the shape of resource policy solely based on the criteria of raw material sufficiency and energy security is unsustainable and does not fit into the concept of sustainable development (Pasqualetti and Sovacool, 2012; Hillebrand, 2013).

Nevertheless, such an approach to building raw material policy is common in intensively developing regions, where economics, sufficiency and economic development are priorities for the whole society. In Asian countries, especially in China, India, and Indonesia (Jiang, 2018; Tagotra, 2018; Zillman and Smith, 2019), the most available resources and the cheapest resources are used because they make a fast path to economic development available. Similarly, resource policies are shaped in Africa and America. Notably, non-renewable energy resources remain the most important source of energy and heat, and their mixes dominate most of the world's economies.

In Europe, including the European Union in particular, the approach to raw material policy-making has been changing very strongly for many years (Bausch et al., 2017; Tvaronavičien⊠ et al., 2015; Vogler, 2013). Practically all regulations and guidelines in this area take into account ecological and social objectives. At the same time, this approach is very restrictive. It was initiated by the 2009 *Climate Package*, which assumed the achievement of the following climate targets by 2020:

- 20% reduction in greenhouse gas emissions (relative to 1990 levels),
- 20% share of energy from renewable sources in total EU energy consumption,
- 20% increase in energy efficiency.

DOI: 10.4324/9781003091110-13

The above-mentioned *Package* is equipped with a number of implementation instruments, including:

1   The Emissions Trading Scheme, which is the EU's primary instrument for reducing greenhouse gas emissions from large power plants and industrial installations and from air transport. The ETS covers about 45 per cent of all EU greenhouse gas emissions.
2   Financial support for low-carbon technologies in the form of the NER300 program for renewable energy technologies and carbon capture and storage, and Horizon 2020, which funds research and innovation.
3   Energy Efficiency Plan and the Energy Efficiency Directive.

The continuation of the goals formulated in the Package is the EU Policy until 2030, which assumes:

- 40% reduction in greenhouse gas emissions (relative to 1990 levels),
- 32% share of energy from renewable sources in total EU energy consumption,
- 32.5% increase in energy efficiency.

By 2050, on the other hand, the main goal of EU energy policy is to achieve a zero-carbon economy, and key priorities include:

- maximising energy efficiency, including making zero-emission buildings;
- maximising the use of renewable energy sources (RES) and electricity to fully decarbonize Europe's energy supply;
- adopting the principles of clean, safe, and connected mobility;
- establishing a competitive EU industry and the implementation of a circular economy as key factors in reducing greenhouse gas emissions;
- developing adequate smart grid infrastructure and interconnections;
- fully exploiting the benefits of the bioeconomy and creating the carbon sinks;
- addressing remaining CO_2 emissions through carbon capture and storage (CCS).
    (Duijndam and van Beukering, 2021; Oztig, 2017; Blesl et al., 2012)

These restrictions create top-down pressure on the energy policies of individual EU countries and force changes in their energy mixes. Table 9.1 provides information on these changes for the European countries analysed in this monograph (Guven et al., 2021; Braun, 2019; Gerhardt, 2017; Sivek et al., 2017; Mez, 2012).

According to the information in Table 8.1, all economies that predominantly used coal in 1990, have seen significant changes in their energy balances. First of all, they have drastically reduced their use of hard coal, in line with the EU's decarbonisation scheme. However, in all analysed countries, the share of coal was first replaced by other non-renewable energy resources, including primarily

Table 9.1 Information on the energy mix changes in coal mining countries in Europe

Country name	Dominant energy source in 1990	Dominant energy source in 2019	Changes in energy policy
Czech Republic	coal, approx. 65%	coal, approx. 38%	using nuclear energy, increasing the use of gas and oil
Germany	coal, approx. 37%	oil, approx. 36%	increasing the share of gas and renewable energy sources, especially solar and wind
Poland	coal, approx. 76%	coal, approx. 49%	increasing the share of oil, gas, and small-scale wind and biomass energy
Spain	oil, approx. 53% coal, approx. 22%	oil, approx. 47% coal, approx. 10%	increasing the share of gas and renewable energy sources, especially solar and wind
Turkey	coal, approx. 34%	coal, approx. 28%	increasing the share of gas and renewable energy sources, especially water and wind

Source: own study based on the data of the BP, 2020

gas, which is a less carbon intensive raw material. The energy balance was significantly supplemented by renewable sources only in Germany and Turkey. Everywhere else, the share of clean energy sources remained rather low, at a level of a few per cent at most.

Thus, the 30-year transition has not led to a revolutionary departure of the above countries from non-renewable energy sources. This reflects the difficulty of the energy transition, which requires significant and capital-intensive investments in the power and heating sectors. It also points to the weaknesses of renewables, such as high cost, lack of storage capacity, or low availability very often dependent on geographical and climatic conditions beyond the influence of those who decide the final shape of energy policy (Silva et al., 2016; Lecuyer and Quirion, 2019).

The energy policy of the CIS countries is based on general principles of energy security, energy conservation, innovative development, environmental safety, development of renewable energy sources (RES), as well as energy availability for consumers through the diversification of sources and suppliers.

The implementation of the energy conservation policy is one of the main prerequisites for ensuring sustainable development of the energy sector and the economy as a whole, and it is also the most important factor in improving the energy and economic security of the CIS countries. Currently, the main elements of sustainable development of the energy industry are improvement and ongoing innovative development. Another important element in the innovative development of the energy sector is government involvement, including investing in policy objectives in the priority areas of energy sector development. Long-term projects for financing production based on using renewable energy sources are expected to play an important role. The development of renewable energy sources will improve environmental safety in the world. Another promising direction is developing intelligent equipment, facilities, power systems, and control systems.

An analysis of the state and prospects of the technological development of the fuel and energy sector of the CIS countries shows that the innovative development of the energy sector is taking place in all the CIS member states but at different rates and in different directions. In the short term and midterm, the main trends in its development will include ongoing modernisation of fuel and energy facilities and replacing foreign technologies, equipment, materials, and services used in activities that are critical for the functioning of the energy sector with national or localised substitutes produced on the territories of the CIS member states. In the long term, it is necessary to ensure the sustainable development of the energy sector of the CIS countries on the basis of new national technologies that are competitive both in the domestic and foreign markets and have high export potential.

Individual energy policy directions in the CIS countries are determined by the existing energy mix, available resources, mid- and long-term opportunities for investment in the development of the energy sector supported by businesses and the state, and the established and developing practices concerning integration with other countries. Table 9.2 presents the energy mix of the CIS countries in 2019, which is followed by comments and an analysis of the energy policies of the countries.

More than half of the Russian energy sector is accounted for by gas. Other elements of the country's energy mix include oil (more than 20%), coal (12%), nuclear power as well as hydroelectric power generation (5% to 6%). The share of renewable energy sources is insignificant. The abundance of fossil fuels has

Table 9.2 Energy mix in CIS

CIS country	Source of energy [%]						
	Oil	Gas	Coal	Nuclear energy	Hydroelectricity	Renewable power	Total
Ukraine	12.00	31.00	32.00	21.00	3.00	1.00	100.00
Azerbaijan	33.86	63.27	0.01	–	2.57	0.29	100.00
Belarus	29.52	66.32	3.53	–	0.28	0.35	100.00
Kazakhstan	21.13	21.68	54.08	–	2.95	0.16	100.00
Russian Federation	21.63	54.47	12.09	6.09	5.68	0.04	100.00
Turkmenistan	22.22	77.78	–	–	–	–	100.00
Uzbekistan	5.09	87.37	4.65	–	2.89	–	100.00
Other CIS	21.87	26.04	10.78	2.29	38.96	0.06	100.00
Total CIS	21.25	54.01	14.28	4.76	5.6	0.06	100.00

Source: calculated by the authors based on BP, 2020

determined the development of the energy sector in Russia in this specific direction. Relatively less attention has been paid to the development of such key energy areas as smart grids, energy management information systems, energy conservation, and decentralisation of energy supply. In the draft version of the Energy Strategy of Russia for the period up to 2035, a course is taken for a profound structural and technological transformation of both the industry itself and all related segments of the energy sector. By 2035, the share of renewable energy sources and hydroelectric power plants in power generation will amount to 16–17%, and renewable energy sources will take up 1.5–2% in the energy mix.

According to the *Strategy of Scientific and Technological Development of Russia until 2035*, which was approved by the Decree of the President of the Russian Federation No. 642 of December 1, 2016, the following are considered to be priority areas for the scientific and technological development of the Russian Federation in the next 10 to 15 years: transition to advanced digital and intelligent production technologies, robotic systems, new materials and design methods; development of data processing, machine learning, and artificial intelligence systems; transition to environmentally friendly and resource-saving energy technologies; improvement in the efficiency of hydrocarbon extraction and processing; development of new energy sources as well as energy transportation and storage methods. At present, new concepts for the development of the energy sector using Smart Grid are being considered in Russia.

In the coal industry, the priority is to upgrade underground coal mining operations, to improve the technologies used in coal preparation, processing, and briquetting, and to produce hydrophobic peat briquettes of high quality.

The energy sector of Azerbaijan is based on the country's hydrocarbon potential. Coal does not play an important role in energy generation. The decree of the President of the Republic of Azerbaijan dated March 16, 2016, established the key directions for the development of the country's industries and the national economy as a whole. The main goals include diversification, the development of non-oil industries, efficiency and competitiveness improvement, etc. In Azerbaijan, a program for the development of the energy sector for the period from 2015 to 2030 is being developed. It provides for annual growth of 4% in electricity consumption.

In the Republic of Belarus, the energy mix is similar. However, coal is also used, and a nuclear power plant has been built. The government of the country approved the Strategy for the Development of the Energy Potential of the Republic of Belarus (*Resolution of the Council of Ministers of the Republic of Belarus* No. 1180 dated August 9, 2010), whose main goal is "innovative and advanced development of the fuel and energy sectors, ensuring the production of competitive products at the level of global standards with reliable and efficient energy supply provided to the population and all sectors of the economy." Its key elements include the diversification of types and suppliers of fuel and energy resources, improving the energy efficiency of energy systems based on upgrading the existing facilities, and involving local fuels and renewable energy sources where it is economically viable.

In the Republic of Kazakhstan, coal-fired power plants account for more than half of the energy mix. Oil and gas provide another 20%. Coal will remain the main feedstock for power plants in the long term. Therefore, much attention is paid to the sustainable development of the coal industry. Solving environmental and technical issues is possible through the introduction of innovative technologies (clean coal technologies, coal beneficiation, combined cycles, etc.). In Kazakhstan, the national energy strategy is embedded in the national strategy of the country's industrial and innovative development. An Action Plan has been developed in order to implement the *Concept for the Development of the Fuel and Energy Sector of the Republic of Kazakhstan until 2030,* which provides for measures in the field of energy conservation and energy efficiency (Government of the Republic of Kazakhstan, 2014).

The foundation of the economy of Turkmenistan is the fuel and energy sector based on oil (more than 70%) and gas (more than 20%). Its development is significantly influenced by massive investments and the latest technologies supplied to the country by the world's leading companies. In 2012, the National Climate Change Strategy of Turkmenistan was approved, whose implementation affects all sectors of the economy but the emphasis is placed on its key segments (industry, transportation, as well as housing and communal services), and the priority areas are the introduction of energy conservation and efficiency technologies, the development of the renewable energy sector, and upgrading in order to ensure the future development and competitiveness of the economy.

In Uzbekistan, gas is the dominant element in the energy mix (over 85%), and the shares of oil and coal are almost equal. The priorities for the development of the energy sector in Uzbekistan are the continuation of the reform of the electric power industry and the coal industry, the accelerated implementation of investment projects for the development and modernisation of energy facilities based on new technologies and equipment, and also the development of energy transmission and distribution systems. The industry's priority is to improve energy efficiency.

The analysis showed that the energy policy in the CIS countries is integrated with the national industrial policy and aimed at the sustainable development of the economy and society. The interaction between the CIS member states in the field of innovative energy development can be carried out in the following areas: energy conservation and efficiency; alternative and renewable energy sources; intelligent systems; scientific breakthroughs in the sector of traditional energy sources. The creation of smart energy systems in the CIS will trigger innovations in other industries, primarily power engineering, which supplies equipment for power generation, i.e. it can have a multiplier effect.

How do governments influence sustainable development in coal mining enterprises? Case studies

This section seeks to answer the question of how resource-based, energy state policy can affect the sustainable development of mining companies in the context of the two leading economies of Poland and Russia.

As it is widely known, the use of non-renewable energy resources is not conducive to the realisation of the concept of sustainable development due to their adverse impact on the environment, thus marginalising the environmental aspects of the quality of life of future generations. Therefore, the state energy policy in the context of the European Union guidelines can take three key directions:

1 Conservative, involving ignoring social and environmental priorities in favour of economic goals and energy security;
2 Adaptive, consisting of gradual and systematic transformation of the energy and heating sectors towards a low- or zero-emission economy;
3 Revolutionary, consisting of the fastest possible implementation of changes and adaptation to the principles of decarbonisation and zero-carbon economy.

In the case of Poland over the last two decades, energy policy has been rather conservative (Sokołowski et al., 2020; Skjærseth, 2018). This was caused by the following circumstances:

- very high share of coal in the energy mix,
- the desire to maintain energy security,
- social pressure to maintain jobs in mining companies,
- fear of pauperisation of mining economic regions in the Upper Silesian and Lublin Coal Basins.

The above-mentioned reasons were the basis for negotiating the climate policy conditions by Poland with the European Commission. Nevertheless, even temporary derogations and reliefs will not prevent Poland from systematically abandoning coal and replacing it with less emitting fuels and/or renewable sources (Budzianowski and Gomes, 2016; Müller, 2018). However, this process will be lengthy and costly, which does not gain full approval in the industry and political-economic community (Marcinkiewicz and Tosun, 2015; Kundzewicz et al., 2019).

The slow change in Poland's energy balance is clearly evidenced by the data on the share of individual energy sources in the energy mix between 1990 and 2018 presented in Table 9.3.

The data shows that Poland has been systematically reducing the share of coal in its energy balance, but this has been achieved primarily by increasing the share of oil and natural gas. At the same time, no crude oil is produced in Poland and Poland's own gas supplies can satisfy approximately ¼ of the demand. This means that the energy transformation is taking place at the expense of energy security. Systematic decommissioning of mines does not allow for prioritisation of social goals, and the low share of renewable sources proves that ecological goals are also not being implemented quickly and effectively.

The answer to the above shortcomings is the *Energy Policy of Poland until 2040*, adopted in 2021. The purpose of the state energy policy is energy security while ensuring the competitiveness of the economy, energy efficiency,

Table 9.3 Changes in the energy mix in Poland in 1990–2018

Energy source	1990	1995	2000	2005	2010	2015	2017	2018
Oil	15.69%	16.28%	23.66%	25.27%	28.10%	28.09%	31.15%	29.82%
Gas	8.59%	9.44%	11.39%	13.33%	13.71%	15.39%	16.21%	15.45%
Coal	75.40%	73.81%	64.31%	60.05%	54.10%	50.97%	47.94%	45.91%
Nuclear energy	0.00%	0.00%	0.00%	0.00%	0.00%	0.00%	0.00%	0.00%
Hydroelectricity	0.31%	0.45%	0.54%	0.54%	0.65%	0.43%	0.57%	0.36%
Solar energy	0.00%	0.00%	0.00%	0.00%	0.00%	0.01%	0.04%	0.09%
Wind energy	0.00%	0.00%	0.04%	0.44%	2.04%	2.75%	2.73%	2.64%
Geothermal, biomass and other	0.01%	0.02%	0.06%	0.37%	1.40%	2.36%	1.36%	5.73%
Total	**100%**	**100%**	**100%**	**100%**	**100%**	**100%**	**100%**	**100%**

Source: own study based on the data from BP, 2019

and reduction of the impact of the energy sector on the environment with optimal use of its own energy resources.

The key assumptions of this *Policy* are presented in Figure 9.1. They show that in the coming years, the energy balance will be shaped in full compliance

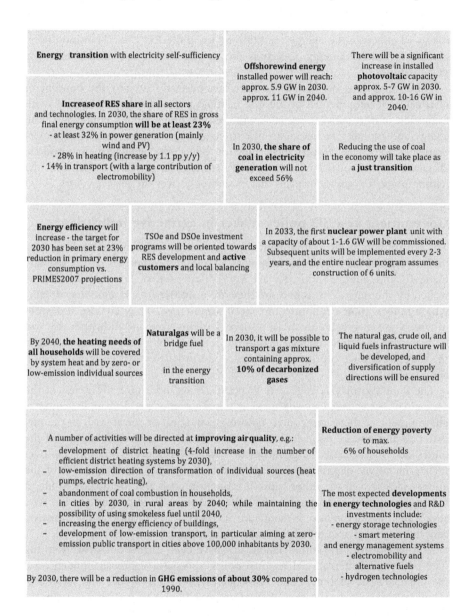

Figure 9.1 Number of mining suppliers in the leading mining countries worldwide in 2018
Source: Ministry of Climate and Environment, 2021

with the guidelines of the EU decarbonisation policy. This is evidenced by the consistent abandonment of coal as the dominant energy fuel and the announcement of an increasing share of renewable energy sources, including primarily wind and solar energy. The *Policy* also assumes the construction and commissioning of a nuclear power plant in 2033.

In addition to changes in the energy mix, the Policy also plans to mitigate the social effects of the energy transition by using the EU's Just Transition Fund granted to Poland. Energy poverty is also to be reduced to a maximum of 6% of households.

The assumptions of the *Policy*, therefore, perfectly fit into the concept of sustainable development. On the one hand, it postulates decarbonisation with mitigation of its negative social effects and, on the other hand, it emphasises clean energy and mobility technologies that strengthen the implementation of environmental objectives. Nevertheless, they are often criticised for their unrealistic character and lack of reference to Poland's current energy situation, which is the starting point for ambitious plans that extend only over the next 19 years.

Government as a SD policy maker in extractive industries

The government plays an important role in creating conditions for implementing the concept of sustainable development in mining companies. Both the raw materials and energy industries are very often owned, co-owned, or controlled by the state. This is because they are industries of strategic importance, which reflects their economic and social importance. They are also industries in which above-average financial resources are invested and industries that can be a source of above-average economic returns. Given these circumstances, the state's influence on their performance in virtually every geographic region is significant.

The state also plays a large role in popularising and raising awareness of the concept of sustainable development in mining companies and in the industry environment of these companies. Ignoring ecological or social goals in the raw materials and energy policies in a way justifies the unfavourable aspects of the mines' activity, because the government – as the authority – officially approves such a hierarchy of priorities and gives consent to the unsustainability of the entire industry. On the other hand, if ecological goals and the quality of life of future generations connected with their realisation are important for the state authorities and expressed in strategic documents, such an attitude must be adopted and implemented also by mining companies.

As it results from the considerations that have been carried out, apart from the state policy, the international regional policy also has a significant influence on the sustainable development and, consequently, on the existence and survival of mining companies. In the case of the European Union, it has been a dominant determinant of energy balances for the last 30 years. In many countries, the EU's decarbonisation agenda has contributed to the complete closure of the mining industry, which demonstrates the strength of this determinant.

It should be added, however, that considering the analysed statistical data, the focus on environmental priorities has led to significant dependence of some European countries on external sources of supply of non-renewable energy resources, which may pose a certain threat to the effective and efficient functioning of their economies. Countries that wished to avoid such a threat decided to use nuclear energy or maximum use. It must be remembered, however, that such a solution requires access to and knowledge of the use of nuclear technology or favourable geographic and climatic conditions, and in both cases a significant capital outlay on the part of the state and citizens, who must accept and partially pay for the proposed energy transition.

Executive and legislative bodies in countries with resource-based economies are making significant efforts to improve their regulatory frameworks and develop organisational and economic mechanisms for regulating sustainable development in the coal industry.

The most important federal-level document for the coal industry in the Russian Federation is the updated Program for the *Development of the Coal Industry in Russia until 2035*, whose purpose is to create conditions for coal companies that will ensure a stable supply of coal to the domestic market and strengthen their positions in foreign markets. This, in turn, will ensure the companies' competitiveness and sustainable economic development. Individual economic measures include:

- development of the railway network with an increase in its throughput; renovation of the Eastern railway routes; extension of the eastern section of the Baikal-Amur Mainline, which will increase the volume of coal supplies from Yakutia and stimulate the creation of new coal mining facilities;
- Project Finance Factory, a project finance mechanism implemented by the VEB Corporation;
- additional mechanisms for investment in the coal industry based on special conditions (special investment contracts, regional investment projects, integrated investment projects).

The Ministry of Industry and Trade has come forward with a timely initiative aimed at fostering the sustainable development of coal companies, which is expected to have an impact on three components: economy, ecology, and society. It proposes to cover up to 20% of the costs that mining companies will pay to replace old excavators that do not meet current safety requirements and need to be disposed of with new mining excavators produced domestically. According to the Ministry, 68% of the excavators used by Russian mining companies today are more than 23 years old, while the average service life is 21 years. This initiative is very important for the coal industry in Russia because open-pit mining accounts for more than 75% (Union of Mining Engineers Mining, 2021a).

A good example of improving federal tax legislation in order to foster the social development of the coal industry is mining tax deductions for companies that implement Occupational Safety & Health (OSH) measures. A special coefficient is used that takes into account coalbed methane contents and the tendency of coal to spontaneous combustion (NK RF, 1998).

Measures at the regional level are aimed at improving the living conditions of the local population. For example, the main impact of large-scale investment projects in the coal industry (e.g., the completion of the first stage of construction of the Sadkinskaya–Vostochnaya coal mine in the Rostov region) with investments of 10 billion rubles manifests itself at the regional level. Such projects make it possible to create hundreds of new jobs and collect more taxes. This is why local authorities have begun to resurface roads and build new housing facilities (Union of Mining Engineers Mining, 2021c).

Examples of more active government involvement in the environmental aspect of the sustainable development of the coal mining industry are the standardisation of implementing best available technology (BAT) at the federal level, as well as legal and organisational efforts on the part of the regional authorities. For example, in the Kemerovo region, whose share in Russian coal production amounts to two-thirds, the regional authorities have recognized the problem of underground fires at abandoned coal mines and are solving problems with mining-induced displacement and resettlement (Metal Mining Info, 2019). Since 2019, coal mining operations have been audited for compliance with the approved documentation, including the implementation of mandatory environmental protection measures.

Environmental, Social, Corporate Governance (ESG) lending, which has emerged in the coal industry, will have a complex impact on sustainable development. Fierce competition and price volatility in external coal markets are forcing companies to save on environmental costs, including efficient equipment for land reclamation and coal dust control. Therefore, ESG loans, the first example of which is a loan agreement between Sberbank, the largest state-owned bank, and the Raspadskaya coal company (EVRAZ), ensure that projects aimed at reducing environmental impact will be implemented. The loan provided is based on sustainable development indicators: the interest rate can be reduced if the company fulfills its ESG obligations, such as having an ESG rating not lower than the industry average and publishing a sustainable development policy including plans to reduce greenhouse gas emissions (Union of Mining Engineers Mining, 2021b).

In general, the efforts made by the federal and local authorities in the CIS countries producing coal are aimed at improving the existing organisational and management tools and developing new ones in the field of sustainable development. A further increase in the volume of coal production and its more efficient use are expected.

The Government of the Republic of Kazakhstan plans to develop its coal industry in a qualitative direction. The main direction is the deep complex processing of coal to produce products with high added value. Coal chemistry and high-tech production will be developed. Relevant projects have been developed in Kazakhstan, and the Government is ready to support this direction. As a result, economic sustainability will increase due to qualitative changes in the consumer properties of products, prices, and going beyond the market of thermal coal. This can significantly affect the efficiency of using Kazakhstan's coal potential and improving the environment. Tax preferences will be granted to new high-tech industries, and special economic zones will be created around large coal enterprises (Metal Mining Info, 2019). It is planned to improve the system of social partnership in the coal industry. Government regulation in the rest of the CIS countries is aimed at ensuring energy independence, "green energy" and renewable energy sources.

Bibliography

Bausch, C., Görlach, B., Mehling, M. (2017). Ambitious Climate Policy Through Centralization? Evidence from the European Union. *Climate Policy*, 17, 32–50.

Blesl, M., Kober, T., Kuder, R., Bruchof, D. (2012). Implications of Different Climate Protection Regimes for the EU-27 and its Member States Through 2050. *Climate Policy*, 12(3), 301–319.

BP (2020). BP Statistical Review of World Energy. https://www.bp.com/en/global/corpora te/energy-economics/statistical-review-of-world-energy.html [access date: 30. 03. 2021].

Braun, M. (2019). The Czech Republic's Approach to the EU 2030 Climate and Energy Framework. *Environmental Politics*, 28(6), 1105–1123.

Budzianowski, M.W, Gomes, J.F.P. (2016). Perspectives for Low-Carbon Electricity Production until 2030: Lessons Learned from the Comparison of Local Contexts in Poland and Portugal. *Energy Sources, Part B: Economics, Planning, and Policy*, 11(6), 534–541.

Christmann, P., Arvanitidis, N., Martins, L., Recoché, G., Solar, S. (2007). Towards the Sustainable Use of Mineral Resources: A European Geological Surveys Perspective. *Minerals & Energy – Raw Materials Report*, 22(3–4), 88–104.

Duijndam, S., van Beukering, P. (2021). Understanding Public Concern about Climate Change in Europe, 2008–2017: The Influence of Economic Factors and Right-Wing Populism. *Climate Policy*, 21(3), 353–367.

Energy Charter Secretariat (2013). Resolution of the Council of Ministers of the Republic of Belarus No. 1180 dated August 9, 2010. In *In-Depth Review of the Energy Efficiency Policy of the Republic of Belarus*. Brussels, Belgium. https://www.energycha rter.org/fileadmin/DocumentsMedia/IDEER/IDEER-Belarus_2013_en.pdf [access date: 31. 03. 2021].

Gerhardt, C. (2017). Germany's Renewable Energy Shift: Addressing Climate Change. *Capitalism Nature Socialism*, 28(2), 103–119.

Government of the Republic of Kazakhstan (2014). Concept for the Development of the Fuel and Energy Sector of the Republic of Kazakhstan until 2030. https://policy. asiapacificenergy.org/node/369 [access date: 31. 03. 2021].

Güney, T. (2019). Renewable Energy, Non-Renewable Energy and Sustainable Development. *International Journal of Sustainable Development & World Ecology*, 26(5), 389–397.

Guven, D., Ozgur, M.K., Kayakutlu, G., Isikli, E. (2021). Impact of Climate Change on Sectoral Electricity Demand in Turkey. *Energy Sources, Part B: Economics, Planning, and Policy*, 16(3), 235–237.

Hillebrand, R., (2013). Climate Protection, Energy Security, and Germany's Policy of Ecological Modernisation. *Environmental Politics*, 22(4), 664–682.

Jiang, N. (2018). Strategic Trends for Future Energy Policy: Evidence from China. *Energy Sources, Part B: Economics, Planning, and Policy*, 13(3), 165–168.

Kundzewicz, Z.W., Painter, J., Kundzewicz, W.J., (2019). Climate Change in the Media: Poland's Exceptionalism. *Environmental Communication*, 13(3), 366–380.

Lecuyer, O., Quirion, P. (2019). Interaction between CO2 Emissions Trading and Renewable Energy Subsidies under Uncertainty: Feed-in Tariffs as a Safety Net Against Over-allocation. *Climate Policy*, 19(8), 1002–1018.

Marcinkiewicz, K., Tosun, J. (2015). Contesting Climate Change: Mapping the Political Debate in Poland. *East European Politics*, 31(2), 187–207.

Metal Mining Info (2019). Budushchee ugol'noj otrasli – za glubokoj pererabotkoj. *Iyun'* 14,. http://metalmininginfo.kz/archives/6289 [access date: 30. 03. 2021].

Mez, L. (2012). Germany's Merger of Energy and Climate Change Policy. *Bulletin of the Atomic Scientists*, 68(6), 22–29.

Ministry of Climate and Environment (2021). Poland's Energy Policy until 2040. https://www.gov.pl/web/klimat/polityka-energetyczna-polski [access date: 31. 01. 2020].

Müller, K. (2018). Mining, Time and Protest: Dealing with Waiting in German Coal Mine Planning. *The Extractive Industries and Society*, 11, 1–7.

NK RF (Nalogovyj kodeks Rossijskoj Federacii) (1998). https://base.garant.ru/10900200/ [access date: 30. 03. 2021].

Oztig, L.I. (2017). Europe's Climate Change Policies: The Paris Agreement and Beyond. *Energy Sources, Part B: Economics, Planning, and Policy*, 12(10), 917–924.

Pasqualetti, M.J., Sovacool, B.K. (2012). The Importance of Scale to Energy Security. *Journal of Integrative Environmental Sciences*, 9(3), 167–180.

Roscongress Foundation (2019). Development of the Coal Industry in Russia until 2035. Russian Energy Week. https://roscongress.org/en/sessions/rew-2019-strategiya-razvitiya-ugolnoy-promyshlennosti-rossii-na-period-do-2035-goda-novyy-vzglyad/about/ [access date: 31. 03. 2021].

Silva, S., Soares, I., Afonso, O. (2016). Tax on Emissions or Subsidy to Renewables? Evaluating the Effects on the Economy and on the Environment. *Applied Economics Letters*, 23(10), 690–694.

Sivek, M., Vlček, T., Kavina, P., Jirásek, J. (2017). Lifting Lignite Mining Limits – Correction of the Czech Republic Energy Policy. *Energy Sources, Part B: Economics, Planning, and Policy*, 12(6), 519–525.

Skjærseth, J.B. (2018). Implementing EU Climate and Energy Policies in Poland: Policy Feedback and Reform. *Environmental Politics*, 27(3), 498–518.

Sokołowski, J., Lewandowski, P., Kiełczewska, A., Bouzarovski, S. (2020). A Multidimensional Index to Measure Energy Poverty: The Polish Case. *Energy Sources, Part B: Economics, Planning, and Policy*, 15(2), 92–112.

Tagotra, N. (2018). Energy Security: How Decision-Making Processes in India's Energy Bureaucracy Shape India's Energy Policy. *Strategic Analysis*, 42(5), 461–475.

Tvaronavičienė, M., Mačiulis, A., Lankauskienė, T., Raudeliūnienė, J., Dzemyda, I. (2015). Energy Security and Sustainable Competitiveness of Industry Development. *Economic Research-Ekonomska Istraživanja*, 28(1), 502–515.

Union of Mining Engineers Mining (2021a). Minpromtorg: esli ne subsidirovat' pokupku rossijskih ekskavatorov v razmere do 20% ot stoimosti, potrebiteli kupyat ekskavatory u inostrannyh proizvoditelej. Industry Portal. http://www.mining-portal.ru/publish/minpromtorg–esli-ne-subsidirovat-pokupku-rossiyskih-ekskavatorov-v-razmere do 20–ot-stoimosti–potrebiteli-kupyat-ekskavatoryi-u-inostrannyih-proizvoditeley/ [access date: 30. 03. 2021].

Union of Mining Engineers Mining (2021b). Ugol'shchikam odobrili pervyj ESG-kredit ot «Sbera». Industry Portal: Mining Industry News. http://www.mining-portal.ru/news/all-news/ugolschikam-odobrili-pervyiy-esg-kredit-ot—sbera—/ [access date: 30. 03. 2021].

Union of Mining Engineers Mining (2021c). V Rostovskoj oblasti stroitsya novaya shahta. K 2023 ona budet davat' bol'she uglya, chem polovina vsej oblasti segodnya. Industry Portal: Mining Industry News. http://www.mining-portal.ru/news/all-news/———v-rostovskoy-oblasti-stroitsya-novaya-shahta–k-2023-ona-budet-davat-bolshe-uglya–chem-polovina-vsey-oblasti-segodnya-/ [access date: 30. 03. 2021].

Vogler, J. (2013). Changing Conceptions of Climate and Energy Security in Europe. *Environmental Politics*, 22(4), 627–645.

Warden-Fernandez, J. (2005). Indigenous Communities' Rights and Mineral Development. *Journal of Energy & Natural Resources Law*, 23(4), 395–426.

Zillman, D.N., Smith, D.C. (2019). The Brave New World of Energy and Natural Resources Development. *Journal of Energy & Natural Resources Law*, 37(1), 3–45.

10 Ecological organisations and associations for or against the existence of a coal mining enterprise

Ecological problems in the lifecycle of a mining enterprise

Coal is a common fuel source that is relatively inexpensive to produce and convert into useful energy. However, the production and use of coal has a largely negative impact on the environment. In this section, environmental problems are presented from three perspectives: (1) General – reporting on the types of environmental hazards associated with coal mining (2) Value – presenting the levels of pollution generated by mining, and (3) Indirect – on the emissions from coal combustion in the power industry.

Coal mining affects the entire local ecosystem. This is because mining activities cause surface degradation, serious disturbances in the hydrosphere and air pollution. The effects of mining activity are intensely felt not only at the stage of establishment and operation of a mining enterprise but also several or even several dozen years after its liquidation. In addition, it is impossible to forget that burning coal, i.e. using this raw material in further production processes, is a source of further environmental hazards, significantly reducing the human life quality. Table 10.1 presents a list of the most important negative environmental effects caused by hard coal mines in their life cycle.

Currently in the European Union, air pollution from mining companies is of particular importance. Thus, the main air pollutants associated with coal mining and processing include:

- Sulfur dioxide (SO_2), which contributes to acid rain and respiratory diseases;
- Nitrogen oxides (NO_x), which contribute to smog and respiratory disease;
- Particulate matter, which contributes to smog, haze, respiratory and lung disease;
- Carbon dioxide (CO_2), which is the main greenhouse gas produced from burning fossil fuels (coal, oil, and natural gas);
- Mercury and other heavy metals, which have been linked to both neurological and developmental damage in humans and other animals;
- Fly ash and slag ash, which are residues produced when coal is burned in power plants.

(EIA, 2020)

DOI: 10.4324/9781003091110-14

Table 10.1 Negative environmental impacts of coal production and combustion

Area	Environmental impact
Land and surroundings	Open-pit mining severely alters the landscape, which diminishes the environmental value of surrounding areas. Open-pit mining eliminates existing vegetation, destroys the genetic soil profile, displaces or destroys wildlife and habitat, alters current land uses, and to some extent permanently alters the overall topography of the mining area. For deep mines, mine collapse has the potential to cause severe above-ground effects that are particularly devastating in developed areas. For example, German deep-coal mining (particularly in North Rhine-Westphalia) has destroyed thousands of homes, and the mining industry has set aside large sums to finance future subsidence damage through its insurance programs and state subsidies.
Water management and pollution	Mining can adversely affect groundwater in a number of ways: by draining usable water from shallow aquifers; by lowering water levels in adjacent areas and diverting flow in aquifers; by contaminating usable aquifers below mining operations through infiltration (see page 21) of poor-quality mine water; and by increased infiltration of precipitation into the tailings piles. Contamination of both groundwater and nearby streams can occur over long periods of time. Deterioration of stream quality results from acid mine drainage, toxic trace elements, high dissolved solids in mine drainage water, and increased sediment loads discharged to streams. Additionally, pollutants discharged from ash basins into surface waters typically include arsenic, lead, mercury, selenium, chromium, and cadmium.
Air emissions	Coal and coal waste (including fly ash, bottom ash, and boiler slag) release approximately 20 toxic chemicals, including arsenic, lead, mercury, nickel, vanadium, beryllium, cadmium, barium, chromium, copper, molybdenum, zinc, selenium, and radium, which are hazardous when released into the environment. During combustion, the reaction of coal with air produces carbon oxides, including carbon dioxide (CO_2, an important greenhouse gas), sulfur oxides (mainly sulfur dioxide, SO_2), and various nitrogen oxides (NO_x). Due to the hydrogen and nitrogen content of coal, the burning of coal also produces hydrides and nitrides of carbon and sulfur in the air. For example, the Mpumalanga Highveld in South Africa is the most polluted area in the world due to the mining industry and coal-fired power plants.
Greenhouse gas emissions	Coal burning is the largest contributor to man-made CO_2 levels in the atmosphere. Electricity generation using coal combustion produces about twice as many greenhouse gases per kilowatt compared to generation using natural gas. Coal mining releases methane, a potent greenhouse gas. Methane is a naturally occurring breakdown product of organic matter as coal deposits form with increasing depth of mining, increasing temperature, and increasing pressure over geologic time.

Source: own work based on: Tiwary, 2001; Hamilton, 2005; Shrader-Frechette, 2011; World Coal Institute, 2015; Flannery, 2015; Jhariya et al., 2016

In Australia, a long-term observation of the effects of coal mines was conducted covering the period 2008–2018. The results of the observations are shown in Table 10.2. They reflect the massive negative impact of mining companies on the environment.

In addition to the pollutants emitted by the mining company, the coal combustion process emits a number of harmful substances that further burden its life cycle environmentally. As provided by the *Union of Concerned Scientists*, a typical coal-fired power plant (500 megawatts in capacity) generates the following amounts of air pollution on average per year:

- 3.7 million tons of carbon dioxide (CO_2), equivalent to cutting down 161 million trees, CO_2 pollution is a major cause of global warming and climate change;
- 10,000 tons of sulfur dioxide (SO_2), which causes acid rain and forms small airborne particles that can cause lung damage, heart disease and other illnesses;
- 10,200 tons of nitrogen oxides (NO_x), equivalent to the production of about half a million cars, NO_x leads to smog, which causes inflammation of lung tissue and increases susceptibility to respiratory disease;
- 500 tons of small airborne particles that can cause bronchitis, reduced lung function, increased hospital admissions, and premature death;

Table 10.2 Air emission from coal mines in Australia in kilograms 2008–2018

Emission	No. of observations	Total amount in kg
Antimony and compounds	741	7,402.5
Arsenic and compounds	985	44,023.9
Beryllium and compounds	902	12,776.9
Cadmium and compounds	866	2,299.9
Chromium and compounds	107	1,565.7
Cobalt and compounds	967	74,179.6
Copper and compounds	1,089	241,099.8
Lead and compounds	1,102	153,289.6
Manganese and compounds	1,161	4,844,927.9
Mercury and compounds	1,114	1,393.3
Nickel and compounds	1,090	281,789.1
Selenium and compounds	667	9,982.4
Zinc and compounds	1,117	1,127,249.7
Total Metals	12	6,801,980.3
PM2.5	1,071	67,361,544.1
PM10	1,082	3,534,238,028.0
NO_x	1,074	83,356 7946.0

Source: Hendryx et al., 2020

- 220 tons of hydrocarbons that contribute to smog;
- 720 tons of carbon monoxide (CO), which causes headaches and has additional negative effects on people with heart disease;
- 170 pounds of mercury (1/70 teaspoon of mercury deposited in a 25-acre lake can make fish unsafe to eat); mercury also causes learning disabilities, brain damage, and neurological disorders;
- 225 pounds of arsenic, leading to cancer in 1 in 100 people who drink water containing 50 parts per billion;
- 114 pounds of lead, 4 pounds of cadmium, and other toxic heavy metals; these toxic metals can accumulate in human and animal tissues and cause serious health problems, including mental retardation, developmental disabilities, and nervous system damage.

(World Coal Institute, 2015; Union of Concerned Scientists, 2017)

Due to the nature of its production operations, the coal industry has a significant negative impact on the environment, especially in regions with a high concentration of coal mining and processing facilities. The degree of this impact varies greatly, depending on the source of pollution (wastewater, emissions, soil disturbance, mining waste). Let us consider the impact of the coal industry on the environment using the example of two countries – Russia and the Republic of Kazakhstan – whose coal production volumes and greenhouse gas emissions are the largest.

Between 2010 and 2018, the volume of wastewater generated by the Russian coal industry decreased by 1.5%, and the specific volume per 1 ton of produced coal decreased by a factor of 1.4. The coal industry accounted for 1.1% of the total volume of wastewater discharge into natural water bodies in Russia and 32.3% of the volume of wastewater discharge from mining facilities (Harionovskij and Danilova, 2020).

Compared to 2010, the Russian coal industry produced 7.0% less gaseous emissions and 36.6% less particulate matter. This dramatic reduction in particulate matter is due to the relative simplicity and lower costs of capturing it compared to gaseous substances. Harmful gases are mainly represented by carbon monoxide (31.3%), sulfur dioxide (23.2%), and nitrogen oxides (11.4%). In 2018, coal producers emitted 1,110.2 thousand tons of harmful substances into the atmosphere.

In Russia, 73.3% of harmful substances released into the atmosphere are captured by filtering. However, this indicator is much lower in the coal sector (30.6%), which is explained by the fact that the methane drained in coal mines is hardly utilised. For the period from 2010 to 2018, the share of the coal industry in the total volume of emissions was much higher than that in the total volume of captured harmful substances. This signals that filters are not widespread in the coal industry.

In 2018, 589.5 hectares of land (5.5%) were reclaimed in the Russian coal industry. The low level of reclamation leads to a steady increase in the total area of disturbed land. The share of the coal industry in land disturbance both all over the Russian Federation and within the mining sector is quite high and amounts to 8.9% and 15%, respectively, whereas the share in reclamation is extremely low (1.0% and 2.5%, respectively). This means that the rate of land reclamation in the coal industry lags behind compared to other industries.

In 2018, the mining sector produced 6,850.5 million tons of waste, or 94.2% of the total volume generated in the Russian Federation. Some 4,381.8 million tons of waste were generated by the coal sector, with the major part being represented by overburden and enclosing rocks (hazard class V). The amount of waste generated annually in the coal industry is growing at an even faster pace than the average value across the Russian Federation. In 2010–2018, the amount of waste generated annually increased by a factor of 2.1. The share of the coal industry in waste generation is extremely high and amounts to 64.0% of the total amount of waste generated by the mining sector and 60.3% of the average indicator in the Russian Federation. The main method of reducing the negative impact of waste on the environment is its disposal.

In 2018, 2,334.9 million tons (or 53.3%) of waste generated by the Russian coal industry were disposed of and rendered harmless. Usually, waste of the second and first classes of hazard (the most hazardous), which is produced to a small extent by the coal industry, is processed and treated. From 2010 to 2018, the annual amount of waste sent for storage in the Russian Federation increased by 55.8%. In the coal industry, it grew by a factor of 1.8. Burial of waste is not used by coal producers. This industry accounts for the biggest share in the total amount of waste sent for storage (52.4% across Russia and 55.8% across the mining sector).

Evaluating the above data, it should be noted that the share of the coal industry in the total negative impact on water bodies, air, and land is very significant, while its participation in environmental protection (wastewater treatment, emissions purification, waste utilisation, and land reclamation) is much lower compared to other Russian industries and mining sectors. In terms of land protection and waste management, it has particularly low indicators.

Most of the coal deposits in Kazakhstan have high moisture content, a relatively low heating value, and also high ash and sulfur contents. Combined with the presence of significant volumes of methane in most of the country's coal deposits, these characteristics result in the fact that the production and consumption of coal in Kazakhstan have a more serious impact on the environment than in many other regions of the world.

In Kazakhstan, coal burning produces approximately 19 million tons of ash and slag per year. More than 300 million tons of waste have been accumulated in ash dumps to date; about 250 million tons of finely dispersed aerosols enter the atmosphere in the form of emissions annually, which can noticeably change the balance of solar radiation at the earth's surface. The energy sector accounts for more than 80% of the total greenhouse gas emissions in Kazakhstan. Kazakhstan is notable for its coal mines with very high methane contents. The concentration of coalbed methane (CBM) reaches potentially dangerous values (18–24 m^3/t on average, reaching 33 m^3/t in some places) in deep mines, in the Karaganda basin in particular. Thus, methane extraction (drainage) is mandatory there to ensure the safety of mining operations. Opportunities for CBM extraction and utilisation are currently being assessed (Kalmykov and Malikova, 2017).

The standards established by the legislation of Kazakhstan are below the requirements that need to be met to achieve significant shifts in the area of ecology.

> In Kazakhstan, it is considered acceptable that during the combustion of one ton of standard coal, 7 to 14 kg of particulate matter (depending on the boiler capacity at the station), 13 to 25 kg of sulfur dioxide, and 7 to 11 kg of nitrogen oxides are emitted into the atmosphere. To compare, the figures in the USA are 0.5 to 1.5 kg of particulate matter, 9.5 to 19 kg of sulfur dioxide, and 4 to 10 kg of nitrogen oxides per ton. An even more striking difference is witnessed in the ash processing sector: less than 8% of ash is processed in Kazakhstan (the rest is stored in ash dumps), while the EU countries process about 90%.
>
> (Forbes, 2012)

In addition, coal mining and combustion in the Republic of Kazakhstan are a source of significant mercury emissions into the environment.

How do societies negotiate their rights and requirements? Case studies

Under the influence of pro-environmental organisations and changes in laws in different countries, mines are taking numerous measures to reduce their negative impact on the environment (Bian et al., 2010). In the European Union countries, a very important factor influencing the necessity of reducing the emission of carbon dioxide to the atmosphere from coal combustion is the decarbonisation policy, which leads to a decrease in profitability of coal production and the need for mines and power plants to invest in modern technologies.

The most important activities undertaken in order to reduce the negative impact of hard coal mining on the environment by mines include:

- Reduction of the quantity of wastes generated from hard coal mining and their maximum possible management on the surface and in underground mine works;
- Increasing the scope of reclamation and development works on coal waste dumps and other areas and land degraded by overuse;
- Minimising the impact of mining overuse on the land surface by conducting mining operations in a manner limiting the deformation of the land surface and applying mining prophylaxis to a large extent;
- Intensifying the repairs of surface infrastructure facilities: bridges, viaducts, roads, railroads and structural facilities damaged as a result of the mining operation;
- Reduction of the impact of discharged mine waters on surface waters, particularly as regards waters with excessive salinity from drainage of the mines;

- Reduction of the emission of dust-gas pollutants into the atmosphere, including reduction of the emission of greenhouse gases;
- Elimination of the sources of excessive noise emission to the environment.

Under the influence of legal changes and activities of pro-environmental organisations, nowadays mines have to include pro-environmental issues in their activities at every stage of the life cycle (Goswami, 2015; Khanna, 2013). This is not an easy process due to the necessity of forecasting the environmental effects in the long term, taking into account a very precise understanding and modelling of the geological structure and hydrological situation. In Europe, including Poland, each coal project must be accompanied by an environmental impact study which is later presented to and accepted by representatives of local communities and environmental organisations. If the environmental impact study is not accepted, it means that investment activities cannot commence. Sometimes it can also lead to the closure of a mine.

As part of the environmental impact, mines must identify all hazards and propose ways to mitigate them. Table 10.3 – as a case study – presents an example of synthesised content of the environmental impact study, which concerns the mining project in the Lublin deposit.

Following the assumptions included in the study of environmental conditions is obligatory and controlled, therefore it can be assumed that the standards of mining activity in Poland are adjusted to the principles of sustainable development. Mining companies are obliged by law to reduce the environmental consequences of their activities during and after the operation. Obviously, these effects will not be eliminated to 100% – as is the case with other industries. Nevertheless, the environmental awareness of government and local government decision makers and environmental organisations is an important element in supporting environmental priorities of sustainable development. Notably, local communities and local ecological organisations are free to express their opinions on mining investments and there are known cases of halting of exploitation or preparation of a deposit due to their protests. Thus it can be stated that in Poland, the representatives of ecological organisations have a real impact on the activity of mining companies and may significantly influence the sustainability of the mining sector.

The nature of the coal mining and processing industry necessitates compliance with the requirements stipulated in regulations concerning resource use (mineral and energy resources, land, water, forests, etc.) and environmental protection.

Coal mining and processing operations must meet general and industry-specific (those relevant for the energy sector) environmental requirements described in the Federal Law No. 7-FZ of January 10, 2002 (*Environmental Protection Law*) and covering all stages of economic and other activities during the placement, design, construction, reconstruction, commissioning, operation, conservation, and abandonment of buildings, structures, and

Table 10.3 Elements of an environmental study for the construction of a mine and the extraction of hard coal from the "Lublin" deposit within the planned mining area and site "Kulik" (Poland)

Area of activities	Range of activities
Noise protection solutions	The main sources of noise are those operating in the open space and cubic sources associated with the installed coal mining support equipment and coal transportation system. The main sources of external noise associated with mine operations will be: • Fan station; • Compressor station; • The mining shaft-skip, hoisting machinery and wheels of the shaft towers; • Coal yard and rail car loading equipment; • Car and rail traffic. The investor plans for all equipment in the mining plant to meet Polish and international requirements related to noise levels. The machinery used in the mining plant on the surface will be mostly located in buildings. The main fans will also be located in the building, which will significantly reduce the level of noise generated. Noise will also be controlled through careful selection of equipment, insulation, and sound-absorbing enclosures for individual pieces of equipment. Acceptable noise levels are not expected to be exceeded either during daytime or at night.
Solutions to protect air quality	For a planned mine, air pollution is mainly linked to the following factors: • Technological processes; • Combustion of fuels for heating purposes; • Transport and storage of coal, including loading on rail cars; • Mine ventilation system exhausting mine gases – post-shot gases, transport; and • Storage of coal and waste, as well as supporting works; • Workshop services. The mine will use all available means to prevent the introduction of pollutants into the ambient air. The rail cars will be loaded using purpose-built loading facilities. Plant shielding when the rail cars are filled will minimise dust emissions and eliminate wind impacts. The design of the loading installation will limit the height of discharge to minimise spoil crushing and reduce noise. Surface stockpiles of excavated material and conveyor belts will also be sources of dust. However, at these locations, it is anticipated that dumpers and conveyors equipped with water sprinkler systems will be used. On the other hand, washdown or water spraying will be used on vehicular haulage routes to de-volatilise dust, if required. The heating plant will be equipped with emission reduction devices required by law. It will be equipped with a flue gas control monitoring system. The level of emissions of harmful gases and dusts will be compliant with the requirements of Polish law and European directives.

(Continued)

Table 10.3 Continued

Area of activities	Range of activities
Waste management	Waste will be generated both at the stage of project preparation, i.e. preparation of land intended for construction of surface facilities, and during the deposit utilisation process. Actions intended to limit the amount of generated waste and limiting the types of waste, including the so-called hazardous waste will depend on the stage of investment. At the stage of preparing the project area the following are planned: • Minimising the amount of demolished objects functioning at present to the necessary minimum; • Segregation of waste produced as a result of demolition and disassembly of existing facilities; • Transferring the waste generated to companies which will primarily subject the waste to • recovery or recycling; It is assumed that transferring waste to landfills will be the last resort.
Earth surface protection methods	During the concession period, mining operations have been designed evenly over almost the entire area of the deposit. The following methods are expected to minimise the impact of mining on the area surface: • Coordination of mining in individual parcels and seams on a spatial-temporal basis taking into account the mining done and designed preventing the aggregation of factors; • Neighboring usage edges, including those by neighboring mines; • Taking advantage of the phenomenon of stress relaxation in surface objects, • Distribution of mining fields as evenly as possible over the entire mining area.

Source: PD Co., 2017

other facilities. General environmental issues in the Russian coal industry are discussed in a number of regulatory documents (Ministry of Energy of the Russian Federation, 2009; State Program, 2014; Strategy of Environmental Safety, 2017; Ministry of Energy of the Russian Federation, 2019; Program for the Development, 2020).

The Program for the Development of the Coal Industry of Russia for the period up to 2035 emphasises that the negative impact on the environment and the risks of introducing environmental restrictions arise due to the following: negative changes in environmental indicators demonstrated by coal producers; the introduction of restrictions on the use of coal for the generation of electricity and heat; more intense competition in the energy market due to the emergence of low-carbon energy sources, which may replace coal in the future. The subprogram named Ensuring the Environmental Safety of the Coal Industry is aimed at reducing the negative impact on the environment from the industrial activities of the coal industry.

The main measures included in the subprogram cover the following areas:

- improvement of the legal and regulatory framework for environmental protection;
- introducing organisational and technological measures aimed at improving the efficiency of environmental protection;
- scientific and technical support aimed at fostering interaction between market participants in the use of new technologies at coal-fired energy facilities;
- implementation of technological and technical measures;
- provision of greenhouse gas emission monitoring services in accordance with the established procedure and assessment of the reduction in emissions as a result of implementing the measures proposed for the long term.

Improving the regulatory and legal framework in the field of environmental protection includes tax incentives and discounts for environmental payment fees to those investing in environmentally friendly technologies; mechanisms for introducing the best available technologies; correction of outdated and development of new industry-specific regulatory and methodological documents.

The most significant organisational and technical measures aimed at improving environmental protection include assessment of the condition and efficiency of environmental facilities; developing solutions regarding mined-out areas that may cause emergencies; development and implementation by coal companies, together with regional administrations, of medium-term programs to ensure environmental safety, and others.

Scientific and technical support is aimed at preparing and justifying technological solutions for the treatment of mine and quarry wastewater; improving the efficiency of treatment facilities; methane drainage and utilisation; ventilation air methane utilisation; developing technologies for the formation of fire-safe waste rock dumps; developing biotechnologies for reclamation.

The implementation of technological and technical measures provides for the introduction of environmentally friendly, waste-free, and low-waste technologies and equipment and making widely used mining technologies and production processes greener taking into account the accumulated environmental damage.

The subprogram is financed by mining operators and the federal budget to complete measures for restructuring the coal industry in several areas: extinguishing waste rock dumps and man-made underground fires at abandoned mines; monitoring environmental impact; land reclamation, waste dump management, and elimination of waste stabilisation ponds.

The program is divided into three stages. The first stage (2019–2025) provides for the development of the regulatory framework, including the adoption of national standards in the coal industry. The second stage (2026–2030) provides for the implementation of innovative projects based on scientific and technical developments in Russia. The last stage (2031–2035) provides for meeting global standards in OSH and environmental protection.

In addition to the legislative regulation of environmental issues, public environmental organisations demonstrate a lot of awareness. For example, the goals of the *All-Russian Society for the Protection of Nature* (VOOP) include carrying out environmental monitoring using both in-house services and those provided by accredited companies and introducing modern high-precision technologies in order to implement effective state control over environmental indicators. The *Center for Environmental Policy of Russia* (CEPR) was established in 1993 as a public environmental organisation for expert support for the environmental movement and the development of recommendations for the legislative and executive authorities. The goal of the Green Movement is to change the attitude of the state and society to the environmental problems of Russia and mankind as a whole through organised political actions.

A number of environmental organisations focus their work on interaction with the population in order to raise environmental awareness and protect human rights to a healthy environment. The Vernadsky Non-Governmental Environmental Foundation has goals in the fields of promoting sustainable development, facilitating interaction between business, government, and society on sustainable development issues, and supporting environmental initiatives and projects. Such NGOs as Green Patrol, Green Cross, and Environmental Protection Teams (EPT) have similar functions.

Some environmental organisations are also involved in massive environmental campaigns. For example, the key task for EPT members is putting environmental ideas into practice. Practical issues are also addressed by the Russian Regional Environmental Centre (RREC), which is part of the network of regional environmental centres operating in Eastern Europe, the Caucasus, and Central Asia to support cooperation between authorities, the business community, and civil society in the field of environmental protection. The mission of the centre is to promote and implement advanced ideas, standards, and methods for the environmental well-being and sustainable development of Russia. Similar functions are performed by the Resource Ecology Public Fund, which carries out public control over compliance with the requirements of environmental legislation and takes into account public opinion in the implementation of the activities of mining companies.

The practical activities of environmental organisations and movements are especially important for mining regions. The first example is that of the Karakan natural reserve. In 2012, for the first time in the history of mining in Russia, a natural reserve was started on the territory that belonged to a mining company (Kuzbass Fuel Company OJSC) with the participation of the Administration of the Kemerovo Region, the scientific and environmental communities. It is located in the immediate vicinity of waste rock dumps and areas where drilling, blasting, and processing operations are performed. One of the key goals of establishing this reserve was to preserve the unique steppe ecosystems (Project of ..., 2015).

Ecologists' role in shaping sustainable development in extractive industries

Creating the right environmental policy for mines requires considering environmental issues throughout the life cycle of a mine, i.e. the following four phases:

- mineral exploration;
- mine development;
- mining operations;
- mine closure.

In each of these phases, implementation of processes must be considered in terms of the least possible negative impact on the environment. This can be achieved by introducing restrictive national legislation on environmental issues, such as the decarbonisation policy implemented by the European Union. Another key solution for shaping sustainable development in mines is implementation of voluntary pro-ecological solutions going beyond the legal regulations in force in a given country.

In 2002, the mining industry commissioned a comprehensive report that critically analysed the problems of sustainable development and identified ways to improve the existing environmental performance (IIED, 2002). The report led to a number of industry initiatives to promote responsible mining worldwide (Liebenthal et al., 2005). Several of these initiatives included standards to address the environmental and social determinants of mining operations. These industry standards have become part of the normative framework in mining because through their use the environmental performance of mining companies can be improved. Examples of these types of industry standards are shown in Table 10.4.

Some standards also have participatory governance principles whereby environmental organisations are also involved in decisions regarding the development of mining companies. Therefore, it can be assumed that the increasing proliferation of such standards along with various metrics can help constitute good practice for the industry as a whole.

Industry standards are usually voluntary and non-binding. However, it is important to note that they have been developed by industry experts with in-depth knowledge of mining. The opportunity for mining companies to gain a positive image as a result of implementing such standards, combined with the need to meet the expectations of their stakeholders – environmental organisations, customers, shareholders or the general public – is a good incentive for mining companies to implement such standards.

A sharp deterioration in the quality of air and water in coal-mining regions is becoming an incentive for the local population to act. Actions in this area are aimed at both the existing coal production facilities and new large investment projects, including those implemented in the coal industry. Mine development

Table 10.4 Examples of international mining sustainable development standards

Standard	Characteristic
ICMM Sustainable Development Framework	The standard was adopted in 2003 and is a key part of the work of the international mining industry body, the International Council on Mining and Metals (ICMM, formerly ICME). The ten principles in the framework cover governance, social and environmental performance. Compliance of member companies with boundaries is ensured by an external auditing body. In particular, Principle 6 deals with environmental performance in mining operations. According to it, it is necessary for mining operations to strive for continuous improvement in environmental issues such as water management, energy consumption and climate change.
Initiative for Responsible Mining Assurance (IRMA)	The Responsible Mining Assurance Standard is a standard first adopted in 2014 and revised in 2016. The standard applies to all types of mines and covers social and environmental responsibility requirements. The standard does not yet have a certification system.
The IFC Performance Standards on Environmental and Social Sustainability	The standard was adopted in 2006 (revised in 2012) and is used as a condition for private sector companies in obtaining loans from the International Finance Corporation (IFC), the private sector lending arm of the World Bank Group. The Principles consist of eight performance standards: assessment and management of environmental and social risks and impacts; labour and working conditions; resource efficiency and pollution prevention; community health, safety and security; land acquisition and involuntary resettlement; biodiversity, conservation and sustainable management of living natural resources; indigenous peoples and cultural heritage.

Source: IFC, 2012; Managing Mining, 2018; ICMM, 2021

operations in buffer zones around towns and cities can result in land subsidence and sinkholes, causing damage to houses.

In some towns of the Kuzbass region, the distance from residential buildings to the edge of the open-pit coal mine is 200 m, which is a violation of the requirements for the minimum buffer zone between industrial and residential areas (a minimum of 1,000 m for objects of the first class of hazard that open-pit coal mines belong to). In some cases, maximum allowable concentrations and land disturbance are exceeded. Also, displacement and resettlement compensations are sometimes not paid. There have been cases of violation of the rights of indigenous small-numbered peoples in connection with the degradation of the territories of their residence and the impossibility for them to continue with the traditional way of life because of coal mining operations.

As a result, Kuzbass, being a coal-mining region with a trend towards increasing coal production, is becoming a place where residents protest and strive to exercise their rights to a clean and safe natural environment, reliable information about its condition, and compensation for damage caused to their property and health. Residents of many cities and towns of Kuzbass are very active and turn to the local authorities in connection with the negative impact of coal companies on the environment (Solov'eva and Slivyak, 2020).

In the regions where mining facilities have appeared only recently, there have also been cases of violation of the rights of the indigenous population with a partial property loss (for example, deer herds of the Evenki people) (Berezhnoj, 2020).

The Ekozashchita environmental group is a successful social institute that is active in coal-mining regions. Environmental activists publish photos and videos, gather signatures, and send letters to the local authorities. The report titled Russia's Coal Industry: Impact on the Environment and Public Health and Prospects for Regional Development published by the group is the first independent assessment of the destructive impact of the Russian coal industry on the environment and population living near mining facilities and coal-fired power plants (Sysoeva and Savvateeva, 2020).

Such forms of activity support local residents, which leads to changes in regulations concerning land use, hinders land withdrawal, and raises public awareness. According to the authors, the main problem is disconnectedness. Actions are taken only at the local level and there is not enough coordination between environmental groups that are focused on individual problems associated with the anthropogenic impact of city-forming enterprises. Bigger environmental organisations and movements are better structured and propose action plans, but the scope of their activities is very wide, and their operations are mainly of an informational and educational nature.

Bibliography

Berezhnoj, S.E. (2020). *Promyshlennye kompanii i korennye narody. Opyt Rossijskoj Federacii.* http://www.pandia.org/text/77/295/81354.php [access date: 30. 03. 2021].

Bian, Z., Inyang, H.I., Daniels, J.L., Otto, F., Struthers, S. (2010). Environmental Issues from Coal Mining and Their Solutions. *Mining Science and Technology*, 20(2), 215–223.

EIA (US Energy Information Administration) (2020). Coal Explained. Coal and Environmenthttps://www.eia.gov/energyexplained/coal/coal-and-the-environment.php [access date: 29. 03. 2021].

Environment and Society Portal (1924). All-Russian Society for the Protection of Nature. https://www.environmentandsociety.org/tools/keywords/foundation-all-russian-society-protection-nature [access date: 30. 03. 2021].

Flannery, T. (2015). *Atmosphere of Hope. Solutions to the Climate Crisis.* London: Penguin Books.

Forbes (2012). Corruption Interferes with Cleaning the Air of Kazakhstan from Hazardous Emissions from Thermal Power Plants. https://forbes.kz/process/probing/pyil_vekov [access date: 30. 03. 2021].

GEM (Global Energy Monitor Wiki) (2020). Environmental Impacts of Coal. https://www.gem.wiki/Environmental_impacts_of_coal [access date: 29. 03. 2021].

Goswami, S. (2015). Impact of Coal Mining on Environment. *European Researcher*, 92(2), 185–196.

Hamilton, M.S. (2005). *Mining Environmental Policy: Comparing Indonesia and the USA*. Ashgate Studies in Environmental Policy and Practice. Burlington, VT: Ashgate Publishing.

Harionovskij, A.A., Danilova, M.Y. (2020). Dolevoe uchastie ugol'noj promyshlennosti v negativnom vozdejstvii na okruzhayushchuyu sredu. *Nauchno-tekhnicheskij vestnik*, 1, 86–93.

Hendryx, M., Islam, M.S., Dong, G.H., Paul, G. (2020). Air Pollution Emissions 2008–2018 from Australian Coal Mining: Implications for Public and Occupational Health. *International Journal of Environmental Research and Public Health*, 7, 1570. doi:10.3390/ijerph1705157.

ICMM (International Council on Mining and Metals) (2021). The Sustainable Development Goals. https://www.icmm.com/en-gb/mining-metals/making-a-positive-contribution/sdgs [access date: 29. 03. 2021].

IFC (International Finance Corporation) (2012). *Performance Standards on Environmental and Social Sustainability*. Washington: The World Bank. https://www.canada.ca/content/dam/esdc-edsc/migration/documents/wps/wcm/connect/115482804a0255db96fbffd1a5d13d27/PS_English_2012_Full-Document.pdf [access date: 29. 03. 2021].

IIED (International Institute of Environment and Development) (2002). *Mining, Minerals and Sustainable Development (MMSD) Report*. Breaking New Grounds January 2002. Routledge. doi:10.4324/9781315541501

Jhariya, D., Khan, R., Takur, G.S. (2016). Impact of Mining Activity on Water Resource: An Overview Study. Proceedings of the Recent Practices and Innovations in Mining Industry. Raipur: India, 19–20.

Kalmykov, D.E., Malikova, A.D. (2017). Zagnannye v ugol'. Obzor ugledobycha i ugol'naya energogeneraciya v kazahstane. *Sostoyanie i perspektivy*. Karaganda.

Khanna, A.A. (2013). *Governance in Coal Mining: Issues and Challenges*. The Energy and Resources Institute, TERI-NFA Working Papers, 9, 4–42.

Liebenthal, A., Michelitsch, R., Tarazona, E. (2005). *Extractive Industries and Sustainable Development: An Evaluation of World Bank Group Experience*. Washington, DC: World Bank. https://openknowledge.worldbank.org/handle/10986/736

Ministry of Energy of the Russian Federation (2009). Energy Strategy of Russia for the period up to 2030. Energeticheskaya strategiya Rossii na period do 2030 goda utverzhdennaya rasporyazheniem Pravitel'stva Rossijskoj Federacii ot 13 noyabrya 2009 g. No. 1715-r.

Ministry of Energy of the Russian Federation (2019). Energy Security Doctrine of the Russian Federation. Doktrina energeticheskoj bezopasnosti Rossijskoj Federacii utverzhdennaya Ukazom Prezidenta Rossijskoj Federacii ot 13 maya 2019 g. No. 216.

PD Co. (2017). *Budowa kopalni wydobywanie kopaliny – węgla kamiennego ze złoża „Lublin" w granicach projektowanego obszaru i terenu górniczego „Kulik"*, Warszawa-Lublin: Multiconsult Polska. http://www.ugcyow.pl/asp/pliki/pobierz/tom_iv_ros_streszczenie_niespecjalistyczne.pdf [access date: 29. 03. 2021].

Program for the Development of the Coal Industry in Russia for the Period Until 2035 (2020). Programma razvitiya ugol'noj promyshlennosti Rossii na period do 2035 goda utverzhdena rasporyazheniem Pravitel'stva Rossijskoj Federacii ot 13 iyunya 2020 g. No. 1582-r.

Project of Biodiversity Conservation in Policies and Programs for the Development of the Energy Sector in Russia (2015). https://docplayer.ru/37424040-Sbornik-innovacionnyh-resheniy-po-sohraneniyu-bioraznoobraziya-dlya-ugledobyvayushchego-sektora-pervaya-versiya.html [access date: 30. 03. 2021].

Shrader-Frechette, K. (2011). *What Will Work: Fighting Climate Change with Renewable Energy, Not Nuclear Power.* Oxford University Press.

Solov'eva, E., Slivyak, V. (2020). *Gonka po niskhodyashchej. Posledstviya shirokomasshtabnoj dobychi uglya v Kuzbasse dlya okruzhayushchej sredy i zdorov'ya naseleniya.* Doklad podgotovlen gruppoj «Ekozashchita!». Kuzbass-Moskva-Kaliningrad. https://ecdru.files. wordpress.com/2020/10/race-to-the-bottom1.pdf [access date: 30. 03. 2021].

State Program of the Russian Federation (2014). Gosudarstvennaya programma Rossijskoj Federacii "Ohrana okruzhayushchej sredy", utverzhdennaya postanovleniem Pravitel'stva Rossijskoj Federacii ot 15 aprelya 2014(a) No. 326.

Strategy of Environmental Safety of the Russian Federation for the Period up to 2025 (2017). Strategiya ekologicheskoj bezopasnosti Rossijskoj Federacii na period do 2025 goda utverzhdennaya Ukazom Prezidenta Rossijskoj Federacii ot 19 aprelya 2017 g. No. 176.

Sysoeva, N.A., Savvateeva, O.A. (2020). Environmental Aspects of the Coal Mining Industry. http://www.mining-portal.ru/publish/ekologicheskie-aspektyi-ugledobyiva yuschey-otrasli/ [access date: 29. 03. 2021].

Tiwary, R.K. (2001). Environmental Impact of Coal Mining on Water Regime and Its Management. *Water, Air, & Soil Pollution,* 132 (1–2), 185–199.

UNDP (2018). *Managing Mining for Sustainable Development. A Sourcebook.* UNDP Bangkok Regional Hub and Poverty-Environment Initiative Asia-Pacific of UNDP and UN Environment. https://www.google.com/url?sa=t&rct=j&q=&esrc=s&source=web&cd= &ved=2ahUKEwjYwNH-69XvAhWGlosKHa5SBtEQFjABegQIBhAD&url=https%3A %2F%2Fwww.undp.org%2Fcontent%2Fdam%2Fundp%2Flibrary%2FSustainable%2520D evelopment%2FExtractives%2FUNDP-MMFSD-LowResolution.pdf&usg=AOvVaw2U Sb1IvAqGd5boT3JG00OX [access date: 29. 03. 2021].

Union of Concerned Scientists (2017). Coal and Air Pollution. https://www.ucsusa. org/resources/coal-and-air-pollution [access date: 29. 03. 2021].

World Coal Institute (2015). Environmental Impacts of Coal Mining. https://web. archive.org/web/20081023173007/http://www.worldcoal.org/pages/content/index. asp?PageID=126 [access date: 29. 03. 2021].

11 The voice of local, regional and national societies in the lifecycle of a coal mining enterprise

Social problems in the lifecycle of a coal mining enterprise

When talking about the impact of social organisations on sustainable development in coal production and the possibility of achieving a balance of expectations of these organisations and coal producers, it is necessary to start from the concept of the so-called social licence to operate (SLO). This concept is defined by the *World Business Council for Sustainable Development* as the ongoing commitment of business to contribute to economic development while improving the quality of life of the workforce and their families as well as communities and society (Riabova and Didyk, 2014). Starting from the concept of social licence to operate during mining operations, social impact assessments of mine operations should be conducted regularly. Social impact assessment can be used to consider the acceptability of a given mining project by the local community. This approach is often combined in practice with the activities of environmental organisations described earlier in this chapter. In essence, SLO assumes that a mining company should seek to minimise the harmful effects of mining activities while maximising the economic benefits to the region. Balancing these components expresses the mining industry's desire for sustainable development. Table 11.1 presents a model of factors affecting SLO levels according to Boutlier and Thomson's concept. This model can be used in practice to analyse specific problems of balancing mining company and community expectations.

According to the information in Table 11.1, mining companies must obtain socio-political approval for a mining project. They must also have international trust. This principle is a green light for approval for mining operations. The absence of any of the defining elements of the model reduces the likelihood of approval for a mining project and increases the risk of local or regional conflict.

Mineral resources serve the entire society, but despite this, local communities are generally sceptical of specific mining projects in their neighbourhoods (Hilson, 2002; Badera, 2010). The reason for this scepticism is the uneven distribution of negative and positive impacts associated with mining activities.

The local and regional community is directly exposed to the negative consequences of mining operations. Its exposure to mining risk is thus much

DOI: 10.4324/9781003091110-15

Table 11.1 Factors constituting social licence to operate in mining enterprises

Level and label	Description	Role in determining SLO
Economic legitimacy	The perception that a particular project or company offers a benefit to the perceiver.	If lacking, most stakeholders will withhold or withdraw SLO. If present, many will grant an acceptance level of SLO.
Socio-political legitimacy	The perception that the project or company contributes to the well-being of the region, respects the local way of life, meets expectations about its role in society and acts in accordance with stakeholders' views of fairness.	If lacking, approval level of SLO is less likely. If both this and international trust are lacking, approval level is rarely granted by any stakeholder.
International trust	The perception that the company and its management listen, respond, keep promises, engage in mutual dialogue and exhibit reciprocity in their interactions.	If lacking, approval level of SLO is less likely. If both this and socio-political legitimacy are lacking, approval level is rarely granted.
Institutionalised trust	The perception that relations between the stakeholders' institutions (for example a community's representative organisations) and the project or organisation are based on an enduring regard for each other's interests.	If lacking, psychological identification is unlikely. If lacking but both socio-political legitimacy and international trust are present, most stakeholders will grant approval level of SLO.

Source: Boutlier and Thomson, 2011; Williams and Walton, 2013; Kokko et al., 2015

higher than that of other natural resource beneficiaries. And, as often mentioned, the full range of mining risks is very complex and multi-faceted. Table 11.2 provides an overview of the typical risks that local communities fear from the operations of mining companies.

Due to the threats listed in Table 11.2, NGOs and local communities remain in opposition to mining. This situation leads to frequent social conflicts regarding the possibility of existence and development of mines (Badera, 2018). At the same time, conflict related to mining activities means the occurrence of such a situation in which the following circumstances occur simultaneously:

- The presence of two or more parties, mutually dependent on each other by taking or not taking action;
- Occurrence of differences of interests, opinions, attitudes, goals in the subject of use of the space where the deposit occurs;
- Inability of the parties to realise their goals, tasks, attitudes, interests in the subject of utilisation of the space, where the deposit occurs, without other parties' participation;

Table 11.2 The threats of mining to humans and the environment

Main elements of the natural and social environment	Threats caused by mining
Humans	Direct and indirect threat to health or life
Air	Natural and blasting gases, dust, radioactive contamination
Potable water	Quantity degradation (drainage) and quality degradation (contamination) of water
Land surface and bedrock	Continuous and discontinuous flooding deformations, para-seismic phenomena
Soils	Total removal or contamination of soil layer
Agricultural and forestry crops, livestock and associated products (food and non-food)	Removal of crops and livestock or contamination of products
Acoustic environment	Noise
Infrastructure (residential, transport, industrial and other)	Decommissioning of infrastructure, mining damage related to surface deformation, stone spreading, etc.
Tourism and recreation values (including nature and culture)	Loss of recreational and tourist functions, especially possibility of contact with widely understood "nature".
Other measurables (e.g. property value, sources and level of income)	Decrease in property value, loss of sources or level of income
Other non-quantifiable factors	Necessity to renovate, change the place of residence and/or lifestyle

Source: Badera, 2010

- Active actions taken by the conflicting parties, blocking the realisation of intentions of the opposing party.

(Ptak, 2019)

Previous studies and observations show that the main and most common causes of mining conflicts include:

- Strong impact of the mining plant on the environment, in particular dust, drainage, and noise;
- Nuisances related to the transportation of excavated material;
- Occurrence of other protected goods;
- Occurrence of large-scale surface transformations;
- Nuisance caused by conducting blasting works;
- Leaving areas devastated and degraded by mining activities.

(Ptak et al., 2020)

In developing countries, the above catalogue is generally somewhat broader and additionally includes:

- anti-extractivism and cultural friction over resources usage,
- short-time decision making applied to long-term challenges,
- weak government capacity, corruption and lack of transparency,
- legacies of state repression,
- poverty and marginalisation of poor local communities,
- demand of greater share of benefits.

(Morrice and Colaguiri, 2013; Haslam and Tanimoune, 2016; Andrews et al., 2017)

The above-mentioned circumstances result from differences in the level of economic and civilisation development between representatives of local communities and owners of mining companies. They result in a number of ethical and moral abuses, which in the long run even more strongly destroy the value and image of the mining industry.

The structure of social conflicts around mining projects is complex in nature. Its major components are shown in Table 11.3.

According to the information in Table 11.3, conflicts can arise from legal differences and gaps that result in insufficient protection of societal interests. They can also result from a lack of communication and proper flow of information between conflicting parties. Finally, they may be of a more serious nature, related to different views. The first two causes can be mitigated and eliminated through legal improvements or negotiations. The third one requires long-term actions and is the most difficult to eliminate. Changing values is not easy and requires, if at all possible, considerable negotiation efforts and many positive experiences of cooperation. In practice, the occurrence of this reason may constitute the most significant barrier to the functioning and development of a mining enterprise.

Table 11.3 Components of conflict in mining

Component	Characteristic
Structural component	It results directly from the applicable law, which differentiates between the various parties to environmental and planning proceedings in terms of the strength of the impact (opinion, consent and decision are not mutually equivalent).
Data conflict	It results from the deficiencies of information policies implemented (or not) by decision-making bodies or companies, and the specific positions from which various types of media, especially social media, operate.
Conflict of tangible or intangible interests	There are conflicting interests in the socio-economic phenomenon among the mining stakeholders. Especially, conflicts of values and conflicts of relationships based on strong emotions are difficult because they are not negotiated.

Source: Badera, 2010

How do societies negotiate their rights and requirements? Case studies

In order to solve social conflicts in the mining sector, negotiations supported by extensive information campaigns are most often used. As for Poland, conflicts concerning mining activities occurred and still occur relatively often. However, it is worth adding at the very beginning that the views of the local community in the course of a conflict are not homogeneous. A mining project neighbourhood often includes both its supporters and opponents living there. However, the former usually do not actively participate in the conflict and tacitly accept the intentions of mining companies. The opponents are definitely more visible and mobilised to protest.

Usually, the consent for operations increases with the distance from the deposit according to the so-called NIMBY (Not In My Backyard) principle (Żylicz, 2007). The voice of the local community is articulated during various meetings, rallies and demonstrations. During the time of widespread access to the Internet, blogs, discussion forums, and in recent years social networking sites have also become a popular form of civic discussion.

Although the voice of citizens does not have to take institutionalised forms, sometimes they form protest committees operating informally or acting as associations for the purposes of conflict (Popa et al., 2016). In some cases, opponents of mining companies become local NGOs operating in the area, established independently of the conflict with mining (Munnik, 2010). Various other economic entities, budgetary units and other types of social organisations operating in the area, whose interests sometimes conflict with those of the mining company, also take part in conflicts (Badera, 2010). An important role in the conflict is also played by the media, including local newspapers, TV, Internet portals and social media. The behavior of these entities and the way of presenting information related to mining investments has a very significant impact on the course and outcome of the conflict.

Other entities participating in conflicts are local authorities at different levels. These authorities, and in particular the local municipal or district administration, are not only a party but also an important decision-maker in conflicts between mines and the local community. The authorities give opinions, agree and issue decisions and concessions for mining companies. Local authorities, aware of certain benefits for their administrative units due to mining activities and realising the risks associated with the activities of mines in the process of making final decisions typically consider the following criteria:

- Their own visions of the development of a given region, resulting from the hierarchy of importance;
- Directions of spatial development imposed by existing documents and local spatial development plans;

- Various types of formal and informal pressure from the investor, other business entities and NGOs;
- Opinions of the local community, which the decision-maker identifies as the voice of the voters.

(Badera, 2010)

In Table 11.4 several examples are presented – case studies – of how different conflict situations between mining companies and the local community were resolved. The examples are from Poland and Germany. Also, to internationalise the topic and to develop the comparative scale, the table also presents an example of mining in Ghana.

The examples presented in Table 11.4 show that conflicts related to mining operations can be effectively resolved by negotiating and offering compensation for the harmful impacts of mining companies. This is possible not only in highly developed countries such as Germany, but also in developing countries (Poland) or those aspiring to faster economic development (Ghana). However, it is notable that the negotiating power of local communities seems to depend on their level of independence, democracy and economic well-being.

The main reasons for the emergence of the "social licence" concept in many countries are: new approaches to local development and self-development, awareness of the place and role of the local community as the main element of the local self-government system, expanding the participation of the local population in the preparation and implementation of decisions (Riabova and Didyk, 2014).

In Ukraine, in 2021, the local population rallied against the development of a zirconium deposit near Mariupol and the extraction of shale gas near Kharkov. The residents of the Zaporozhye region are currently protesting against kaolin mining. The main problems and concerns of the Ukrainians are a significant technogenic impact on land and water resources and alienation of inhabited lands, where the population density is quite high (Karachun, 2021).

Residents of the Alai region of Kyrgyzstan are against the development of a coal deposit, which is located two and a half thousand metres from their village. The reason for the rallies is the protection of territories from cutting down trees and pollution of the Gulcho River (Radio Azartyk, 2020).

Many mining sites in Kyrgyzstan were targeted by local residents in 2020 amid political protests. During the days of mass protests in October 2020 in Bishkek, several large deposits of coal, copper and gold were seized. In the Naryn region, the Kara-Keche coal deposit in the Naryn region was seized, which threatened to disrupt the heating season in the capital, since the coal from this deposit is supplied to the Bishkek thermal power plant (Interfax, 2020).

Three mining companies – "Bereket-Ken", "Nark-Too" and "Open pit Min-Kush", which mined coal in the Naryn region of Kyrgyzstan, were forced to stop operations because local residents blocked the roads leading to the deposits they were developing. The main complaints of the local population of Kyrgyzstan are the total impoverishment of the population against the use of

Table 11.4 International examples of conflicts in the mining industry

Conflict	Characteristics
Problems with former mining areas in Saxony	In the geological conditions of Lusatia, former mining areas may become unstable due to the large-scale re-elevation of groundwater even if further opencast mines are closed in the vicinity. German mining law is not in agreement as to whether a newly established mining company can also be held liable for the consequences of this renewed rise in groundwater.
	The Federal Republic of Germany, as the entity responsible for the reclamation of coal mining in the former GDR, and the Free State of Saxony have therefore agreed on the removal of such risks in former mining areas, financing these measures 50–50.
	The Saxon State Mining Authority, as the police authority responsible for the prevention of hazards in connection with old spoil heaps and excavated areas, orders the necessary measures, which are then implemented by the federal mining rehabilitation authority.
	Due to the need to implement appropriate safety measures and the fact that the owners (or users) of the unprotected areas cannot use them during this period, including buildings, crops, etc., the Saxon Police Act stipulates that they must be paid property damage compensation for this period. In this particular case, after reclamation and the expiration of the ban on use, the land can be used again by its owners, since neither the sale nor the expropriation of the properties in question took place here.
	Both the subject matter of the compensation and its amount were disputed in the present case, and thus the case went to court without waiting for the conclusion of the formal administrative proceedings.
	Before proceeding, the court recommended an amicable settlement between the owners of the affected land and the Saxon State Mining Authority in Freiberg. The parties agreed to this and proceeded to settle the dispute amicably. Through mediation, an agreement was reached that spared the parties from tedious and lengthy court proceedings.
Transport route from the mine in Poland	The mine is adjacent to a town. Over the years, the transport of ore from the mine has taken place by rail and road. The road of wheeled transport of aggregate export from the mine passed through the centre of the town in the vicinity of the kindergarten, school, and municipal office. Periodically, when no railroad transport was available, it was the only way of transporting aggregate from the mine. A large part of the road was in a bad technical condition. The additional nuisance of this transport was the frequent congestion of cars waiting for loading in front of the mining plant. This situation caused dissatisfaction among the residents. According to them, the nuisance posed a threat to life and health. In this conflict situation, the local authorities decided in 2011 to move transport from the city centre to the outskirts of the city by a roundabout. This was only possible with the cooperation of the municipality, which prepared the land for the road construction in cooperation with the mine. The mining company built the new road in 2012 using its own funds and then donated it to the municipality. In addition, the company repaired a section of a damaged municipal road, which had previously been used for transportation from the mine.

Conflict	Characteristics
Particulate matter nuisance to the community – Poland	The mine has been the target of numerous complaints regarding nuisance emissions. Among the complainants were the local residents who also included employees of the mine. As a result of numerous meetings, the mining entrepreneur together with the local authorities developed alternative transport routes. As of 09/2016, truck transport has been shifted to the bypass road (partially financed by the mine). From the organisational and ad hoc actions that contributed to solving the problem, it is necessary to mention the orders of the mining supervisory authority on: • Regular road cleaning; • Spraying the access roads to the mine and in the mine; • Inspection of the technical condition of the de-dusting plant and wheel washers; • Regular cleaning of the processing plant yards; • Spraying of finished products storage yards; • Greening of redundant areas.
Land ownership – Ghana	Land ownership is also a key issue in conflicts in African countries. For example, in Prestea, Ghana, a local mining group was in conflict with the local community over mining concessions. While the mining company claimed to have exclusive rights to the land, having obtained the required permits and leases, the local community believes that it should have the right of final decision regarding the land proceedings. On the other hand, the government's opinion is that it has the right to decide on mining concessions arguing the good of the country as a whole. The conflict was resolved through mediation with local authorities. It is typical of African countries where there are often no clear land tenure rights.

Source: based on Abuya, 2018; Ptak et al., 2020

labour migration from China, the deterioration of the environment in the mining areas, the seizure of land used for cattle breeding and agriculture (CSR Central Asia, 2021).

In the countries of Central Asia, the government is not involved in the process of providing companies with access to mining fields; therefore, in the event of a conflict with the local community, the solution of the problem directly depends on the company itself. Foreign companies that develop deposits in Central Asia are largely interested in the loyalty of the local population, and therefore strive to conduct educational activities on the interaction of companies and local communities. In 2017, the German Society for International Cooperation (GIZ) issued Guidelines for Mining Companies "Establishing good community relations", which provides information on the legal framework for regulating social licences, procedures for holding public hearings and methods of interaction between local communities and mining companies (IBC, 2018). The Guidelines are based on the realities of Kyrgyzstan and offer practical solutions for building strong relationships between companies and local communities. The main problems of the interaction were identified through interviews, the results of which were analysed against the international best practices. Based on the results, recommendations were developed for the implementation of approaches that help to establish strong and respectable relations between companies and local communities in Kyrgyzstan.

The project for the development of the Elegeskoye coal deposit in Russia has been keeping the local population in suspense for 10 years due to the constantly changing plans of investors. Despite the fact that a licence, including a social one, for development has been obtained and the local population has been promised a developed railway infrastructure, the population of the republic still has a negative attitude towards the project, fearing "a noticeable change in the ethnic makeup" (RIA Federal Press, 2020).

In Russia, an acute situation is developing in the Kemerovo region, where the company SDS-Ugol plans to develop the licenced areas "Chernigovskaya Mine Field" and "Yuzhny". The local population protests against these projects, since the documentation explicitly states that "the seizure of a land plot for mining coal reserves in an open way will affect the natural environment," in particular, "the recreational function will be reduced, bioproductivity will decrease, surface pollution by coal dust and wind erosion products of rock dumps will increase" (Stepanova, 2020).

In the Primorsky Territory of Russia, the problem of using coal terminals is also acute: closed technologies for handling coal and ores are not used in the country, while the turnover of coal is constantly increasing. Plans for the construction of new handling terminals cause a direct conflict of interest. The relatively small length of the coastline of southern Primorye, free from environmental restrictions in the areas of reserves, sanctuaries and natural monuments, is in the sphere of interests of several potential investors at once. Situations arise when mutually exclusive industries, such as a fish processing plant and an open terminal for handling coal, lay claim to one area of interest (Morvesti.ru, 2015).

In Russia, there are factors that increase the importance of a social licence not only for companies, but for residents of single-industry towns that were founded and exist only in connection with the activities of mining companies, especially in the Arctic regions, where the development of alternative types of economic activity is extremely difficult (Masloboev et al., 2015). In these conditions, the requirements of the local community should be considered; otherwise the likelihood of a serious social conflict increases significantly.

Anglo-Saxon case law gives more favourable conditions for the practical application of the concept of social licence (Thomson and Boutilier, 2011). In countries where legislative norms of civil law prevail (e.g. Russia) only official authorities can provide a licence for entrepreneurial activity. Many companies consider a government-granted mining licence as a single and sufficient authority. Although a social licence is an informal institution, as world practice shows, it is one of the most important additional conditions for the implementation of mining projects with minimal socio-political and financial risks (Riabova and Didyk, 2014).

Societies in shaping sustainable development in extractive industries

To summarise the considerations in this chapter, it can be said that conflict resolution activities in the mining industry can be divided into two groups: (1) preventive, i.e. conflict prevention and (2) causal, i.e. conflict resolution. Table 11.5 shows both

Table 11.5 Conflict prevention and resolution in the mining industry

Conflict prevention in the mining industry	Conflict resolution in the mining industry
• Clarification of legal and environmental regulations, which are the basis for defining the rights and obligations of the parties and their mutual relationships • Taking care of a high quality of communication with establishing e. g. rules of information, procedure or exchange of information • Disclosure of interests, opinions, goals in an unambiguous way by the conflicting parties • Focusing on the issue and not on the person; • Looking to the future, not the past, without seeking blame • Educating at every level about the raw material needs of the economy • Avoiding blocking behaviour in communication, such as judging or moralising.	• Listening to the complainant, their expectations and the nature of the problem • Establishing facts based on documents, expertise, available analyses, inspections and reports • Appointing trustworthy people with authority, knowledge and personal skills for interviews • Maintaining good public relations for a good image, good press and media, including the organisation of e.g. meetings for children, young people or inhabitants, familiarising them with the profile and nature or the mine • Engaging in the life of the local community • Informing in a language understandable for the group of recipients about the plans and program being implemented • Transparent environmental reports as part of corporate social responsibility • Constantly monitoring the fulfillment of promises and commitments made to the local community • Taking preemptive actions, resulting from the current situation of the company in the context of the time needed to prepare information campaigns or preventive actions • Building human potential through employment of the region's residents • Presenting several options of solutions in case of the most difficult situations and their joint analysis to strengthen the feeling of participation in the decision-making process among all the parties involved

Source: Hilson, 2002; Kramer et al., 2005; Ptak et al., 2020

groups of activities. It specifically includes those activities that work particularly well in resolving conflict situations in the mining industry.

All of the activities listed in Table 11.5 are transparent, communicative, and ethical. Without these features, an effective dialogue with local communities is not possible. In such a case, it becomes impossible to balance economic and social priorities, so important for the concept of corporate social responsibility (CSR).

Conflict resolution in the mining industry is a very complex process; nevertheless its success is determined in particular by the following factors:

- Changes in legislation, on the one hand aimed at simplifying it and on the other hand enriching it with the so-called social impact assessment;
- Improvement of the industry's image through appropriate creation of the information policy and changes in the way of education from the youngest age;
- Valorisation of deposits and granting selected sites the status of public purposes in the legal sense (exploitation of these deposits as a public purpose investment);
- Assigning greater importance to social consultations, e.g. by realistically including local opinion leaders in the decision-making process and increasing the role of mediators (specialising in mining industry issues);
- Further research on the role of emotions, in order to develop methods to improve relations among stakeholders;
- In the case of African countries with land tenure issues, it is important to carefully define these issues in local law.

(Suopajärvi, 2013; Belzyt, 2017; Dutkowski, 2017;
Abuya, 2018; Badera, 2018)

Mining companies are increasingly accepting community expectations and trying to meet them as part of their corporate social responsibility strategy. In response to the expectations of the local community, mining companies often implement or finance initiatives for its development. In doing so, they seek to build good relationships with local communities and gain a social licence to operate. Such initiatives usually focus on areas such as health, education, infrastructure and business development.

Social activities aimed at building good relations with the local community carried out by mining companies can take the following forms of activities (UNDP and UN Environment, 2018):

- Philanthropic activities for the benefit of various social groups, taking various forms: cash or in-kind assistance; equipment and supplies.
- Funding and implementation of social campaigns and programs such as social welfare programs, skill and capacity building programs for example among children and awareness campaigns.
- Funding and construction of social infrastructure such as schools, hospitals and housing.
- Funding development programs through grants to local organisations.

- Payments to third parties or government funds used for social purposes such as improving education and health outcomes.
- Large mining companies sometimes recruit community relations officers or specialised corporate social responsibility units to implement local development initiatives and engage local communities. Companies may also partner with NGOs and international organisations. This type of activity helps to establish good relations with the local community and helps to reduce the occurrence of conflicts between the community and the mining company.

In underground mining enterprises, which are potentially hazardous, accidents can have an impact on the population, urban infrastructure, buildings (objects), and on the environment in general. Sometimes the extraction of minerals has catastrophic consequences due to insufficiently studied geological anomalies in the deposit structure, an accidental combination of natural and man-made factors, and errors in the engineering of mining operations and exploitation of deposits. Given these circumstances, obtaining a "social licence" to operate or develop new deposits largely depends on the effectiveness of the interaction between mining companies, the population and authorities at different levels.

Jonek-Kowalska's work (Jonek-Kowalska et al., 2018) reveals that the key external stakeholders in long-term mining projects are the local population, state authorities of various levels and local self-government. The local population has a varying interest depending on the type of territory being developed: in old industrial regions, the local population has a high interest in the environmental compliance of project implementation, the development of urban infrastructure, the creation of new jobs; in regions of new development, the local population is identified as expecting stakeholders.

The interests of each specific stakeholder do not meet the requirement to maximise overall economic benefits, hence conflicts may arise. Federal authorities require strict compliance with legal requirements in terms of the integrated and rational use of mineral resources and industrial safety. Regional authorities aim to comply with legal requirements related to the environment and construction of facilities. The local population strives to protect the environment of the region and is interested in creating jobs and developing social infrastructure. Investors are eager to develop their companies, and at the same time they have to comply with the requirements of the federal and regional authorities, the local population.

Many social initiatives of mining companies do not produce the desired results. Therefore, the traditional approaches to working with local communities and government should be reconsidered. Total automation and robotisation of mining work processes intensify the problem with employment of the local population. One of the terms of contracts concerning the relationship between mining companies and local communities was creation of jobs. As digitalisation spreads, the content of such a "social contract" may change. Mining companies will have to analyse the needs of the local community, develop a strategy for additional education for workers and try to involve local suppliers in their production chains.

The task of mining companies will be, not only the assessment of the key stakeholders, but also entering into partnerships with industry trading groups, identifying the urgent needs of the local population and finding common interests shared by the authorities and the community. For mining companies, it is possible to move from compensating for negative impacts (in the form of donations, charity or providing benefits when giving employment) to active interaction at the level of co-investment in business (Calam, 2018).

Bibliography

Abuya, W.O. (2018). Mining Conflicts and Corporate Social Responsibility in Kenya's Nascent Mining Industry: A Call for Legislation, Social Responsibility. *IntechOpen*, https://www.intechopen.com/books/social-responsibility/mining-conflicts-and-corporate-social-responsibility-in-kenya-s-nascent-mining-industry-a-call-for-l [access date: 29. 03. 2021].

Andrews, T., Elizalde, B., Le Billon, P., Oh, C.H., Reyes, D., Thomson, I. (2017). The Rise in Conflict Associated with Mining Operations: What Lies Beneath? *Canadian International Resources and Development Institute*.

Badera, J. (2010). Social Conflicts on the Environmental Background Related to Development of Mineral Deposits in Poland. *Mineral Resources Management*, 26(1), 105–125.

Badera, J. (2018). Geneza konfliktów społeczno-środowiskowych związanych z górnictwem. *Górnictwo Odkrywkowe*, 3, 28–30.

Belzyt, J.I. (2017). The Relationship with the Other as a Platform for Discussion about Conflicts. Comments on the Orzesze Coal Mine Project. *Environmental & Socio-economic Studies*, 5(2), 19–26.

Boutilier, R.G., Thomson, I. (2011). Modelling and Measuring the Social License to Operate: Fruits of a Dialogue between Theory and Practice. Social license.com. http://socialicense.com/publications/Modelling%20and%20Measuring%20the%20SLO.pdf [access date: 29. 03. 2021].

Calam, C. (2018). 2018 Deloitte Report – Mining Industry Trends and Challenges. *Thermo Fisher Scientific*. https://www.thermofisher.com/blog/mining/2018-deloitte-report-mining-industry-trends-and-challenges/ [access date: 31. 03. 2021].

CSR Central Asia (2021). Publications. http://csr-ca.com/publications/ [access date: 30. 03. 2021].

Dutkowski, M. (2017). Ekologiczne konflikty emocji. W: Badera, J. (Ed.), II Interdyscyplinarne Seminarium pt. Konflikty w gospodarowaniu przestrzenią i zasobami Ziemi. Sosnowiec, 28–29 września 2017.

Haslam, P.A., Tanimoune, N.A. (2016). The Determinants of Social Conflict in the Latin American Mining Sector: New Evidence with Quantitative Data. *World Development*, 78, 401–419.

Hilson, G. (2002). An Overview of Land Use Conflicts in Mining Communities. *Land Use Policy*, 19, 65–73.

IBC (2018). GIZ Guide To Building Successful Mining Companies' Interactions with Local Communities. http://www.ibc.kg/ru/analysis/articles/3063_rukovodstvo_giz_po_postroeniyu_uspeshnogo_vzaimodeistviya_gornodobyvayuschih_kompanii_s_mestnymi_soobschestvami_ [access date: 30. 03. 2021].

Interfax (2020). Media Reported on the Seizure of Deposits of Gold, Copper and Coal in Kyrgyzstan. October 6, 2020. https://www.interfax.ru/world/730257 [access date: 30. 03. 2021].

Jonek-Kowalska, I., Ponomarenko, T.V., Marinina, O.A. (2018). Problems of Interaction with Stakeholders during Implementation of Long-Term Mining Projects. *Journal of Mining Institute*, 232, 428–437.

Karachun (2021). Shale Panic Near Svyatogorsk. *Region news*. February 28, 2021. https://ka rachun.com.ua/slantsevaya-panika-pod-svyatogorskom-chego-boyatsya-zhiteli-donbassa -i-est-li-realnaya-ugroza-19894 [access date: 30. 03. 2021].

Kokko, K., Buanes, A., Koivurova, T., Maslobeov, V., Pettersson, M. (2015). Sustainable mining, local communities and environmental regulation. *Barents Studies*, 2(1), 50–81.

Kramer, M., Urbaniec, M., Kryński, A. (2005). *Międzynarodowe zarządzanie środowiskiem Tom I: Interdyscyplinarne założenia proekologicznego zarządzania przedsiębiorstwem.* Warsaw: C.H. Beck, Studia Ekonomiczne.

Masloboev, V.A., Vinogradova, S.N., Didyk, V.V., Klyuchnikova, E.M., Korchak, E. A., Mingaleva, T.A., Petrov, V.N., Ryabova, L.A. (2015). Mining in the Arctic in the Context of Ensuring Sustainable Development of Local Communities. *Bulletin of the Kola Scientific Center of the Russian Academy of Sciences*, 4(23), 82–89.

Morrice, E., Colaguiri, R. (2013). Coal Mining, Social Injustice and Health: A Universal Conflict of Power and Priorities. *Health & Place*, 19, 74–79.

Morvesti.ru (2015). Coal Port and Ecology: Compromise or Opposition?http://www. morvesti.ru/analitika/1692/31901/ [access date: 30. 03. 2021].

Munnik, V. (2010). *The Social and Environmental Consequences of Coal Mining in South Africa. A Case Study.* https://static1.squarespace.com/static/5a7859a10a bd0477ecb31301/t/5c5d88fbe5e5f0151ead5a97/1549633797101/2010Jan_-_Coal_ in_SA_Social_and_Env_Impacts.pdf [access data: 29. 03. 2021].

Popa, A., Menon, A.D., Walentynski, B., Young, J.R., Ching, H.Y., Cairone, L., Brito, M.B., Yung, W.Y.K. (2016). *The Challenges of the US Coal Industry and Lessons for Europe.* https://unece.org/DAM/energy/se/pdfs/cmm/pub/Challengs_US.Coal.Ind_ LessonsEurope.pdf [access date: 29. 03. 2021].

Ptak, M. (2019). *Górnictwo Odkrywkowe - Uwarunkowania prawne i środowiskowe Stan Analiza – Ocena.* Wrocław: Politechnika Wrocławska.

Ptak, M., Belzyt, J.I., Badera, J. (2020). *Rozwiązywanie konfliktów w górnictwie. Polskie i saksońskie doświadczenia w ramach projektu Życie z górnictwem.* Saksoński Wyższy urząd Górniczy we Freibergu and Wyższy urząd Górniczy w Katowicach. https://www. oba.sachsen.de/download/2020-03-13_OBA_MineLife_Konfliktleitfaden_PL.pdf [access date: 29. 03. 2021].

Radio Azartyk (2020). In the Alai Region, Residents Opposed the Development of a Coal Deposit. February 10, 2020. https://rus.azattyk.org/a/30426247.html [access date: 30. 03. 2021].

Riabova, L. and Didyk, V. (2014). Social Licence to Operate for Mining Companies in the Russian Arctic: Two Cases in the Murmansk Region. *Arctic Yearbook*, 527–537.

RIA Federal Press (2020). One Way Road. Will the Project of the Kuragin-Kyzyl Railway Line be Revived. *Finance Rambler.* https://finance.rambler.ru/other/ 43795727/?utm_content=finance_media&utm_medium=read_more&utm_source= copylink [access date: 30. 03. 2021].

Stepanova, A. (2020). Popular Anger to a Critical Level: What Is Happening in the Coal-mining Kuzbass? *Regnum.* https://regnum.ru/news/2842621.html [access date: 30. 03. 2021].

Suopajärvi, L. (2013). Social Impact Assessment in Mining Projects in Northern Finland: Comparing Practice to Theory. *Environmental Impact Assessment Review*, 42, 25–30.

Thomson, I., Boutilier, R.G. (2011). The Social License to Operate. In: Darling, P. (Ed.), *SME Mining Engineering Handbook*. Littleton Co., 1779–1790.

UNDP and UN Environment. (2018). *Managing Mining for Sustainable Development. A Sourcebook*. Bangkok: United Nations Cevlopment Programme. https://www.google.com/url?sa=t&rct=j&q=&esrc=s&source=web&cd=&ved=2ahUKEwjYwNH-69XvAhWGlosKHa5SBtEQFjABegQIBhAD&url=https%3A%2F%2Fwww.undp.org%2Fcontent%2Fdam%2Fundp%2Flibrary%2FSustainable%2520Development%2FExtractives%2FUNDP-MMFSD-LowResolution.pdf&usg=AOvVaw2USb1IvAqGd5boT3JG00OX [access date: 29. 03. 2021].

Williams, R., Walton, A. (2013). The Social License to Operate and Coal Seam Gas Development. A Literature Review Report to the Gas Industry Social and Environmental Research Alliance (GISERA). Canberra: CSIRO. http://www.gisera.org.au/publications/tech_reports_papers/socioeco-proj-5-lit-review.pdf [access data: 29. 03. 2021].

Żylicz T. (2007). Syndrom "NIMBY". *Aura*, 4, 8–9.

Part IV

Summary of research and considerations

12 Comparative analysis of examined coal mining industries

Differences and similarities of extractive industries from the examined perspective

The last part of the monograph opens with a comparative analysis of the impact of individual stakeholders on sustainable development in hard coal mining. Due to the fact that the authors of this monograph focused on the countries belonging to the European Union and the countries belonging to the CIS, the analysis will be presented in a comparative system concerning the behaviour and conditions associated with individual stakeholders in the two groups mentioned. The most important observations and conclusions regarding the impact of stakeholders on sustainable development are presented in Table 12.1.

The analysis of the data collected in the table shows that in many points the expectations and attitudes of stakeholders towards mining companies in the EU and CIS countries are similar. Most of the significant differences result from the application of a very restrictive environmental policy in the European Union and a much greater emphasis on sustainable development than in the countries belonging to the Commonwealth of Independent States.

In the case of **owners**, both in the EU countries and in the CIS countries, there are state-owned and private mining enterprises. Nevertheless, in the last 30 years, in both groups the number of privatised mining enterprises has increased, enabling them to be marketed and completely focused on achieving economic efficiency. This is especially true in CIS countries where the mining industry is characterised by a significant concentration of capital and an emphasis on maximising economic returns in order to guarantee dividends to owners. The strategic orientation of mining companies operating in the CIS is long-term due to the long-term sufficiency of the deposits and the lack of legal and environmental restrictions related to their extraction. This orientation is fostered by the multitude of available energy resources, which facilitates their diversification and prevents dependence on external suppliers.

European mining enterprises are in the final stage of maturity or are in the phase of decommissioning due to the depletion of deposits and/or the lack of economic profitability of mining. Their existence is mainly supported by the need to maintain energy security, as well as the long duration and difficulties

DOI: 10.4324/9781003091110-17

Table 12.1 Comparison of the role of stakeholders in mining enterprises in the European Union and the Commonwealth of Independent States

Stakeholder	EU	CIS
Owners	There are open pit and deep pit mines – there is a domination of deep mines. High extraction costs, problem with depletion of ressources. Countries with a large amount of hard coal production are also main consumers of hard coal. In some countries (Bulgaria, Czech Republic, Germany, Poland and Serbia) coal is the main energy source. There is a balance between privately owned and state-owned mines. In Western EU countries they are generally privately owned and in the Eastern part of the EU state owned companies dominate. After 2010, in Eastern EU countries the privatisation process accelerated because of a ban on co-financing mines from the state budget. Short term orientation. State owned companies are oriented towards social values and energy security.	There are open pit and deep pit mines – open pit mining dominates. Low current costs due to use of open mining method. Countries with a large amount of hard coal production are also main consumers of hard coal. Coal is not a main energy source in all CIS countries except Kazakhstan. There is balance between privately owned and state-owned mines – in Russia they are privately owned, in other CIS countries ther is a dominance of state-owned firms. Russian mining companies provide much information for stakeholders because of the attitude of IPOs and SPOs. There is a high concentration of equity. They are generally long-term oriented. They focus on economic values – on market capitalisation and maximising value. It is also the reason for trying to ensure sustainable development in key areas. Emphasis on regular dividend payment.
Board	There is a fairly large number of positions in the management board. Positions are mainly filled by way of competition and run by a supervisory board to guarantee the highest level of knowledge and experience. They focus a lot of activities on social goals and CRS. Many companies publish extended integrated sustainable development reports. Reports are prepared according to GRI international guidelines. Managers have a good knowledge about CSR principles but they are not fully convinced about the need for application of restrictive CSR requirements in the mining industry.	There is a fairly large number of positions in the management board. Quality of board is ensured by corporate legislation and management norms. They mainly concentrate on economic goals. Companies rarely publish sustainable development reports. If companies report CSR activities they mainly do it according to country guidelines or sometimes the UN Global Compact guidelines. Managers have a good knowledge about CSR principles but they are not fully convinced about the need for application of restrictive CSR requirements in the mining industry.

Stakeholder	EU	CIS
	Management board main priorities are: safety of mining crews, economic goals, environmental goals, social goals. Managers did not notice an impact of the implementation of CSR on the financial results and value of mining.	Management board main priorities are: safety of mining crew, social and environmental goals, economical goals. There is a very large polarisation of opinions on the importance of CSR issues – managers either strongly agree with it or strongly disagree. Managers notice a moderate impact of the implementation of CSR on the financial results and value of mining.
Employ-ees	The number of people employed in the mining industry decrease year by year. We can observe an increase in labour productivity. We can observe a slight decrease in the number of accidents. Employees have a strong awareness of economic and social needs and goals. Sustainable development is noticed by employees as an important factor but it does not contain all factors connected with CSR. Employees are guaranteed full employment rights with social benefits and this is also the case with the liquidation of a mine.	The number of people employed in the mining industry decreases year by year. We can observe an increase in labour productivity. We can observe a decrease in the number of accidents. Employees have a strong awareness of economic and social needs and goals. Sustainable development is noticed by employees as an important factor but it does not contain all factors connected with CSR. Employees are guaranteed full employment rights with social benefits and this is also the case with the liquidation of a mine.
Trade unions	Trade unions are important but we can observe a decreasing number of employers participating in them. One of the causes is the fact that they are financed from membership fees. A moderate number of workers participate in trade unions. The level varies among countries. Reasonable guaranties to union leaders and members of unions. In previous years we can observe a decrease in the popularity of trade unions in society. Trade unions operate on a national level. Sometimes trade union activity can be a barrier to sustainable development and can destroy the image of an extractive industry.	In the late 1990s trade unions ceased to be a significant institutional structure. A moderate number of workers participate in trade unions. The level varies among countries. Low guaranties to union leaders and union members. There is a freedom to form trade unions. Trade unions in previous years are consolidated on an international level in CIS countries. The trade unions are not well perceived by a lot of workers. Trade unions have a lower strength than in EU countries. Trade unions are ineffective and can sometimes be a barrier to sustainable development.

(Continued)

Table 12.1 Continued

Stakeholder	EU	CIS
Suppliers and recipients	Recipients are adapting to growing requirements in terms of social responsibility and especially environmental protection. Considerable pressure of EU consumers to supply clean energy. Mining is excluded from the right to receive sectoral state aid. Significant pressure on the implementation of more advanced and environmentally friendly technologies. Significant influence of mining suppliers on the development of the region due to coefficient of multiplication of jobs by mining enterprises. Suppliers have problems with diversification or a complete change of their business due to the specificity of the mining industry. Key suppliers are manufacturers of mining machinery and mining equipment. Recipients have a strong position in the value chain due to the nature of the product.	Lower pressure on adaptation to growing requirements in terms of social responsibility and environmental protection due to big domestic market. Lower but still important pressure of consumers to supply clean energy. Medium pressure on the implementation of more advanced and environmentally friendly technologies. Significant influence of mining suppliers on the development of the region due to coefficient of multiplication of jobs by mining enterprises. Suppliers have problems with diversification or a complete change of their business due to the specificity of the mining industry. Key suppliers are manufacturers of mining machinery and mining equipment. Recipients have a strong position in the value chain due to the nature of the product.
Competitors	Strong emphasis on the increase of production form of renewable sources. There are many producers of various types of green energy.	Lower emphasis on the increase of production form of renewable sources. Renewable energy sector exists and is growing but is much smaller than in EU countries.
Government policy	Government plays an important role in creating conditions for sustainable development. Strong emphasis on decarbonisation. Goal to become zero-carbon economy by 2050. The percentage of energy from renewable sources in EU countries is growing year by year.	Government plays a moderate role in creating conditions for sustainable development. Very low emphasis on decarbonisation – emphasis is on energy security and energy availability. Medium emphasis on green energy in long-term policies. Very small amount of energy consumption from renewable sources.

Stakeholder	EU	CIS
Ecologi-cal orga-nisations	Coal industry has a significant negative impact on the environment. Strong impact of ecological organisation on EU policies and the mining industry. Mining enterprises are implementing international mining sustainable development standards. Balance between environment, production end economy.	Coal industry has a significant negative impact on the environment. Moderate impact of ecological organisation on EU policies and the mining industry. Very few mining enterprises are implementing mining sustainable development standards. Emphasis on production and economy.
Local, regional and national societies	Mining companies must obtain socio-political approval from mining operations. Local communities are generally sceptical of specific mining projects in their neighbourhoods. Local community is directly exposed to the negative consequences of mining operations. There are social conflicts connected with mining industry operations. The automatisation and digitalisation of production can change the "social contract" between mining companies and the local community due to the fact that companies will not generate too many workplaces.	There is a lesser emphasis on obtaining socio-political approval from mining operations. Local communities are generally sceptical of specific mining projects in their neighbourhoods. Local community is directly exposed to the negative consequences of mining operations. There are social conflicts connected with mining industry operations. The automatisation and digitalisation of production can change the "social contract" between mining companies and the local community due to the fact that companies will not generate too many workplaces.

Source: own study

accompanying the energy transformation towards a low and zero-emission economy. Social goals are an important priority for their existence in the form of securing jobs in industries of high economic importance and preventing the pauperisation of mining regions.

In the case of the **management board**, both in the EU and in the CIS countries, there are regulations that entrust the management board with well-educated, experienced and prepared to work mining staff. However, it has a different view of the importance of sustainable development and the legitimacy of implementing this concept in mining enterprises. European managers show greater commitment to achieving social and environmental goals. Mining companies in EU countries often implement CSR reporting standards in line with the international guidelines included in the Global Reporting Initiative (GRI). In CIS countries, reporting on corporate social responsibility is very rare in mining enterprises, including in relation to international standards in this area.

In the EU countries, the management staff declares knowledge of CSR practices, but is sceptical about the necessity of their wider implementation. In the case of CIS countries, the opinions of the management are similar; however, they are highly polarised, as some managers consider CSR practices to be very important, and some to be completely irrelevant. Most likely, this results from the fact that in both groups of countries, the impact of the use of the principles of sustainable development on the financial results of enterprises and the value of mining enterprises was not apparent. Therefore, the Management Board does not see a significant impact of the CSR policy on the goals for which it was established and for which it is first assessed. The above mentioned circumstances are certainly not conducive to the implementation of sustainable development in the extraction industry.

It seems that sustainable development is also not a priority for **employees** of mining enterprises, neither in the CIS nor in the EU. This group of stakeholders primarily focuses on profitable goals, which partially justifies the hazardous and physical nature of miners' work. Employees also strive for work safety, thus protecting their lives and health against geological and mining hazards characteristic of the mining industry. In this way, however, the social dimension of sustainable development is realised, in which it is important to respect human and employee rights and to prevent abuse in the workplace. Environmental goals exist and become firmly established in the minds of mining enterprise employees, mainly as a result of their exposure by mining enterprises in corporate social responsibility reports. The employee awareness increases with the level of environmental awareness of a given society.

In the last 20–30 years both in the EU and CIS countries, the importance of **trade unions** has been decreasing. It is also worth adding that in EU countries trade unions mainly operate at the national level, while in the case of the CIS they are linked at the international level. In the CIS countries, trade unions have little influence on the functioning of the extractive industry due to legal conditions that do not give large guarantees to trade union leaders, e.g. in terms of employment or working conditions. In the case of EU countries, these guarantees are greater and hence there is a greater power of trade unions, giving them a dominant role in negotiations between the government and mining enterprises. However, despite this, fewer and fewer workers belong to mining unions even in European countries.

It should also be added that despite the fierce struggle for workers' rights, currently mining unions, both in the EU and in the CIS, do not have a positive social image, as they are perceived as entities defending industry privileges at the expense of the non-mining part of society. Additionally, in the CIS countries they are also considered to be ineffective.

Recipients have a very strong influence on the mining industry, both in the EU and CIS countries. The difference concerns the much greater pressure of EU recipients on environmental issues and the need to adapt to this in the mining industry. In the case of the CIS countries, this type of pressure also occurs, but it is much weaker due to the extensive local market, where recipients do not emphasise pro-ecological requirements so much. It can therefore be concluded that the impact of consumers on European mining companies in terms of sustainable development is significantly greater than in the CIS. The energy and heating sectors in the EU must reduce carbon dioxide emissions due to high and growing fees for emission permits. Therefore, they expect coal supplies of the highest quality, and more and more often they decide to use less emitting fuels, e.g. natural gas. In CIS countries, where the above restrictions do not apply, domestic and foreign recipients do not have such a direct and radical impact on the functioning of the mining industry.

In the context of hard coal recipients, it is also worth referring to the homogeneity of the extracted raw material, the specificity of which makes it practically impossible to change the sector or diversify production. The size of the demand and market of customers is therefore a key determinant of the survival and development of mining enterprises.

The **suppliers** of mining enterprises are also in a similar situation, as they provide fixed and current assets that are mainly used in the mining industry. Therefore, they have a limited ability to disperse production and sales risk. For this reason, their impact on the functioning of mining enterprises is not significant. The negotiating position of suppliers in relation to the mining industry is very weak. There were no major differences in this respect in the EU and CIS countries. The role of suppliers in shaping the sustainable development policy is therefore negligible in both cases.

In the case of **competitors**, their importance is much greater in the EU countries. This is due to the strong emphasis on the use of renewable energy sources and the existence of numerous producers providing renewable energy from various sources. At the same time, the year by year share of energy from renewable sources in the energy balance of all EU countries makes competitors gain in importance and poses a great threat to the existence of the mining sector. In the case of the CIS countries, this kind of competition also exists and is still developing, but it is currently too weak to threaten the extractive industries in the coming years. This is largely due to the created and desired environmental policy, which in the EU is conducive to the competition of mining enterprises.

In light of the above, **state and regional policy** plays a significant role in the absorption of the principles of sustainable development by mining enterprises. In the EU countries, a very restrictive decarbonisation policy is implemented, the aim of which is to achieve a zero-carbon economy by 2050. This poses a great threat to the mining industry, which is forced to invest in modern, pro-ecological technologies in order to be able to adapt to the requirements. In the case of the CIS countries, the emphasis on the production of environmentally friendly energy is beginning to appear, but it is still not very intense with regard to affecting the functioning of mining enterprises. However, it should be noted that the decarbonisation policy pursued by the EU and some other countries in the world may adversely affect the ability of the CIS countries to export coal. Therefore, in the globalised world economy, the policy of individual regions begins to play an increasingly important role, shaping the principles of extraction and the use of natural resources, and thus influencing the possibilities of implementing individual priorities of sustainable development.

As the mining industry has a significant negative impact on the environment, **ecological organisations** are trying to reduce this impact through numerous protests and lobbying for environmental protection at the political level. Such organisations exist both in EU and in CIS countries, but in the EU countries their impact is greater due to the greater importance and awareness of pro-ecological issues.

Environmental organisations in both groups very often cooperate **with local and regional communities** to reduce or eliminate the harmful effects of mining. This cooperation allows attention to be paid to the social and environmental threats caused by hard coal mining in both open and deep pit mines. In many cases, the protests of local and regional communities contribute to making mining more sustainable by putting pressure on the limitation and liquidation of mining damages and taking measures to prevent their occurrence. The attention of the community also enables the effective revitalisation of post-mining areas and prevents the long-term effects of mine closures. In this way, it becomes possible to achieve a balance between the goals and needs of residents of mining regions and mining enterprises. It is worth emphasising that the mining industry is sometimes a local and regional economic driving force, it creates jobs and helps to improve individual and budget incomes. So, it is not only a threat to the lives of the residents.

Typology of mining enterprises in terms of the strength and influence of stakeholders

The considerations carried out in the previous section let us identify the practical differences between the strength and influence of individual stakeholders on sustainable development in mining enterprises operating in the EU and the CIS. The key factor shaping this influence is the regional energy policy and the related environmental policy. First of all, decarbonisation in the EU means that it is possible to intensively implement environmental priorities, which, however, pose a serious threat to the existence of mining enterprises. The lack of such restrictive conditions in the CIS countries does not limit the development of mining enterprises, but it does not mean that environmental priorities are not noticed and implemented there. However, their implementation is slower and less exposed.

The pro-ecological policy of the EU makes mining enterprises very dependent on the recipients, i.e. the energy and heating sectors. The market for non-renewable energy fuels is systematically shrinking, which threatens the existence of the mining sector. The geographical distance to countries outside the EU makes it difficult, and sometimes even impossible, to export hard coal to other regions of the world. This problem does not much affect the mining enterprises operating within the CIS, for which the local and international market of raw materials remains open and receptive, as it is not blocked by environmental restrictions, including fees.

Among the significant differences between the CIS and the EU, it is also worth mentioning that workers and the trade unions representing them play an important role in European countries. The social goals of sustainable development then become important and are often foregrounded. In the CIS countries, neither workers nor trade unions play such an important role. Therefore, social goals are not the primary issue. In the case of mining enterprises operating in the CIS, however, the economic goals emphasised by the management boards of companies and by the state systematically privatising the mining sector are much more important.

The above observations prove that there are significant differences between the functioning of the mining industry in the EU and the CIS. Depending on

Table 12.2 The criteria of the typology of mining enterprises in terms of the strength of the influence of stakeholders on individual dimensions of sustainable development

Stakeholder	Assessment of the impact on a given dimension
Owners	**1: positive** **0: neutral** **-1: negative**
Board	**1: positive** **0: neutral** **-1: negative**
Employees	**1: positive** **0: neutral** **-1: negative**
Trade unions	**1: positive** **0: neutral** **-1: negative**
Suppliers	**1: positive** **0: neutral** **-1: negative**
Recipients	**1: positive** **0: neutral** **-1: negative**
Competitors	**1: positive** **0: neutral** **-1: negative**
Government policy	**1: positive** **0: neutral** **-1: negative**
Ecological organisations	**1: positive** **0: neutral** **-1: negative**
Local, regional and national societies	**1: positive** **0: neutral** **-1: negative**

Source: own study

the strength and role of stakeholders in mining enterprises, the arrangement of priority areas of sustainable development also changes. Such observations enable the development of a theoretical typology of mining enterprises, which takes into account all possible cases of the influence of individual stakeholders on the implementation of the principles of sustainable development. A proposal for such a typology is presented in Table 12.2.

The system of stakeholders (10 cases of stakeholders – first column in Table 12.2) and the possibilities of assessing their impact on sustainable development (3 degrees of assessment of the impact on a given dimension – second column in Table 12.2) presented in Table 12.2 creates 30 possible cases. In order to present the principles of operation of the adopted typology, Figures 12.1 and 12.2 present exemplary holistic assessments of such impact for Poland and Russia, as representatives of the EU and the CIS, respectively.

The assessment of the impact of stakeholders on sustainable development was made on the basis of detailed analyses presented in this monograph. According to its final results, in Poland, the actions and attitudes of recipients, competitors, local and regional societies and ecological organisations favour the sustainable development of mining enterprises. In Russia, due to the lack of centralised environmental policies and the universal obligation to prepare reports on corporate social responsibility, it is mainly ecological organisations and local and regional societies that act for sustainable development. The competition that uses less emission and renewable energy sources also contributes to changing the behaviour of mining enterprises. The figures presented also show a greater

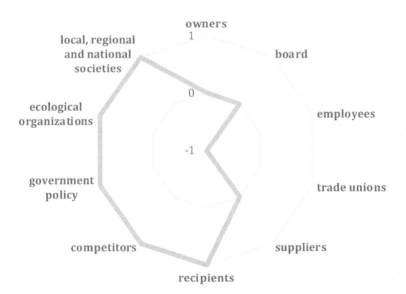

Figure 12.1 Distribution of the impact of mining enterprises' stakeholders on sustainable development in Poland (EU)
Source: own study

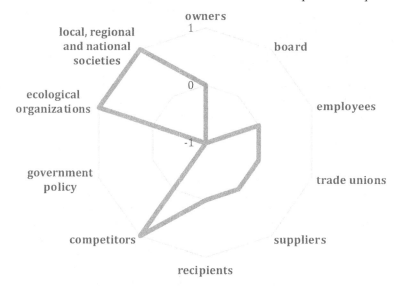

Figure 12.2 Distribution of the impact of mining enterprises' stakeholders on sustainable development in Russia (CIS)
Source: own study

balance in the Polish hard coal mining industry, which is largely due to the restrictive environmental and energy policy of the EU and the adoption of its principles by the Polish government.

In the next chapter, the general principles of the adopted model will be described in a universal manner, taking into account activities for a more sustainable hard coal mining.

13 Universal model of managing stakeholders towards supporting sustainable development implementation

Conceptual framework of proposed model – towards real sustainability in mining industries

The previous chapter presents a preliminary assessment of the role of individual stakeholders of mining enterprises in shaping sustainable development for two countries representing the main groups described in this monograph: European countries and countries belonging to the Commonwealth of Independent States. In this chapter, the authors present the idea of the assessment and general guidelines concerning the attitudes of mining enterprises' stakeholders towards the implementation of the principles of sustainable development.

Hard coal mining – as has been emphasised many times – is an industry in which the implementation of the principles of sustainable development is very difficult due to the somewhat primary, irremovable and extremely harmful influence of mining enterprises on the natural environment and the life and health of local and regional communities. Nevertheless, the authors believe that this is not an impossible task due to two key circumstances. Firstly, as is shown in the course of the considerations conducted in various regions of the world, hard coal mining is characterised by a different attitude to the principles of sustainable development and a different level of their acceptance by individual stakeholders, and thus a different level of final implementation of these principles in mining enterprises. Thus, it is possible in practice to shape and achieve various effects of implementing the effects of sustainable development, which clearly suggests the possibility of their modification and improvement.

Secondly, whether we like it or not, hard coal mining, like other enterprises extracting natural resources, will operate in the world for at least several dozen years more. Most countries, including the most developed and intensively developing countries, predominantly use non-renewable resources such as coal, gas and oil in the energy and heating sectors. The process of replacing them with renewable energy sources is very slow, and, in the current technological and economic conditions, full or even a majority substitution of non-renewable resources by renewable ones is not possible.

Taking into account the above circumstances, attempting to balance the activities of mining enterprises – in the opinion of the authors – is fully

DOI: 10.4324/9781003091110-18

justified. It can bring measurable environmental and social effects, and the dissemination of recommendations in this area contributes to the increase in environmental awareness and the requirements set by individual stakeholders for mining enterprises.

The proposed model for assessing the influence of individual stakeholders on the sustainable development of mining enterprises is generally based on the following two assumptions.

1   There are 10 groups of stakeholders influencing the activity and sustainability of mining enterprises, which include:

- owners,
- management,
- employees,
- trade unions,
- suppliers,
- recipients,
- competitors,
- the state,
- local and regional communities,
- environmental organisations.

2   These groups and their influence on sustainable development in the researched countries are described in detail in earlier chapters of this monograph. They include both internal stakeholders directly involved in the activities of the mining enterprise (owners, management, employees, trade unions) as well as those related to the closer environment (suppliers, recipients, competitors) and farther one (the state, local and regional community, environmental organisations). Therefore, the model covers all market participants in the hard coal mining sector.

3   The assessment of the influence of individual stakeholder groups on sustainable development is carried out on a three level scale, taking into account the following notes:

1: positive influence, which is understood as knowledge of the principles of sustainable development and taking active measures for its implementation in the mining enterprise;
0: neutral influence, which is understood as knowledge of the principles of sustainable development, but no action to implement it in the mining enterprise;
− 1: negative influence, which is understood as the lack of knowledge of the principles of sustainable development or the deliberate disregard for them and striving for unsustainability by focusing on individual aspects related to the realisation of benefits only for a given group of stakeholders.

Taking into account the above assumptions, the radar chart used in the previous chapter for the initial assessment of the influence of stakeholders on the sustainable development of hard coal mining in Poland and Russia is an excellent illustration of the assessment. In a universal approach, the model can take two extreme forms as presented in Figures 13.1 and 13.2.

With the first option, it is assumed that all stakeholders know, understand and implement the principles of sustainable development and do not put individual goals above the interests of other groups. It is an idealistic assumption which economies and sectors in countries that are highly developed in terms of civilisation and economics can approach. Then, a high degree of satisfaction of individual needs enables a broader, participatory view, as well as perceiving and taking into account collective needs.

With the second option, all stakeholders have a negative influence on the sustainable development of mining enterprises, which may result from not knowing or ignoring sustainability principles. Then, individual goals constitute the only point of reference and complete imbalance occurs, usually accompanied by a series of intergroup tensions and conflicts.

Apart from the presented options, which define the maximum and minimum of the model, there are a number of indirect models reflecting the degree of involvement of individual stakeholders in the development of mining enterprises. Thanks to their use, a given region can carry out a general and detailed (descriptive) assessment and designate those areas (relations between stakeholders) that require improvement in order to approach the option reflecting the ideal, model state.

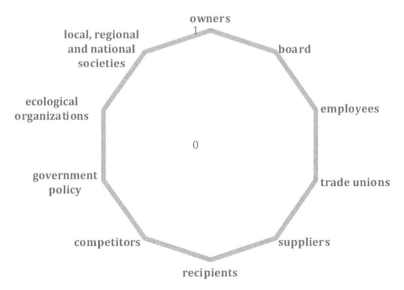

Figure 13.1 Model for assessing the influence of stakeholders of mining enterprises on their sustainable development – the most beneficial option
Source: own study

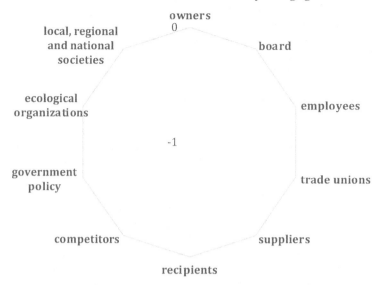

Figure 13.2 Model for assessing the influence of stakeholders of mining enterprises on their sustainable development – the least beneficial option

Source: own study

A refinement of the model may be the use of a multi-level assessment scale instead of only the -1;0;1 levels. Then, apart from the direction of stakeholders' influence on sustainable development, it will also be possible to take into account the strength of this influence. An example of a scale for this model version is presented in Table 13.1. The graphical representation of the model may still remain the radar chart, synthetically and graphically representing the level and scale of imbalance.

Paths of transforming identified existing relations towards the universal model of managing stakeholders for supporting SD implementation – rules and methods

In the process of improving the influence of individual stakeholders on the sustainable development of mining enterprises, it is necessary to

1   Identify relations assessed as negative, and then define the causes of the existing state of affairs, which should be systematically eradicated until their complete elimination;
2   Identify relations assessed as neutral and attempt to transform them into positive ones through actions raising awareness of the benefits of sustainable development; as a last resort, these relationships can remain neutral in the case of weak stakeholder influence on sustainability;
3   Identify positive relationships, monitor them and look after their behavior; they can also be used as an example of good practice for less involved stakeholders.

Table 13.1 An alternative scale of the model that also takes into account, apart from the direction of the influence, the strength of stakeholder influence

Direction of influence	Strength of influence
Negative (-)	1: low 2: average 3: high
Neutral	0
Positive (+)	1: low 2: average 3: high

Source: own study

In the above activities, communication between individual stakeholders is of great importance, which favours the exchange of information, negotiations and cooperation for sustainable development, which is why the role of institutional mediators and education, in particular pro-ecological and pro-social education, are so important.

In order to present the above improvement mechanism, Table 13.2 presents the categorisation of stakeholders in Poland and Russia regarding the influence they exert on the sustainable development of mining enterprises.

Table 13.2 shows that both in Poland and in Russia, the activities of the local and regional community as well as environmental organisations that work together to highlight environmental priorities, most often omitted or ignored in the activities of hard coal mining, have a positive influence on sustainable development. In Poland, these activities are supported by state policy and recipients from the energy

Table 13.2 Categorisation of stakeholders in Poland and Russia regarding the direction of influence on sustainable development

Direction of influence	Country	
	Poland	*Russia*
Positive (+)	recipients state policy competition local and regional communities environmental organisations	competition local and regional communities environmental organisations
Neutral (0)	owners management suppliers	owners employees trade unions, suppliers recipients
Negative (-)	employees trade unions	management state policy

Source: own study

sector, who expect mining enterprises to implement clean coal technologies and raw materials of the highest quality guaranteeing the lowest environmental pollution. It is a derivative of the European Union's climate policy. Due to the lack of such a policy and central environmental conditions, the state and customers were not included among the stakeholders positively influencing the sustainable development of hard coal mining in Russia.

Owners and suppliers are in the group with a neutral influence on sustainability in both countries. The former try to find a balance between economic, environmental and social goals. It seems that the latter are treated by them in terms of image and are implemented as part of corporate social responsibility. In Poland, this view of the priorities of sustainable development is shared by the management board, which has also been qualified as neutral stakeholders. In turn, in Russia, this group also includes trade unions and employees, who are most probably looking for a balance between economic and social goals, but their influence on the decisions of mining enterprises is much smaller than in Poland. Moreover, in Russia, customers in the heating and energy sectors do not have to worry about environmental restrictions, and therefore their influence on sustainable development is weaker and voluntary.

In the group of stakeholders negatively affecting the sustainable development of mining enterprises in the current conditions in Poland, there are trade unions and employees who mainly prioritise social goals in the context of earnings, ignoring the efficiency goals of the sector. Additionally, they very often do not see the environmental risks associated with mining activities. The research conducted so far indicates a very low awareness of the need to balance mining activities in social and economic groups. This is reflected in the use of force, a very common solution of disputes and conflicts in the form of strikes or protests. The driving force of these stakeholders practically overpowers the activities of other groups. Such an imbalance could pose a serious threat to the functioning of the entire sector.

In Russia, the management boards of mining enterprises and the state were included in the group of stakeholders negatively affecting the sustainability of hard coal mining. The listed stakeholders strongly focus on economic priorities and – similarly to Poland's trade unions and employees – have a considerable power to influence the activities of mining enterprises. With such a system of influences, and taking into account single aspect interests, achieving a balance is very difficult, negatively affecting the process of awareness and implementation of the principles of sustainable development.

When looking for methods to improve the diagnosed situation in Poland, one should focus on reducing the negative influence of trade unions and employees on the sustainable development policy. Unfortunately, this process, which has been going on for many years, does not bring the desired results, despite its side effects in the form of closure of many unprofitable mines. In turn, in Russia, the sustainable operation of mining enterprises would certainly be facilitated by an increase in environmental awareness and the introduction of more restrictive environmental regulations.

14 Conclusions and directions for further research on SD in extractive industries

Theoretical and practical conclusions

In this chapter, a summary of conclusions resulting from the research and analyses described in this monograph will be presented. It uses the stakeholder theory to analyse the prospects for the functioning of the mining industry in the context of sustainable development. The monograph uses the division of stakeholders into the following ten categories: owners, management board, employees, trade unions, recipients, suppliers, competitors, the state and regional policy, ecological organisations, and local and regional communities. The use of the stakeholder theory is related to the fact that this theory determines the use of the concept of corporate social responsibility (CSR) in an organisation. The use of both concepts – stakeholders and CSR – determines the change in the way of thinking about the functioning of the organisation, from an approach only focused on the interests of shareholders towards a multi-faceted approach, trying to balance the expectations of various types of entities towards the implementation of sustainable development in the organisation.

The conducted research used both the macro-analysis of statistical data describing the researched issues at the level of the European Union and the Commonwealth of Independent States, and the micro-analysis perspective, which consists in examining case studies from individual countries, in particular from Poland and Russia.

The issue of sustainable development is currently extremely important, due to the progressing climate crisis, and there is growing interest in it around the world. In particular, these issues are important in organisations operating in European Union countries, as the EU is very strongly committed to conducting a pro-ecological sustainable development policy. This has a significant impact on the operating conditions of the entire industry, in particular the mining industry.

A very significant threat to the functioning of mining enterprises is the decarbonisation policy pursued by the European Union, according to which it is planned to achieve complete emission neutrality by 2050. The data collected in the monograph for Poland and other European Union countries shows that the percentage of energy derived from renewable sources is growing in all countries.

DOI: 10.4324/9781003091110-19

In the long run, this is a major threat to all mining enterprises, as they may lose their main markets. This type of policy is not only implemented in the European Union countries, but also in other countries. An example of one suchpolicy is the American RECLAIM Act.

The policy implemented by governments has a very strong influence on the process of implementing sustainable development solutions in mining in the given countries. This situation occurs because mining enterprises are often owned or jointly owned by the public and also because legal solutions imposed by the authorities, in particular in the field of ecology, have a very strong impact on the entire mining industry.

As the mining industry is one of the industries with the strongest negative impact on the environment, there seems to be a contradiction between its operation and the implementation of a sustainable development strategy. Nevertheless, due to the fact that the transformation of the energy sector towards renewable energy sources will not be quick and due to the need to ensure energy security, it will still be necessary to use non-renewable fuels such as hard coal for a long time.

When considering the issues involved in sustainable development, it should not be forgotten that the mining industry – in countries such as Poland, for example, where a large part of the energy comes from burning coal – ensures national energy independence. This is important from the point of view of the country's strategic energy security, and therefore is an issue that must be taken into account when planning energy policy.

Currently, fossil fuels are still the main source of energy in the world, including hard coal. The development of the renewable energy and nuclear energy market is insufficient on the world scale to be able to replace energy from fossil fuel combustion in the near future, especially as total energy consumption in the world is showing an upward trend. In this context, it is important that the continued operation of this industry can be carried out in the most sustainable manner. This is not easy due to the aforementioned very large negative environmental impact of the mining industry. Nevertheless, it is worth paying attention to the fact that the mining industry should function but limit the following: the consumption of resources and waste, in particular hazardous waste, the impact of mining activities on the surface, energy consumption by mines, and noise emission.

Currently, the largest hard coal producers in Europe include countries such as Poland, Germany, Turkey, the Czech Republic, and Serbia. In the case of CIS countries, the largest producers are Russia, Kazakhstan and Ukraine. Among these countries, the highest level of production in the CIS countries is in Russia and Kazakhstan, while in the European Union it is in Poland and Germany. In the case of the European Union countries, coal is the main energy source in the Czech Republic, Germany, Poland and Serbia. In other countries, it is often also an important source of energy, however, it does not have a dominant position. In the CIS countries, only Kazakhstan has coal as the dominant energy source. In other CIS countries it is not the dominant energy source.

In the countries under study, there is a diversified ownership structure in the mining industry. There are both state owned and private mining enterprises. State ownership usually occurs in former socialist countries, but this is not a rule, as with the example of Russia where private ownership dominates in this industry. The form of ownership, as the results from our research show, has an impact on the structure of the mining enterprise's goals. In the case of private ownership, focus on the economic result and the needs of shareholders is dominant, while in mining enterprises with public ownership, the focus is on the implementation of social, employee and energy security goals. The analyses carried out in the monograph have shown that in the case of private mining enterprises, more attention is paid to issues related to sustainable development due to the need to care for a positive image of the organisation. In the case of state ownership, the main problem is the marginalisation of environmental goals. The conducted analyses show that, neither in the case of private nor public ownership structure, are ecological issues a priority in the mining industry.

The monograph also presents the results of research conducted among members of the supervisory boards of Polish and Russian mines. In the case of research conducted in Poland, the analysis of priorities in the field of CSR showed that the highest rated priority was issues related to employee safety, followed by economic goals, and environmental and social goals. The surveyed members of supervisory boards in Poland did not notice any significant impact of CSR implementation on financial results, the value of the mining enterprise or employees' attitudes. In Poland, mining enterprises implement CSR principles, but they are not completely convinced of their importance and impact on the functioning of their organisation.

In the case of research conducted in Russia, the safety of employees was also recognised as the most important factor of CSR, with successive places awarded to social, environmental and economic goals. The surveyed members of supervisory boards in Russia notice a moderate relationship between the implementation of CSR and the financial, environmental and social performance of mining enterprises.

Research has shown that the increasing level of mechanisation of mining activities and restructuring of the industry lead to an increase in productivity and thus to a decrease in people employed in the mining industry, even if the level of mining remains unchanged. For example, in Poland in the years 1995–2019, employment in the mining industry decreased from 274 thousand to 83 thousand people. In the case of the European Union countries, Poland has the most people working in the mining industry, and for this reason, the industry is of great social importance as an employer. There is a similar situation in Silesia, a region traditionally very strongly associated with the mining industry. If we look at work safety, measured by the accident rate, this has for many years remained at a similar level, as shown in the detailed analyses presented in the monograph. Most of the injury and serious accident rates in Poland are constant over time. In the case of Russia, it can be seen that we have observed a decreasing trend in the accident rate since 2005. The main causes of accidents in mining are fire and explosions, especially those associated with coal dust and methane explosions.

In the case of the studied countries of the European Union and the CIS, employees are guaranteed full rights, including an appropriate level of remuneration and additional social benefits. In many countries, they receive special remuneration in the event of mine closure.

Traditionally, trade unions played an important role in mining enterprises. In particular, in the 20th century, their role was very important and in many countries mining trade unions were among the largest and strongest unions. This is related to the very large number of employees employed in the mining sector and the strategic importance of coal as a raw material. At the end of the 20th century and in the 21st century, the importance of mining trade unions began to decline significantly. There are significant differences in this regard between the individual EU and CIS countries – the trade unionisation level ranges from 12–25% of employees in the EU countries and 16–69% of employees in the CIS countries. The weaker position of trade unions in the mining industry also results from the limitation of legal privileges of employees and activists belonging to trade unions. This phenomenon can be observed, for example, in Russia where, despite the highest level of unionisation among the surveyed countries, the role of trade unions is small due to the lack of legal protection of union activists. Mining strikes and demands for privileges by trade unions are usually negatively perceived by the societies of the surveyed countries, which additionally limits the influence of trade unions.

In the case of the mining industry, the important role of suppliers results, inter alia, from the fact that the so-called mining related companies are very important in generating jobs in the vicinity of the mine. In Poland, it is assumed that for one place in mining there are about 3–4 places in companies that are its suppliers and cooperators. Similar values for the job multiplication factor are also achieved in other countries around the world. A major threat to suppliers is the strong dependence of the condition of mining enterprise suppliers on the condition of the entire sector. In the event of problems in the industry and sales restrictions, mining related companies may face a big problem.

In recent years, processes of vertical or horizontal consolidation have also been observed in the mining industry. In particular, there is often a phenomenon of vertical consolidation, which consists in consolidating activities along the entire supply chain of the energy market.

Due to the aforementioned decarbonisation process and the growing share of renewable sources in the energy balance of countries, the mining industry faces very strong competition. This competition is made up of producers of energy from renewable sources such as water, wind, solar radiation, biomass, radioactive decay and gravity. This is a particularly significant threat in the case of European Union countries due to the fact that, in accordance with the new energy policy, in 2030 the share of renewable energy sources in the energy balance is required to be 23%. In the CIS countries, this type of risk is much lower, but also in these countries the share of energy from renewable sources is showing an upward trend.

Changes in the field of sustainable development policy implemented by the government are often forced under the influence of various types of pro-ecological organisations operating in a given country. These organisations are lobbying for solutions that will be more environmentally friendly, which poses a threat to mining enterprises. Usually, the most restrictive pro-ecological regulations occur in those regions where the strength of pro-ecological organisations is the greatest, such as in the European Union countries. Under the influence of pro-ecological organisations, international standards for the implementation of sustainable development in the mining industry were also created. They include, but are not limited to: ICMM – Sustainable Development Framework, IRMA – Initiative for Responsible Mining Assurance and OFC Performance Standards on Environmental and Social Sustainability.

An important factor influencing the activities of mining enterprises are also non-governmental organisations and local communities. The analyses show that they usually have a negative attitude towards mining, which may lead to the occurrence of social conflicts. Proper resolution of this type of conflict is necessary for the mining enterprise to conduct its operations in a safe manner.

The main theoretical contribution of this monograph to science is the development of a typology model of mining enterprises from the point of view of the strength of the influence of stakeholders on individual dimensions of sustainable development. The monograph has developed an original concept of assessing the impact of individual stakeholders that may be positive, neutral or negative. On this basis, models were developed for two countries – one European Union country – Poland, and one CIS country – Russia. Data compiled in individual chapters of this monograph was used to develop the models. The models were developed in a static system for 2021.

The second important theoretical contribution is related to the comparison of the functioning of sustainable development in the mining industry in two groups of countries – European Union countries and CIS countries. Analysing the similarities and differences between them in Chapter 12, two highly different approaches to the issue of sustainable development and the resulting implications are shown.

Another theoretical contribution of this research results from the fact that the analysis of case studies carried out allowed us to propose three patterns of influence of mining enterprises' employees on their functioning:

- The first formula occurs when employees of mining enterprises are treated as an easily replaceable workforce. Working conditions in mines are usually poor and workers are deprived of legal protection. The influence of employees on the functioning of the organisation is very small. The model is valid for low developed countries.
- The second formula occurs when there are decent working conditions in the mine and miners are an important social group with a clearly defined character, often with a system of mining traditions and customs. Trade unions and industrial organisations play a strong role. Employees have a great influence on the functioning of mining enterprises.

- The third formula occurs when employees not only think about the potential earnings and risks associated with the work of a miner and about ensuring satisfaction with their other economic needs, but also pay attention to environmental issues. There is a very strong influence of employees on the functioning of the mine as a result of the simultaneous influence of employees, local communities and environmental organisations.

Comparing the two areas analysed – the European Union countries and the CIS countries – it can be concluded that the general requirements of individual stakeholder groups are similar in both of them. The differences mainly concern sustainability issues. In this case, the decarbonisation policy and strong emphasis on ecology related issues that occur in the European Union countries result in a much higher level of restrictiveness of the requirements for sustainable development imposed on mining enterprises.

The second area in which there are significant differences are issues related to the priorities of mining organisations. In the case of European Union countries, social and sustainable development issues are dominant. However, in the case of the mining industry in CIS countries, the main emphasis is on the implementation of economic goals with little role for social issues.

Research amongst members of supervisory boards of Polish and Russian mining enterprises also showed that Russian experts more often agree that CSR has a positive impact on the financial results of the mine and the attitude of employees to work.

A very important practical conclusion is also that the decreasing market demand for non-renewable fuels is a significant threat to the functioning of the entire mining sector. This is particularly important in the case of European Union countries, especially as there are few export opportunities due to the high cost and distance. In the case of CIS countries, this is much less of a problem due to the large internal market and the ability to sell coal on the world market.

Policy recommendations

On the basis of the research conducted, the following recommendations can be made regarding the sustainable development policy in the mining industry and its future functioning in the field of the surveyed stakeholders:

- Organisations in the mining industry should adapt to the increasingly restrictive requirements in the field of environmental protection. This is particularly important in the case of mining enterprises operating in the European Union, due to increasingly restrictive regulations. They should adapt their policy to the requirements and legal regulations, in particular those related to decarbonisation.
- Management board members in the mining industry should have extensive knowledge of mining issues as well as sustainable development. In order to ensure an appropriate level of competence of management board members,

in particular in state owned enterprises, special state exams should be applied to check the competences of potential supervisory board members. It is also worth creating specialised job positions in mining enterprises, enabling the participation of highly specialised staff in management.

- It is worth introducing modern normative solutions regarding sustainable development and corporate social responsibility in mining companies. Mining enterprises should use these guidelines much more often than is the case right now. Currently, only a few mines in the European Union and CIS countries submit annual CSR reports. Changing this state of affairs will allow the industry to better adapt to the requirements of sustainable development. In particular, companies from the mining industry can be recommended to prepare sustainable development reports, preferably in a standardised version, in accordance with the requirements of the GRI Guidelines or the UN Global Compact Communication of Progress. It is also worth paying attention to the GRI non-financial reporting guidelines contained in the appendix on reporting of enterprises from the mining and metallurgical sector. In this case, special indicators on mining and metals are added to the standard measures, allowing for much more accurate and detailed reporting of corporate social responsibility by enterprises in this industry. This type of approach, based on the standardisation of the reported indicators, will allow for better compatibility and comparability between individual mines and countries and will enable overcoming typical emerging problems of CSR reporting in mining, described, for example, in the work of Boral and Henri (2015).

- In addition, it is also worth considering the implementation of international standards regarding CSR in mining enterprises, such as, for example, ISO 26000 or SA 8000. This is important as mining organisations have a dubious reputation for corporate social responsibility in many countries, especially in developing countries. The implementation of appropriate normative requirements may improve this situation and lead to the improvement of the image of mining enterprises in society.

- The involvement of mines in the implementation of social goals may consist in a wider implementation of Industry 4.0 solutions in them, consisting in obtaining a higher level of mechanisation and robotisation of mining activities, especially in those places where there are conditions harmful to the health of employees.

- It is recommended to use the developed model of the strength of influence of stakeholders in the mining industry as a tool for identifying those stakeholders who have the strongest impact on mining enterprises in a given country. Then, the obtained results should be used to enhance the impact of stakeholders who have a positive impact on the mining industry and weaken the impact of those who have a negative impact. In this way, the developed model can be used as a strategic management tool at the managerial level, as a "compass" allowing for better planning of the policy and strategy of mining enterprises in order to achieve their goals.

- Mines should implement modern technologies enabling more environmentally friendly production. One of them is a technology that allows the production of so-called low emission carbon containing a low amount of particles such as PM2.5, PM10 and an almost complete reduction of Benzo[a] pyrene emissions during combustion. Another type of technology worth implementing in mining enterprises is the coal gasification process. In this process, the coal is converted to a gaseous form. The product obtained in this way is more environmentally friendly than classic coal.

- Suppliers of the mining industry, i.e. the so-called mining related companies, should strive to diversify their sales and limit the very strong dependence of their operations on the condition of the mining industry. Otherwise, industry problems could contribute to their financial troubles and even bankruptcy.

- Vertical consolidation is worth considering, in particular between energy enterprises and mines. This will allow mines to obtain additional capital, which will enable the implementation of newer technologies. At the same time, the use of vertical consolidation allows power plants to maintain continuity of supply.

- In order to reduce the negative environmental impact of the entire industry, coal based power plants should invest in technologies that let them operate with lower carbon dioxide emissions. This type of effect can be achieved, inter alia, as a result of: improving the efficiency of electricity generation, the use of new types of boilers, the introduction of combustion in oxygen or the use of chemical looping combustion. Such technologies can reduce carbon dioxide emissions by 30–50%.

- Mining enterprises should implement sustainable development standards such as ICMM – Sustainable Development Framework, IRMA – Initiative for Responsible Mining Assurance and OFC Performance Standards on Environmental and Social Sustainability. Such standards are voluntary and non-binding. Nevertheless, their use allows mining enterprises to obtain a positive image and better adapt to the principles of sustainable development.

- In order to improve the conflict resolution process in the mining industry, in particular between the local community and the mining enterprise, appropriate negotiation procedures should be developed that will take into account the interests of all social stakeholders of the mine. It is also worth using solutions such as public consultations or valorisation of deposits and granting selected facilities a public status in order to improve relations between social stakeholders and mining enterprises.

Bibliography

Boral, O., Henri, J.F. (2015). Is Sustainability Performance Comparable? A Study of GRI Reports of Mining Organizations. *Business & Society*, 56(2), 1–30. doi:10.1177/0007650315576134.

Index

Note: **Bold** page number refers to tables and *italics* page number refers to figures.

Printed in the United States
by Baker & Taylor Publisher Services